SPEAK, OKINAWA

ALFRED A. KNOPF   NEW YORK   2021

Speak, Okinawa

· · · A MEMOIR

Elizabeth Miki Brina

THIS IS A BORZOI BOOK PUBLISHED BY ALFRED A. KNOPF

www.aaknopf.com

Knopf, Borzoi Books, and the colophon are registered trademarks of Penguin Random House LLC.

Portions of this work first appeared, some in slightly different form, in the following publications: "Worse Than the Dog" in *Hyphen Magazine* (May 25, 2018); "Erizabesu" and "Miki" as "Both Names" in *Crab Fat Magazine* (May 2018); "One Percent" in *New Delta Review* (May 2018); "Without Being Taught" in *River Teeth* (August 9, 2019); and "Missing Ghosts" in *The Sun* (September 2020). An earlier version of "How They Met" won first place in the summer contest issue of *So to Speak* (2018).

Library of Congress Cataloging-in-Publication Data
Names: Brina, Elizabeth Miki, 1981– author.
Title: Speak, Okinawa : a memoir Elizabeth Miki Brina.
Description: First edition. | New York : Alfred A. Knopf, [2021]
Identifiers: LCCN 2020030710 (print) | LCCN 2020030711 (ebook) |
    ISBN 9780525657347 (hardcover) | ISBN 9780525657354 (ebook)
Subjects: LCSH: Brina, Elizabeth Miki, 1981– | Brina, Elizabeth Miki,
    1981—Family. | Brina, Elizabeth Miki, 1981—Travel—Japan. | Japanese
    American women—Biography. | Japanese Americans—Ethnic identity. |
    Japanese Americans—Biography. | Ryukyuans—New York—Biography. |
    Intercountry marriage—New York—Syracuse. | Okinawa-ken
    (Japan)—Biography
Classification: LCC E184.J3 B75 2021 (print) | LCC E184.J3 (ebook) |
    DDC 305.48/8956073—dc23
LC record available at https://lccn.loc.gov/2020030710
LC ebook record available at https://lccn.loc.gov/2020030711

Jacket photograph: Author's own / Asata Photography, Kadena
Jacket design by Janet Hansen

Manufactured in Canada

First Edition

To my mother and father

SPEAK, OKINAWA

WORSE THAN THE DOG

I asked my dad why all the great stories were sad ones. "Most good stories are mysteries," he said. "The author is like a detective trying to get to the bottom of some truth, and happiness is a mystery that can come apart in your hands when you try to unravel it. Sadness, on the other hand, is infinitely more resilient. Scrutiny only adds to its depths and weight."
—Bliss Broyard, "My Father's Daughter"

*M*y first memory: a dog bites me, on the arm, not hard, but just enough to jar me into consciousness. His name is Shiro, which means "white" or "castle" or "generation" in Japanese, depending on how it is written. Shiro has long white hair, blue eyes, and a grayish-pink nose. I am three years old and he is just above my height, but I can still look him in the eyes. I believe we understand each other, our arrangement. I believe, at age three, I've earned his subservience. He carries himself proudly. Majestic, like a horse.

So one day, when no one else is around, in the backyard, beside the cinderblock fence, as he lowers his head to drink from a shiny porcelain bowl of water, I try to mount him. He growls and bites me. He doesn't frighten me. He embarrasses me, shames me. And as a small child, an only child, accustomed to endless doting, I wouldn't tolerate these strange emotions. I cry and run to my mother. I don't tell her why I'm crying. I'm afraid that if I tell her she'll scold me worse than the dog did.

Shiro is not to be ridden like a horse.

.

Shiro was my obaasan's dog. Obaa, my grandmother, my mother's mother, found Shiro when he was still a puppy, eyes closed, curled up into a ball, quivering on a pile of garbage.

Often at night, Obaa pushed a cart through the streets of Kadena, a town located on the island of Okinawa, where my mother was born and raised, where I lived for six months when I was three years old. Often at night, when the air thinned and cooled, when the sounds of jets, helicopters, and gunfire coming from the nearby military bases quieted, Obaa pushed a cart through the streets and rummaged through trash heaps, searching for cans and bottles to sell, scraps of wood and metal to reuse. She lived in a house with a rusted tin roof, a rusted tin gate, a floor raised from the mud by cinder blocks, with a single room for cooking, eating, drinking, sleeping, and playing cards, a backyard for bathing and growing sweet potatoes, which she ate for every meal. She lived almost all her life in this house, the house where my mother grew up, the house my grandfather built after their previous house was destroyed during the battle.

.

The Battle of Okinawa. That is how most of us have heard of Okinawa. But as a battle fought and won, and quickly disregarded. Not as a battle on which our entire contemporary history depends, from which we are still recovering.

It began in April of 1945 and lasted eighty-two days. In Japanese, the battle is referred to as "tetsu no ame." In English, the phrase means "rain of steel." The Okinawans simply refer to it as Okinawa no Sensho, "Okinawan War." Although a conquered nation for many centuries—first as a tributary of China, then as a colony of Japan—Okinawa had never known such carnage. For eighty-two days, thousands of planes dropped hundreds of thousands of bombs on the island, crushing and burning countless creatures, plants, houses, and buildings. For eighty-two days, hundreds of thousands of troops invaded the island, wielding tanks and guns, throwing grenades, and shooting into hiding places. One hundred forty thousand Okinawans, a third of the population, were killed. That does not account for all those who died of injury, illness, starvation after the battle. That does not account for all those who were forced to commit suicide. Of those killed, some were conscripted soldiers called Boeitai, boys as young as twelve, ordered to fight in the front lines. Some were nurses or members of relief teams called Giyutai, girls as young as fourteen, ordered to cook and tend to the wounded. The rest were civilians. One hundred twenty thousand civilians. Who died in a war they didn't choose, sacrificed to protect Japan, the precious mainland. Many Okinawans believe that those who died had died in vain. Or, rather, what they refer to as "a dog's death," inujini.

When news spread that Okinawa would soon be attacked, Obaa was living by herself with her four children, my mother's older brother and older three sisters. My grandfather, conscripted four years earlier, was somewhere in Korea, being held prisoner. When the sirens blared, days before the troops landed, before the ships could be seen from shore, Obaa and her four children— her son, age four, and her three daughters, ages three, five, and seven—grabbed sacks of potatoes they had been gathering and storing for months. They hid in caves while the ground shook with each explosion, while their island, their home, crumbled and turned to ash. They fled from cave to cave, while their sacks emptied, while their clothes loosened and unraveled from their shrinking bodies. For two years after the war, they wandered from camp to camp, slept in tents or under tarps. They bathed in the ocean. They ate what they could scavenge. They collected rain and drew from low muddy wells for drinking. When my grandfather returned from Korea, he was a different person. He returned, but he was gone.

Somehow Obaa kept herself and her four children alive and unharmed through one of the most horrific battles in history. A story I wish she could have told me.

Yet these memories are impossible to forget, regardless of whether we actually lived through them. I believe they stay in our bodies. As sickness, as addiction, as poor posture or a tendency toward apology, as a deepened capacity for sadness or anger. As determination to survive, a relentless tempered optimism. I believe they are inherited, passed on to us like brown eyes or the shape of a nose.

.

I had not learned this history, my mother's history, my history, until I was thirty-four years old. Which is to say that I grew up not knowing my mother or myself.

.

Three years after the war, my mother was born. She was born into poverty and chaos. She was born into a family, an entire people, stunned by violence and grief. When my mother was born, Okinawa was still considered an "enemy territory." This meant that the occupying U.S. military was under no obligation to restore the battered landscape, and Okinawa was still a vast ruin of decay and rubble. This meant that the occupying U.S. military guarded and patrolled the wreckage of an island, and Okinawans relied on bare subsistence rations of bread and milk, cans of red chili, popcorn, and candy. Some of the troops gave the prettiest girls bright new clothes to wear and called them "honeys." Some of the troops broke into homes, robbed and raped Okinawans inside homes, because there were no laws against it, no laws at all.

In 1952, three years after my mother was born, around the age she would have formed her first memory, Japan officially relinquished rule of Okinawa to the United States. My mother witnessed the U.S. military devouring the island, constructing immense complexes of bases. She witnessed forests and fields, wetlands and beaches becoming concrete. She witnessed farmers and fishermen, carpenters and potters, cooks and shopkeepers becoming mere labor. Her brothers were hired to help build the bases. Her sisters were hired to serve food in the cafeterias. Obaa cleaned barracks. My grandfather also cleaned barracks, but mostly he just stayed in bed, too sick with grief, humiliation, and alcoholism to do much of anything else.

For many years after the war, in order to supplement her income, Obaa cooked breakfast and lunch for a few of her neighbors; a couple of them were orphans, older than her youngest children, old enough to work, but still needing someone to care for them. She cooked on a portable gas stove while they drank tea and played cards in the same room. They paid her one dollar to sit on her floor and eat food she prepared. Not much, just potato and broth.

Not long after her own children moved out and moved away, after my grandfather gambled and drank himself to death, Obaa found Shiro on a pile of garbage and brought him to her home.

She held him like a baby and fed him with a bottle. Then he grew older and bigger, and they would sit together at the same table, which was already low to the floor, perfect for a dog, and share from the same bowl. One piece of potato for her, one piece for him. She would slurp some broth and give the rest to him. Back and forth. For every meal.

Shiro trotted beside her as Obaa pushed a cart through the streets.

Shiro was not to be ridden like a horse.

.

My first memory of Shiro biting me is all I remember of the time I lived in Okinawa. There are many photographs of my aunts and uncles holding me and smiling, my cousins holding me and smiling, Obaa carrying me on her back and smiling. We are not just posing for photographs. We are smiling because we are happy. I am a small child and I don't know what sadness is yet, and therefore I make everyone happy.

There is a photograph of me at a beach, lying on my stomach on the sand, wearing a red-and-white polka-dotted swimsuit and sunglasses much too large for my face. I am laughing, probably because the person behind the camera is laughing.

There is a photograph of me in the park, standing on a pair of giant bronze statue boots, each boot bigger than my whole body, wearing braids and bow-shaped barrettes in my hair, arms crossed and brow furrowed, trying to look tough, probably because the person behind the camera is showing me how to look tough and I am mimicking her. We are having fun, pretending and playing together, because I am happy and everyone loves to play with me.

But I do not remember any of these moments. They are just photographs my mother had taken and framed, and hung on walls or put on shelves around the house. They do not belong to my life. They belong to hers.

What I do remember is walking through Newark Airport. I am walking with my mother, staying very close to her, holding her hand. A man walks beside us. He smiles a lot and wants to hold my hand, too, but I won't let him. I won't let him because I don't know him. I don't remember him because my first memory is of Shiro biting me. My mother tells me the man is my father. She tells me that he stayed behind, here, where we are now, in the United States. She tells me that he was traveling, looking for a better job and a better place for us to live. That is why we had to live with my aunt on Okinawa for six months. That is why we have returned. Because the man is my father and her husband. We belong with him. She says "Otosan . . . Otosan . . . Anata no otosan." *Father . . . Father . . . Your father.* She tells me in Japanese, because back then I could understand and speak Japanese. I hold my mother's hand tighter, hiding from him behind her.

And for a long time, that is the closest I ever felt to my mother. When I was still in her world.

.

What my mother and I share now is an understanding that precedes words. It is an understanding that comes from being the same body, being fed, bathed, clothed, held in her arms every day, loved every day, then becoming separate, growing apart, then remembering how much that hurt, remembering and being grateful for the distance we traversed, the distance we were able to recover. It is an understanding that comes from forgiveness.

My mother and I communicate through layered small-talk, subtexted chitchat, a shorthand that took years and years to develop, and satisfies our desire to be close.

But will that ever compensate for the years and years of silence, for the time we missed, the time I squandered?

*   *   *

My mother was born in 1948, three years after the war, three years after the bombings of Hiroshima and Nagasaki. She was born and raised in Kadena, the sixth child of a fisherman and a fisherman's wife, both from Miyako, one of the many smaller islands that surround Okinawa. I don't know much about their lives before the war, because they were never able to tell me. They were never able to tell my mother. They worked hard with their bodies every day to feed themselves and their children, and when they didn't work, they were too tired to talk to their children about such trifles as their lives when they were younger.

My mother quit school before she finished eighth grade. She worked for fifty cents an hour in a factory that manufactured bento boxes until she turned sixteen, old enough to work at a nightclub as a waitress. She worked as a waitress for the rest of her life, at nightclubs in Okinawa, then at Japanese restaurants in the United States. When she moved to the United States, she dreamed of climbing the social ladder to the status of secretary or accountant, of wearing pressed suits and blouses and typing reports, but disillusionment quickly settled. She couldn't speak English. She couldn't learn English fast enough, well enough. Working hard with her body was all she knew. Working hard with her body was her rightful place, and the restaurants became her retreat, a backdrop of wood-and-paper paneled screens, rock ponds filled with koi fish, the strumming of three-stringed guitars heard through stereo speakers, which so faintly reminded her of home. She always gave some of her paycheck to her mother and younger sister, even long after she left Okinawa. Sometimes she still gives some of it to her spoiled daughter.

.

According to Japanese legend, if you make a thousand paper cranes you are granted three wishes. My mother made a thousand paper cranes once, shortly after she became a waitress. Her three wishes were to marry an American, an American who would buy her a big house, and together they would have a child—a daughter, fingers crossed—who could eat as much as she pleased and sleep on a bed in her very own room.

.

My father was born in 1948, three years after Victory Day, three years after the Cold War commenced. He was born in Brooklyn and raised in Manhattan, the first child of a wealthy Italian immigrant and an English-Irish-Scots woman who could trace her lineage back to Jamestown. My grandfather salvaged a small portion of his family's wealth despite the Great Depression. To prove his loyalty to his new country, he enlisted in the army and swiftly ascended the ranks as a translator. He could speak Italian, Spanish, French, German, and English, fluently. He studied philosophy at Columbia University, then founded one of the first telephone-answering services in New York City. My grandmother was his receptionist. A recent graduate of Hunter College, twenty-two years old, fifteen years younger than my grandfather, when they married. They bought a corner condo on the Upper West Side, where they raised three boys.

My father and his two younger brothers went to Loyola, a prestigious Jesuit high school at Eighty-eighth Street and Park Avenue, not too far from where they lived. My father was taught

Latin. He was taught St. Thomas Aquinas. He read every play by Shakespeare, every book by Dickens, Conrad, Hemingway, and Fitzgerald, by the time he graduated from Fordham University, another Jesuit institution. After he enlisted in the army, following in the footsteps of his father, he read *The Communist Manifesto* by Karl Marx and *The State and Revolution* by Vladimir Lenin because he "sought to understand the mind of the enemy." His exact words. My father became an Airborne Ranger, a Green Beret, then a captain. He fought in the Vietnam War. He fought to save the Vietnamese from communism, from tyranny. When he returned to the United States, he dreamed of keeping up the good fight, of solving the nation's economic problems, but he couldn't keep a job for very long. There was always a boss to rebuke, a partner to contend with, a devious consumer policy he refused to abide. There was always a layoff, a bankruptcy, a recession, persecution for being a veteran. Eventually, the narrative shifted, and the culprits included the Women's Movement, Affirmative Action, and the "Jews in charge of Wall Street." I cringe to admit that's what he believes, but that's what he believes. Writing it feels like betrayal, because he is my father and he means so much more to me than his bigotry.

.

My father believes in the code of heroes, of men, of strong men who protect the weak. He believes in honor and sacrifice. If my mother or I asked for anything, needed anything, he would do anything. He wouldn't sleep or eat, he wouldn't stop fighting, wouldn't surrender.

.

I was born in 1981, the year Ronald Reagan was inaugurated as the fortieth president, the year MTV began broadcasting. I was born in Elk Grove, a suburb of Chicago, the first and only child of an aspiring entrepreneur and an expatriate. Around the time I was born, my father graduated from Northwestern University with an M.B.A. in operations management and my mother started taking ELL classes. My mother hated those classes, she confided years later, when I became old enough to care enough to ask her.

"Too hard. I want to stop going, but your father not let me. He make me study. He study with me. He help me."

Good for him, I thought to myself. Not yet comprehending the unfairness, the very lopsided power dynamic. Not yet aware of the ease with which she conceived and uttered the word "let," the ease with which I heard and processed it. We accepted the word without resistance, with a nod of approval.

We always listened to my father. We trusted him.

Because my father was the parent who knew what to say when I asked about thunder and lightning or jumping off a diving board, about the girls who teased me or the boys who ignored me. He knew what to say to teachers and gymnastics coaches. He knew what to say, and he said it so well. His pronunciation was perfect.

Why didn't I learn Japanese? Why didn't my father learn, and require me to learn, like he required my mother to learn English? Perhaps ethnocentrism is to blame. Perhaps learning a language that wasn't European wasn't very popular in the 1980s. Perhaps my father heeded what the psychologists were claiming at the time, that learning two or more languages at once would confuse children. Perhaps he remembered my grandfather, who was fluent in five languages but didn't graduate from high school until he was twenty-one years old. Perhaps my father, as a man, an American man who grew up in the 1950s, couldn't quite empathize, couldn't quite anticipate the isolation of his wife, the strain on the relationship between her and her daughter. Perhaps part of him enjoyed being everything for her, doing everything for her. Or perhaps he tried and failed or tried and gave up, couldn't surmount the challenge without such a massive imperative, without a spouse and a child and in-laws and friends and neighbors and co-workers and customers and cashiers who understand and speak only English.

Even now, as I try to learn, listening to a Pimsleur lesson every day (well, almost every day; sometimes every other day or every other week) for going on two years, I can barely utter more than a few words and phrases. It is too hard to retain, to pay attention, to think and speak in a language that isn't mine, isn't *necessary*. I am too dependent on English. I am too American.

*　　*　　*

In 1972, Okinawa reverted, or, rather, was "sold," back to Japan for the sum of six hundred eighty-five million dollars.

The Okinawans who were skeptical held their breath. The Okinawans who were hopeful celebrated. They sang and danced. They marched in parades and waved Japanese flags. They thought they were done with the U.S. military, done with the bases.

The bases remain.

Since 1972, nearly nine thousand crimes—including murders by shooting, by stabbing, by strangulation, vehicular homicide, theft, arson, rape, sexual assault—have been committed by U.S. military personnel stationed in Okinawa. One hundred sixty-nine court-martial cases for sexual assault—a higher record than at U.S. military bases in any other nation—have occurred in Okinawa.

Today, twenty percent of Okinawan land mass is still controlled by the U.S. military. More land controlled by a foreign military than in any other nation.

·

Okinawa became known as an "R&R island," a place where troops could relax and recuperate between stints at war. My father was stationed on Okinawa after he fought for four years in Vietnam. He met my mother in Kadena, just outside the army base, at a club called the Blue Diamond, where she worked as a waitress, getting paid one dollar for every drink she got a serviceman to buy for her.

And here is where history becomes mine, alive in me.

He sits on a stool. He is strong, confident. He is handsome, movie-star handsome, Elvis handsome. He smiles with straight white teeth and flashes a wad of crisp cash. He orders a bourbon on the rocks in a language and accent that signal power. She sits next to him. She is petite, slender. She is beautiful, exotic. She smiles and twirls a few strands of her dark dark hair, as smooth as silk, flowing down to her waist like water.

Is love possible in a place like this, in a situation like this, between two people from separate worlds, on opposite sides of war and conquest?

I will never know how the story began, only how it ends.

Perhaps to someone who had grown up eating sweet potatoes for every meal, sleeping in the same room as her mother, father, and six siblings, he must have seemed like a way out. Perhaps to someone who had just spent four years in combat, she was too vulnerable to resist. He had to save her.

And so, a year later, in 1974, two years after the reversion and one year before the Vietnam War ended, they married on the island. Marriage to locals was discouraged, but as a commanding officer my father granted his own approval.

It was a small ceremony. Only Obaa attended. My grandfather was too sick. My uncles were too angry. My aunts were too sad, scared, maybe jealous, that their sister was marrying an American, a soldier, that their sister was leaving. Obaa managed to scrounge enough money to rent two traditional wedding kimonos and hire a photographer to document the event.

My mother has seen her mother three times in the forty-five years since she left.

* * *

While my mother and I lived in Okinawa, Obaa carried me on her back, walked the streets carrying me on her back, and pointed. "Ie" for house, "ki" for tree, and "tori" for bird. She taught me how to say "taberu" if I was hungry and "nomu" if I was thirsty. She taught me how to say many words I can't remember. My mother was grateful to spend this time with Obaa when neither of them had to work so hard. Back then, she believed she could have both: her life in Okinawa and her life in the United States. Back then, she believed she would return more often, enough to keep these separate worlds, Okinawa and the United States, her mother and her daughter, connected.

But even the best intentions dilute from routine and convenience. As I grew up, as I became more and more American, so did my mother. Visits became once a decade, and then once every two decades. Phone calls became once a month, and then once every three months.

.

While my mother and I lived in Okinawa, my father looked for a better job and a better place for us to live. A job and a place befitting his expectations and potential. He traveled to Brazil. He traveled to Singapore. He traveled to Tokyo and Osaka. He traveled to Texas and California and Washington, D.C. He was offered a job at the CIA but was told my mother would be a liability; he declined the offer. My father finally found a job as a management consultant for a financial firm called the Princeton Group. He found a place for us to live in Plainsboro, New Jersey, in a condo, in a complex of condos. Each building uniformly square, uniformly painted gray and blue, enclosed by parking lots and fences. The complex of condos shared a playground, two tennis courts, and a pool.

In many ways, it resembled a military base.

There was a process, I'm sure, but in my memory, almost immediately I joined my father's world. A world in which my mother was never entirely welcome, could never fully participate.

I remember she dressed up as a clown for Halloween once, but only once. I remember she helped us decorate the Christmas tree, but she wanted to wrap the lights too close around the trunk, not dangling closer to the edges of the branches.

I remember an older little girl from the neighborhood flung a shoe at my chest, knocking the wind out of me, and a sharp pebble at my face, slicing the bridge of my nose. I cried and ran to my mother, but she could see I wasn't hurt too badly and did nothing. My father came home from work, and after I told him what had happened, he went on a hunt for this older little girl. He charged through the neighborhood, wearing his three-piece suit, searching every alley and alcove of the complex. When he spotted her on the playground, swinging on a tire swing by herself, he yelled at this older little girl until his skin reddened and his veins bulged, until she trembled with terror, until she cried and ran to her mother, and then her mother came pounding on our door, clamoring for an explanation. My father told her that he would have struck this older little girl if she were his own child and if she were a boy. He told her that bullies must be bullied; otherwise, they will never learn.

My father believed it was his duty to bully the bullies. He possessed an irresistible certainty, the assurance of someone who knew how it felt to do more than survive.

He always made me feel safe and protected in his world.

.

We lived in Plainsboro, New Jersey, for a year and a half. During that time, my father would travel to Manhattan on business trips for days, sometimes a week. I saw my father on weekends. I ached from missing him.

When my father was home, he would take me to the pool and we would swim laps. I clung to his shoulders, and his body held me above the water. My mother didn't want to go to the pool. The water was saturated with chemicals, and the neighbors showered after—not before—they swam in the pool. The neighbors asked my mother to repeat herself, which annoyed her and seemed to frighten her. And her fear scared me, too. She didn't belong. That meant I didn't, either.

My father would watch *Bugs Bunny* cartoons with me. We sat on the couch together, eating carrots whole, as if they were plucked from the ground. My mother would peel and slice the carrots. She couldn't understand why I preferred to eat the carrots whole, like an animal.

My father would sit in a chair beside my bed and read to me until I fell asleep. My mother couldn't understand why I was so afraid of the dark, so afraid of this giant empty room that I was lucky enough to have all to myself.

Sometimes I would cry and cry from missing my father, and my mother would have to call him at work, because only his voice calmed me. His voice. The voice that read *Cinderella, Sleeping Beauty, The Ugly Duckling,* and *The Velveteen Rabbit* to me whenever I asked and so often I had memorized the words. I remember one day, when I was four years old, I asked my mother to read these stories with me. I wanted her to listen and watch. I wanted to show off. We sat on the floor of my bedroom with the books spread between us. I recited the words and turned the pages.

"You don't need me," my mother said, bitter and accusing.

I didn't bother to deny it. Even at that age, we both knew it was true.

.

I spent most of that year and a half with my mother, but my recollections of her are vague. She was a ghost who suddenly appeared in rooms, carrying a stack of carefully folded laundry or pushing a vacuum. She swept and mopped the floors, scrubbed the countertops, while I played with dolls that didn't look anything like me and looked even less like her. She bought me a Mariko doll, the Asian-looking Barbie doll, but I was not amused.

She taught me how to fold paper into the shape of a bird.

.

Sometimes my mother got very drunk. She would call her mother and sisters in Okinawa, talk on the phone for hours, then hang up and burst into tears. For a long time, I thought my mother was weak. Because she couldn't speak English very well or read. Because she was afraid of pools and neighbors. Because she got drunk and sobbed unconsolably, and had to be carried, sometimes dragged, to bed.

I didn't realize then that she couldn't change history, that history wasn't her fault. That she could never escape the legacy of defeat, of trauma, perpetuated by her very own husband and daughter. That I could never escape, either.

Now, whenever I try to comprehend her loneliness, I am completely overwhelmed by her strength. She must have longed for that small child in the photographs. She must have ached from missing me.

.

My mother told me I used to understand and speak Japanese. She told me that, after we returned to the United States, she would speak to me in Japanese, and at first I responded, but then I stopped answering, and then, eventually, I stopped listening. Everywhere around me, English. Everywhere around my mother, English. I adapted. She could not. So I abandoned her.

My mother told me Obaa came to live with us for two months when I was four years old. She was supposed to come live with us permanently, but the United States, even just the sliver of it called Plainsboro, New Jersey, was too big and cruel for her.

I remember when Obaa took me to the pool. She wore a flimsy floral-printed button-down shirt and a skirt, and white sandals with white socks. She looked so odd and out of place in my world. She sat on a plastic lawn chair at the edge of the pool while I swam by myself in the shallow end and ignored her. Because she couldn't speak English. Because she was old and wrinkled. From pushing a cart through the streets and rummaging through trash heaps. From watching a husband gamble and drink himself to death. From watching a daughter die of pneumonia, a daughter die of cancer, and another daughter move far away to another world.

I wish I could have made her feel more welcome back then. "Please stay with us, Obaa," I would have said. "My mother needs you. I need you. Teach me Japanese."

.

I imagine poor Shiro for those two months while Obaa was with us. Probably eating outside with the other dogs.

.

Shiro died shortly after Obaa returned to Okinawa, and Obaa never returned to the United States.

I wish I could be there," I tell my mother over the phone, after she tells me she is going to be baptized in two weeks.

"Oh, would you?" she pleads, with such unabashed eagerness and expectancy, I am forced to feel that familiar pang of guilt.

I am thirty-three years old. I am a full-time graduate student and a part-time adjunct instructor. I live in New Orleans. My mother and father live in Fairport, a suburb of Rochester, New York. I have lived in many cities since I moved away from them, and I have visited as seldom as possible. I stand in front of a calendar, rearranging events and deadlines. I don't wish I could be there. I don't have time to spare. I am about to recant my statement, but then she says to me, "I prayed to God you would come."

At sixty-seven years old, my mother has found religion, now believes in God and Jesus Christ. To my knowledge, she had never believed in God or Jesus Christ or Buddha or practiced any religion before. She used to scoff when my father and I would discuss and theorize about the Big Bang and Intelligent Design. She used to slap her palm on the dining room table and scream "Stop it!" in a shrill voice I interpreted as fear of concepts too large, too formidable, for her to understand. She didn't think or care much about a life beyond this life, a world beyond this world, though I do remember she made quite a fuss when my pet hamster died, and insisted that we bury him. I ask her why she wants to become Christian. She gives a blanket statement: "Good things happen when you become Christian." I cringe at her naïveté. But I also concede that no harm is being done. She seems happy. Happier than she has ever seemed, in fact. Her voice is brighter, lighter. My mother hasn't called me drunk and sobbing once in eight months, since she started attending church with the Japanese Christian friends she met at the restaurant. She used to call me drunk and sobbing a lot. I can't remember exactly how often. Once every two weeks. Once every two months. Often enough that if she called late at night I would roll my eyes and wait a few rings. Sometimes I would answer and check my email or unload the dishwasher while I listened to her gurgle and slur and repeat the same incoherent phrases over and over. And sometimes— with that familiar pang of guilt—I would shove the phone away from sight and refuse to answer. Two missed calls. Three missed calls. Sixteen missed calls. I hoped she wouldn't remember in the morning.

I don't believe in the kind of God who answers prayers, but I do believe in the powers of positive reinforcement. Yes. Of course I will be there for her baptism.

•

At five o'clock on a Sunday morning, my mother wakes up to begin soaking the rice. The rice needs to be soaked for at least an hour, then rinsed several times, until the water runs clear, then steamed, then seasoned with sweetened vinegar. She must clean and scrub the scales off the tuna, salmon, and yellowtail she bought from the market yesterday, then slice the fillets into long ribbon-wide chunks. She must wash, peel, and chop the vegetables. She must beat the eggs, then add mirin and soy sauce, then pour them into a skillet to make an omelet. The eel must be broiled in the oven. The shrimp must be battered and fried. She plans to prepare enough sushi to feed fifty fellow members of the Rochester Japanese Christian Congregation for the post-sermon meal, scheduled for two o'clock this afternoon. She usually brings a dish to pass, usually something simple, like inari or gyoza, but today is a special occasion.

I wake up in the master bedroom, her bedroom, to the sound of the door to the guest bedroom, where she sleeps when I'm visiting, open and close. The thought of getting up to help her occurs to me, just briefly, just before I fall back asleep.

My father wakes me three hours later to tell me that it's eight o'clock in the morning, and would I like to wake up yet, or should he check again in an hour. I try to contain the irritation in my voice as I thank him and tell him I'm getting out of bed now. For most of my life, my father's voice would be the first sound I heard each day. He would knock on my bedroom door and shout the time just minutes before my alarm went off. After I moved away, he would call, and when I answered, he would inform me of the time, the temperature, the chance of precipitation, as well as the percentage of cloud coverage. If I didn't answer, he would call again, and then again. Two missed calls. Three missed calls. I almost always answered. Because he was my father and I trusted him. But also because he was much more persistent than my mother, and if I avoided him for too long, he would call roommates or friends or even mere acquaintances, numbers that were the most recent in my cell-phone log, which he accessed through the T-Mobile Web site.

I walk downstairs to join my mother in the kitchen. I sit on a stool at the counter where she slices, peels, and chops. She pours me a cup of coffee. She pours herself a cup of green tea.

My mother's dark dark hair, straight and luxuriously soft, is now streaked with gray. She keeps her hair bobbed, just below her chin, with a square curtain of bangs. She has brown, oval-shaped eyes, slightly darker brown and more oval-shaped than my eyes, a pug nose, same as my nose, and plump lips, same as my lips. My mother is five feet and two inches tall and weighs one hundred pounds. She is much smaller than me, has been much smaller than me for most of my life. At five feet six inches, I feel like I tower over her. At one hundred and sixty pounds on a good day—on a very good day—I feel more like her personal bodyguard than her daughter. She is shy, sometimes comes off as meek and unsure of herself to strangers—English-speaking strangers—though the more appropriate term might be "modest." Yet she always appears strong and confident when she holds a heavy metal pot with one hand and scrapes the hot steamed rice into a large wooden bowl with the other.

"Here." She hands me a fan.

"Like this?" I wave the fan lazily above the bowl.

"A little bit faster."

I wave the fan faster.

She pours vinegar into the bowl with a swift circular motion. She mixes the vinegar into the rice, jabbing, lifting, and folding the rice with a small wooden paddle, while I wave the fan so fast my arm gets sore.

"What does fanning the rice do?"

She laughs. "I don't know."

According to a nice-looking blonde lady on the website *La Fuji Mama*, fanning the rice increases the rate of evaporation, so that the rice becomes sticky and a glossy sheen forms.

My mother pours more vinegar, then mixes more, then pours more, then mixes more.

"How do you know how much vinegar?"

She laughs again. "Depends on how much rice."
I laugh, too.

.

I ask my mother obvious questions. I ask her how finely to grate the ginger. I ask her the exact proportions of soy sauce, mirin, sake, and dashi needed for a sauce. I ask her how many minutes to let it simmer. I ask her how to sew a button, how to tie the knot at the end. I ask her how she sews a hem, with each stitch of thread perfectly round and equidistant from the next. I follow her around the house as she waters her fifty-eight plants, dusts off their leaves with a cloth, and rubs them with her fingertips. Some of these plants she has kept alive since before I was born, and I ask her how, but she doesn't know.

I ask my mother obvious questions, the same questions again and again, because this is the necessary nature of our interactions. The only way we know how to talk. About the concrete, the immediate, the here and now. Otherwise, there is mostly silence between us.

What did you have for dinner?
Beef curry. Your father loves beef curry.
What did you put in it?
Onions, potatoes, peas, and carrots.
With rice?
Of course, with rice. What about you?
I ordered pizza.
You eat too much pizza.
You're right.
Did you get a microwave?

Not yet.
You should get a microwave. Easy to reheat leftovers.
I will, I will. Pause. What's Dad doing?
He's watching Yankees. He's sad because Yankees losing.
What's the score?
I don't know. I can just tell.
Pause. *Did you work today?*
Yes. Every day except Wednesday.
What time?
Eleven-thirty to nine.
Every day?
Yes. Every day. Except Wednesday.
Pause. *Did you go for a walk before work?*
Yes. Four miles. I try to walk four miles every day.
That's good.
You should walk, too.
I try.
Pause. *Did you gain more weight?*
Pause. *Yes.*
I think you eat too much pizza.
You're right.
Did you get a microwave?
Not yet.
You should get a microwave. Easy to reheat leftovers.

.

There are answers I want, but questions I don't know how to ask. Or maybe I'm too afraid, too lazy to ask.

.

My mother and I speak different languages. Her native language is Japanese. My native language is English. This might seem like a mundane fact about us. It's not. It dictates everything.

Because even though my mother understands and speaks English at a highly functional level, there are places inside me she can't reach, nuances of thought and emotion I can't express in words that make sense to her.

I don't understand and speak Japanese. I know nothing more than a list of words. "Kudasai" for "please" and "arigato" for "thank you." Ichi, ni, san, yon, go, roku, shichi, hachi, kyu, ju for the numbers one through ten. The words for private parts— "chin-chin" for "vagina" and "oshiri" for "buttocks"—which I still remember from when I was child, words used as euphemisms when my mother needed to confirm that they were properly washed.

Sometimes I believe the cruelest injustice my mother has had to suffer, surpassing the war that ravaged her homeland, surpassing the poverty, surpassing the beatings from her oldest brother, the negligence of her father, the ongoing yet forgivable distractions of Obaa, is the fact that she can't communicate with her daughter in her native language. The Japanese I don't understand and speak measures the enormity of her inner world that is impenetrable, blocked, hidden from me.

.

And there is more to a language barrier than mere lack of shared vocabulary. There is a clash of history and culture. There is an imbalance of power.

I grew up in the United States, a nation of triumph and abundance. My mother grew up in Okinawa, a colony, a pawn, subjugated and impoverished.

I grew up eating pancakes and cereal for breakfast, frozen

pizzas or macaroni and cheese for my second lunch. My mother grew up starving.

I grew up speaking English, "standard" English, an international language, an exalted language, a language I learned in highly ranked public schools, from classic literature, classic movies, and popular sitcoms on television. My mother grew up speaking a dialect that is purely indigenous, shamed, and belittled, a dialect of Okinawa called Uchinaaguchi ("Okinawa Mouth"), also known as Hogen—a language that was forbidden and outlawed by the conquerors from Japan, a language that is now endangered, on the brink of extinction.

Obaa and my grandfather spoke Hogen. When my mother speaks Japanese to people who are from Japan—not from Okinawa—she is reluctant, embarrassed. Because she has an accent, traces of her degraded heritage in her voice.

I grew up correcting my mother's pronunciation and grammar, feeling frustrated when my mother stammered, paused, pushed out the words too slowly, or blinked and stared and said nothing if I spoke too quickly.

.

When two people with different histories, different cultures, interact with one another, they may very well get along. They may become friends. They may fall in love. They may marry and become family. But often, more often than perhaps we're willing to observe and decipher, our ingrained histories and cultures will confront each other, potentially misinterpret and upset each other. No matter how unintentional, an offensive thought, a tactless remark, a moment of condescension inevitably slips out.

.

My mother spreads the rice on sheets of seaweed. The rice must cool, so she takes a break to feed the birds and squirrels. Or "skwars," as my mother pronounces it.

She opens the screen door, and two fat squirrels scurry to the edge of the patio deck.

"Hi, skwars," she says cheerfully.

"These squirrels are humongous!" I shout in protest.

"You can thank your mother for that!" my father bellows from the living room. He has been watching Fox News on the television while checking stock-market stats on his laptop.

My mother refills the bird feeder with seeds, then discovers that she has run out of shelled peanuts. She reaches for a bag of roasted almonds in the cupboard. We usually eat these roasted almonds with an assortment of cheeses and Maker's Mark Manhattan cocktails before dinner, a strict tradition from my father's side of the family.

"No, Mom. What a waste." I grab the bag from her.

"Oh. Okay." She shrugs. "I feed them later."

That's a bad habit I still have. Treating my mother like I'm the boss, like I know best.

I dig into the bag of roasted almonds and scatter a handful onto the patio deck.

.

It took too long for me to admire my mother's common sense and practical knowledge. Her ingenious reuse of excess food packaging. Her ability to transform a can of tuna fish and a carrot into a deftly flavored stir-fry dish. It took me too long to accept and appreciate my mother's English. Her simplicity and directness. Her words for household items, such as "remako" (remote control) and "reku puraiya" (record player). The way she mixes up the pronouns "he" and "she." Eventually I realized that the world is certainly big enough for her English, for all Englishes, for all the languages and dialects, each one another history, another journey, another map by which we discover ourselves. Eventually I realized that it is my responsibility to understand her, not her responsibility to make herself understood.

But it took too long.

III

NO NAME ISLAND

At first, in the old time, in the beginning,
the great sun god,
beautifully shone,
and looked far down,
and bent down, looked down,
far away,
(there was something floating)
and said, "Let there be islands"
and said, "Let there be good people."
—*Omoro Soshi*

*W*e can't remember our name. The one we gave ourselves in the beginning. Maybe we never had one. Maybe we didn't need one, back then, when we were left alone. A name offers power and prominence. Both, we didn't want. Today we call ourselves Uchinaa, which is how we pronounce "Okinawa," which means "a rope in the offing." Because if you look at us on a map, we look like a knotted rope tossed carelessly from the sky onto the sea. We are the largest of an island chain called Ryukyu, which is how the Japanese pronounced Liu Chiu, which is what the Chinese called us many centuries ago.

We are made of mountains, marshes, coral reefs, and beaches of white star-shaped grains of sand. We are made of mangroves, laurels, deigo trees with flowers that bloom like fire, and gajimaru trees with roots that climb above the ground and weave themselves through their own branches. Our water is clear and blue and green. Our summer is hot. Our rain is heavy. Our wind is strong, but so are our trees, which keep their leaves through the winter. We are the home of wild orchids and wild violets, frogs and snakes that shine like jewels, giant crabs and even bigger turtles, long-beaked birds with ruffled chests that look like waves of water, and fish that could feed us for a thousand years. And they have. And they will.

.

We are islands and we are people. We are people who can't remember how we got here. Or why we came here. Some of us came with the current and some of us came with the winds. Some of us came from the north, from Japan. Some of us came from the west, from China and Korea. Some of us came from the south, from the Philippines and Formosa. Maybe we came because we were hungry. Maybe we came because we were curious. Maybe we came because we were exiled. Or maybe we got lost in a storm and stayed because we were happy or because there was nowhere else to go. Beyond us, to the east, there is only ocean. Miles and miles of endless ocean.

.

In the beginning, we worshipped groves. We found groves of palm or citrus or plum or ginger, and we settled. The first who settled, neya, the founding family, lived closest to the grove. The oldest brother was named chief, nebito, and the oldest sister was named priestess, negami. When the rest of the family joined, we called ourselves makyo, and when other families joined, we called ourselves mura. We always honored the family who came first. We always listened and obeyed. The nebito resolved disputes, and the negami told us stories of our ancestors, delivered messages from our ancestors, and kept the fires in our hearths burning. Fires that were kept alive and burning for generations.

We rarely argued over land, because we rarely grew food. We picked fruit from trees and caught fish with our weirs and our nets. We didn't make weapons because we didn't hunt. We didn't make weapons because we rarely argued over land. We built houses out of clay and grasses and branches, with roofs shaped like the backs of turtles. We built canoes out of pine to feed the living. We built shrines in the groves to honor the dead. The living spent our hours fishing, cooking, eating, weaving, singing, dancing, birthing and raising children. The living wore dresses and long hair tied in knots on the top of our heads, held in place by wooden pins. The dead spent our hours heating the sun, shining the moon, swaying the trees, and stirring the ocean. The dead gave warmth and light, fruit and fish. The living and the dead were the same, just as the gods and the people were the same.

.

Then, one day, early in the fourteenth century, men from China, wearing garments as hard as stone, carrying long, pointed knives, came looking for gold and silver. They came looking for immortality. Instead, they found us. They pointed at us, barked and squawked in a language we didn't understand. "You are part of China now." We didn't understand. So we just laughed and shrugged and nodded and said "Okay."

They pointed at us and called us Liu Chiu, which means "friendly" or "easy."

·

The Chinese showed us how to grow food: rice, sweet potatoes, and bitter melon. For that, we are grateful. They showed us
how to carve up the land with fences and lock up the land with
gates, and build castles on rocky mountaintops to protect these
portions of land known as "kingdoms." They showed the nebito
and negami how to wear robes and move into castles. Some of
the nebito became anji, lords, and some of the anji became kings.
Some of the wives became queens, and some of the sons and
daughters became princes and princesses. Some of the negami
became noro, high priestesses, who built shrines and kept fires
burning in the courtyards.

We were divided into three kingdoms: Hokuzan, "Northern
Mountain"; Chuzan, "Central Mountain'"; and Nanzan, "South-
ern Mountain." We became Sanzan, "Three Kingdoms." The
leader of these three kingdoms was Chuzan, because of the harbors, and the capital of Chuzan was called Shuri, which means
"first village," built on the highest mountaintop, with views of
the sea from every direction.

In the hills and forests and shores, most of us still shared the
land. Most of us still caught fish. We all still wore our long hair
tied in knots on top of our heads, held in place by wooden pins.
Those were our crowns.

·

Whether king or lord, high priestess or humble negami,
farmer or fisherman, merchant or peasant, we all still bowed to
China. Once a year, for five hundred years, we paid tribute.

They let us borrow ships, and we sailed to their capital,

bringing woven cloths, pottery, urchin, conch, and miyako uma, our native horses. Small, sturdy, docile, eager to be trained and ridden. The Chinese greatly admired our horses.

In return for our tribute, we received many gifts. Lodging in the palace, banquets, fans, umbrellas, trinkets. They offered us silk, but we preferred iron. Also gifts of knowledge. We were able to look upon the paintings, hear the instruments, read the books about law and religion. They taught us how to be civilized.

Impressed with our skill at seafaring, the Chinese let us retain a few ships for ourselves, and we sailed to ports in Japan, Korea, Vietnam, Cambodia, Siam, Malacca, Djambi, and Gresik. We traded rice. We traded pigs and onions. We traded gold, silver, bronze, and copper. We traded fine lacquerware, porcelain, and paper. We earned a reputation for honesty and for refusing to buy men and women, or sell anyone of our own for any amount of profit. When asked, we would tell them, "We'd rather die."

As a license to partake in the privilege of trading with China, a nation is required to kowtow. Each time we arrived and departed at the port, each time we entered and exited the capital, they required us to bend and stretch our bodies flat on the ground, facedown, and then stand upright, nine times, and then bow three times in the direction of the Emperor. We performed this ritual with such graciousness, such sincere precision, that we became known as the "Land of Propriety."

.

Japan refused to kowtow, and therefore trade between Japan and China was forbidden. Therefore, Japan needed us. Japan needed us as mediators.

.

So, one day early in the seventeenth century, men from Japan came, wearing armor and carrying swords. They commanded us to join them and attack China. Attack Korea. Attack our friends. We refused. The men from Japan kidnapped our king at Shuri. They looted our castles. They pointed their swords at us. We had never fought before. We had never owned weapons before. We had always defended ourselves with diplomacy.

But diplomacy couldn't save us any longer.

We were forced to swear allegiance to Japan. We were forced to keep our allegiance a secret from China. We pretended not to understand or speak Japanese. For the next three hundred years, we paid tribute to China, traded with China as if we were independent, yet we belonged to Japan. Almost everything we owned went to Japan. The rice. The onions and pigs. The gold, silver, bronze, and copper. The lacquerware, porcelain, and paper. We became poorer than we had ever been. We would never know prosperity or independence again.

Japan still ruled from afar. So we farmed and fished. We celebrated harvests and the coming of seasonal schools of fish so large they changed the color of the water. We brought guitars and drums to the fields and shores. We sang and danced while we worked. In the evening, we drank wine around our hearths, and the noro told us stories of ancestors who defied foreign kings, ancestors who would rather burn in a fire or drown in the sea than surrender. We spoke our own language. We were still ourselves. We survived typhoons, earthquakes, floods, and famines by ourselves. Without any help from Japan. Or China.

·

In the middle of the nineteenth century, men coming from the east, referring to themselves as the West, came to the island to explore. They coveted our proximity to Japan and China, which they meant to visit more often and gain influence. We welcomed them. We appreciated their interest. We paddled to their ships and brought gifts. Sacks of potatoes, and herbs for the sick. They thanked us. They asked us who we were. We didn't know whether to say Liu Chiu, or Ryukyu, or Sanzan. They asked if they could stay with us for as long as they wanted. We didn't know what to say.

These men from the east, who referred to themselves as the West, made Japan very nervous.

Toward the end of the nineteenth century, some men from the east, called Americans, tried to claim us. They did not know we were already claimed.

.

In 1879, we were officially annexed to Japan. Our kings and queens were exiled to Tokyo. Our kingdoms were dismantled. The land we shared was given to Japanese lords and government officials. Many of us became farmers of sugarcane and pineapple. Crops that were sold, not eaten. Our anji banished. Our noro banished. Our history banished. Our language banished. We were mocked for our accents when we spoke Japanese.

We became an event in a more powerful nation's history. A place for more powerful nations to attack and act against each other.

We became Okinawa, a prefecture of Japan.

IV
ERIZABESU

*M*y name is Elizabeth, which means "God's Oath" in Hebrew. It means I speak the truth. It means God can swear by me. I am named Elizabeth after my father's mother, after my father's mother's mother, after my father's mother's mother's mother, and so on. It is a family name, a queen's name. It is Anglo. It is Western. It is White. Like my father.

I can't remember exactly when I began to notice that my mother didn't pronounce my name the same way as my father. That my father pronounced my name the same way as my neighbors, teachers, classmates, friends, and friends' parents, so therefore correctly. Therefore, my mother's pronunciation was wrong.

*   *   *

I am four years old. I am waiting for my mother to pick me up from preschool. Some of the children sit in circles on the lawn, but I prefer to wait on the porch, where all the lunchboxes are stacked in a row along the banister. I lift each lunchbox, one by one, and look at the lids: Sesame Street . . . Star Wars . . . Strawberry Shortcake . . . Transformers . . . Jem. I carefully select the lunchbox to hold while I sit on the steps of the porch and wait. Not because I don't care for my own lunchbox, which is Cabbage Patch. I just want to hold something new, pretend to be someone else. When my mother arrives, I return the borrowed lunchbox and retrieve my own. No one ever seems to mind. Or I never get caught. My mother is usually the first to arrive, and she hurries me into the car without lingering for a few minutes to have a quick chat with the other mothers.

"Goodbye, Elizabeth! Goodbye, Mrs. Brina!" the teacher says, and waves.

My mother nods and bows.

.

I see her face. I see the faces of the other mothers. I hear her voice. I hear the voices of the other mothers. I compare.

.

These are the first lessons we are taught in preschool. *Which one is not like the others?* We are taught to match. Colors with corresponding colors, shapes with corresponding shapes, fruits with other fruits, a tree does not belong in the group labeled "animal." We are taught that sameness is correct. Sameness is desired.

.

One afternoon when my mother picks me up from preschool, I notice that she has changed. Or rather, her hair has changed. She used to have hair flowing down to her waist like water. She used to brush it a hundred times, twist it in a coil, tie it in a knot on top of her head, and then hold it in place with a wooden pin. I see her step out of the car with her new hair, chopped at her shoulders, blow-dried, curled, and sprayed. She smiles, and when I don't smile, her smile fades. I shake my head. That was her most beautiful part. *Her only beautiful part.* This isn't how my mother is supposed to look. This isn't how women who look like my mother are supposed to look. *Nice try, Mom.*

She is still different. She can't really change.

When my father comes home from work that day, I ask him if he likes her new hair, and he says yes, of course he likes it if she likes it. But I know that means he doesn't. All three of us know that means he doesn't.

.

I don't know what I expect from her, what I want from her. I guess I just want her to be . . . *American.* A White, English-Speaking, Correctly-Pronouncing American.

.

My mother saves her hair in a bright red box, where she also saves a pair of the first socks she knitted for me when I was a baby and the wristband I wore at the hospital on the day I was born.

*   *   *

When I was a child, my mother called me "baby" or "munch-kin" ("man-chu-kin") instead of my name. As I got older, I asked her to stop, to call me by my name. I was still very young, but I wasn't a baby anymore.

.

I sit in the middle of the backseat as she drives me home, as we pass by the freshly cleared fields of corn and newly constructed houses. I can see the inground pools in their backyards through the windshield.

I ask her to say my name, again and again. I ask her to say it, and each time she says it, I laugh. Each time she says it, I laugh, until she realizes I am mocking her. I can see the corners of her mouth tighten and turn down in the rearview mirror.

I didn't mean to hurt her. Or maybe I did.

"Erizabesu . . . Erizabesu . . ." is how she pronounces it.

.

When I was a child, my mother pronounced my name "Erizabesu" because the English sounds were unfamiliar, uncomfortable to her. The textures were off. Because she had to concentrate just a breath of a second longer.

As a child, I made fun of the way she said it. My friends made fun of the way she said it. My friends' parents made fun of the way she said it. We thought it was her fault.

I am five years old. I am sitting in the front part of a big truck, in between my father, who is driving, and my mother, who leans her head against the window. We are moving to a new town, a new state. My father has found a better job, a better place for us to live. He loves the future. He craves newness and possibility and adventure. He is happy. He is always happy when he is taking care of his family. So he drives. My mother has no choice but to follow him. She already made her choice when she married him. She doesn't love the future. She accepts it. She has moved from Okinawa to the United States, as his wife, the wife of a soldier. She has moved from Manhattan to Phoenix to Chicago to Plainsboro, following his jobs, his dreams. She knows she can't go back to her poor island, her poor family. She is not happy. But maybe she is more relieved than resigned. So she leans her head against the window.

And I don't mind in the slightest, staring out the windshield at my old house, my old neighbors, who are waving goodbye, as we pull out of the driveway and turn around. Past and future have no meaning for me. I don't know what it means to miss a place. I just want to be wherever my father is.

Now we live in Fairport. My father has chosen Fairport because it boasts the finest public-school district in the western region of New York State. Well, second best, after Pittsford, the neighboring district, but he can't afford for us to live there. At least, he hopes, not yet.

My father owns a business, a chain of video stores called Shows to Go! . . . During the weekends, I make sure the cassette tapes are inside the right covers. My father pays me three dollars a day until I can save a hundred dollars and then I buy a bicycle, which costs much more than a hundred dollars. During the weekends, I watch movies all day. In the office or on the big TV in the front of the store. One of my favorite movies is *Karate Kid II*, which takes place in Okinawa. I know my mother is from Okinawa, but that doesn't make sense to me. Okinawa is a piece of fiction, as foreign and exotic to me as it is to any other five-year-old kid growing up in the United States. My mother is from Okinawa, but when I have questions about their strange practices, like catching flies with chopsticks, I ask my father, who is the smartest person in the world because he is from Manhattan. I watch the dancing and tea ceremonies with fascination, but I feel no pride, no connection. Mr. Miyagi is also a piece of fiction. A character, a caricature. He is like Yoda, like a doll. He talks funny, like my mother.

.

Fairport has a population of roughly six thousand people, ninety-nine percent white and one percent everything else. The only other Asians I know work at Fuji-Ya, the restaurant where my mother works as a waitress, owned and managed by a Chinese couple, Mr. and Mrs. Lee, staffed by more Chinese, Korean, Japanese, and a couple Okinawans, who work the dining service, as well as Vietnamese, Thai, and Laotian, who work the kitchen service. I can't tell the difference between them. Here, in the United States, Asians are all the same. The details of our histories, languages, and cultures are negligible. Here, in Fair-port, in 1986, Asians/Blacks/Latinos/part-Asian/part-Black/part-Latino are all the same. We are simply Not-White. I don't understand, and I won't, not for a very long time, why I will try to stay as far away from the rest of the one percent as possible. For much of my life I won't want to be associated. Or too visible.

During the week, after school, I sit at a table at the restaurant and roll towels, which will be heated in a big rice-cooker, and I feed the koi fish and fetch pennies from a slate-rock fountain plugged into the wall. I watch the waitresses wrap themselves in kimonos and tie their sashes in elaborate knots. They speak to each other in languages I can't understand, and when they speak to me, they talk funny. Sometimes I still can't understand.

After my father closes the store, he picks me up from the restaurant. He takes me to McDonald's, Wendy's, Burger King, Pizza Hut, or Boston Market for dinner. We watch the news for a while, and then Nick at Night together. We watch *Bewitched, Mr. Ed, My Three Sons,* and then *The Patty Duke Show.* Sometimes I stay up late enough for *Donna Reed,* but that's my least favor-ite. We laugh, and when I don't laugh, he explains the jokes. By the time my mother comes home from the restaurant, I'm already asleep. Sometimes I pretend to be asleep.

•

Sometimes my mother drives me twenty minutes to Penfield, another suburb of Rochester, to visit the dishwasher's daughter. She is Vietnamese. She thinks and speaks in Vietnamese. I think and speak in English. We don't know what to say. We don't know what to do together, except sing karaoke. I sing Whitney Hous-ton, and she sings songs I've never heard before. I sing in English. She sings in Vietnamese. She makes me uncomfortable, because

I see the ways we resemble each other, and I find her quite ugly. She has short black hair, a "flat" face, and "slits" for eyes. She wears glasses. Her clothes are cheap. She lives in The Pines, an apartment complex, where poor people live. I hate how her apartment smells. Like fish.

Sometimes my mother drives me thirty minutes to Irondequoit, another suburb of Rochester, to visit the waitress's daughter. Her mother is also Okinawan. Her father is also White. She also thinks and speaks in English, but she doesn't look like she thinks and speaks in English. She is a "half-breed," a "twinkie," just like me. When I come over, all I want to do is hang out in her basement. We watch *Parent Trap* twice, play fifty rounds of *Super Mario Brothers* and *Duck Hunt*, eat a large pizza and two bags of Doritos. We leave grease and powdered cheese on the controllers. We are fat. We are gross.

I don't understand why my mother wants me to spend so much time with these people. I don't want to understand what we have in common.

.

My father tells me that at school I will finally make friends. But instead, I'm hardly noticed. Except sometimes some of my classmates stretch their eyelids with their fingertips and sing the song "We Are Siamese" from the Disney movie *Lady and the Tramp*. Sometimes they call me Data, the "booty-trap" setter from the Donner/Spielberg movie *The Goonies*. Sometimes they call me Tinker Bell, because of my slanted eyes, or Miss Piggy, because of my pug nose. I don't understand that these names they call me are racist. I am not yet aware of the damage this daily teasing will cause. It seems harmless. Lots of other kids who are uglier and poorer—many of them happen to be my fellow one percent—get teased just as much if not more than me. For much of my life, I will feel as if I have no right to complain. Because being ignored and belittled isn't so bad. I am not feared or hated or oppressed.

.

I start to drop things a lot. I can't open the tiny cartons without spilling milk all over my desk. I can't carry the lunchtrays without splattering food all over the cafeteria floor. As punishment, my teacher says I must stand at the sink to drink my milk, or at the trash can to eat my lunch. For the rest of the week. I become known as the "girl who is clumsy," and this pleases me. Because I am known for something that is cross-cultural, non-restrictive. I start to drop more things. I knock over chairs and bookshelves. I make myself trip and fall. Kids laugh. Teachers yell. And this pleases me. I relish the attention.

Very often in the movies, kids who get laughed at or yelled at turn out okay in the end.

.

When my mother looks at me, she sees her daughter. She sees the part of me that is like her, the part of me that is Okinawan. My hair, my eyes, my nose, my lips, my skin tone, my reserved and deferential temperament. She sees the onigiri, ramen, and miso soup she feeds me every day, unique family recipes I can't help but find delicious. She sees the time I got sick with pneumonia and had to be taken to the hospital, but the doctors were too slow and indifferent, so she fed me a stew of seaweed, green tea, and herbs until I'm cured. She sees the time Obaa carried me on her back, how natural and at ease I looked, pointing and just starting to mumble words in her language. It does not cause her shame or aversion or confusion to see me this way. Because I still come from the same place as her. She just wants to be close. She just wants to be home. She doesn't understand, and I don't either— I won't, not for a long time—why I feel so different from her, why I want so desperately to be so different from people like her.

.

When my father sees me, he sees his daughter. He sees the part of me that is like him, the part of me that is the mind he is trying to shape. My imagination, my proneness to daydreaming. He sees the books he reads to me every day: *Peter Pan, Alice's Adventures in Wonderland, Grimm's Fairytales,* and *The Little Mermaid.* He sees the time he took me to a showing of *Fantasia* at the theater and I was so exhilarated, so grateful, as if he had taken me on a hot-air balloon ride. He sees the time he played Beethoven's *Moonlight* Sonata on the record player and I lay down on the floor so I could get my head closer to the speaker. It causes him pride and adoration and reassurance to see me this way. Because race and ethnicity are incidental, external peculiarities that I can transcend, that he will help me transcend. He will help me be like him, a cultivated American. He will protect me, prevent me from becoming more like her, an outcast, an interloper. He doesn't understand, and I don't either—I won't, not for a long time— how his rearing of me will complicate how I see myself, how I see my mother, and distance me further from her.

.

On Saturday and Sunday mornings, after cartoons, before we go to work at the video store, my father and I make pancakes from scratch, because that is what his father made with him when he was a child. We make a dozen pancakes. My mother sleeps while we make breakfast. She shuffles into the kitchen while we set the table. My father pulls out a chair and kisses her on top of her head. "I'm glad you came to join us!" he says. Sometimes my mother smiles, and sometimes she squints and stares straight ahead. "Would you like one pancake, or two?" he asks. Sometimes she says "one" and sometimes she groans. "Okay, we'll start you off with just one," he says. He sets down a plate and a cup of coffee. "Here you are, my dear." He addresses us both as "my dear," and sometimes this makes me jealous. She wraps her palms around the cup, warming herself with the steam, letting my father be the pleasant one, the gracious one. I kneel and wriggle in my chair, waiting for my plate, looking at my father, asking my father for three pancakes, not looking at my mother, not asking her how she slept, how she feels, how was work last night, not wondering how many days have accumulated before she let herself give up and just hushed. We spread butter and pour maple syrup. My mother is exhausted or hung over, and barely eats more than a few bites. I prefer to lick the batter from the bowl, and barely eat more than a few bites. My father eats six pancakes by himself and throws the rest of them out. He doesn't mind.

.

When we don't have to work at the video store, my father and I spend our weekends at the YMCA in Pittsford. He drives us twenty minutes along the Erie Canal. We catch glimpses of brown water through the trees and talk about what time of year the locks will open or shut. We listen to the radio and talk about the songs we recognize. I can remember titles and the artists who sing them now, and my father is very impressed. We park in the parking lot, outside a big brick building with a neon "Y" sign. We check in at the front desk and are greeted by our names, Mr.

Brina and Elizabeth, father and daughter, because we come here almost every weekend. He goes upstairs to run on the treadmill and lift weights. I stay downstairs and go to gymnastics class. I learn cartwheels, then back walkovers, then back handsprings; then I learn how to do each move on the balance beam. Halfway through class, my father walks through the door and stands against the wall. I wave. He waves. He is the only father who watches, the only father who cares.

At first, the coaches and classmates ask, "Is he your father?" and I say "Yes."

At first, I don't notice their expression, and then I will not understand what it means, and then some of my coaches and classmates will ask, "Are you adopted?" and I will say "No." And then they will pause for a moment to figure out what to ask next.

.

I start going to gymnastics class every day after school. My mother drives me twenty minutes out of her way on her way to work. She drives while I nap. She drops me off at the curb. She doesn't check in at the front desk and isn't greeted by her name. Halfway through class, she doesn't walk through the door and stand against the wall. She doesn't watch. I don't mind.

.

About once a month, one of the YMCAs hosts a competition. My father drives us thirty minutes to Palmyra, forty minutes to Henrietta, an hour to Auburn and Batavia. He sits on the bleachers for hours, chatting with the other parents and pointing at my name on the bulletin board. My coaches and classmates know him. They know he helps pay for the new leotards and the pizza parties. When it's my turn, he watches. Sometimes I win second place in floor, fourth place in beam, eleventh place in vault, but there is no award, no ribbon for eleventh place. On the way home, we dream about training with Bela Karolyi and competing in the Olympics. My father knows this is impossible, but he lets me dream.

.

About twice a year, it's the YMCA in Pittsford's turn to host a competition. If my mother doesn't have to work, she attends. She sits on the bleachers for hours, blinking and nodding, surrounded by the other parents, who are asking her questions and talking too fast. Eventually, they will give up. She smiles at me, but I think she looks a bit odd and out of place, as if she wishes she didn't have to be there, as if she wishes she could just go home. And, to be honest, I also wish she would just go home. I feel bad for wishing she would just go home.

.

Her fear embarrasses me. Her fear is always embarrassing me. At the grocery store, at the mall, she asks me to read signs and where to find things. When cashiers and clerks ask her to repeat herself, sometimes I have to interrupt and speak for her. I'm afraid to let her speak. I'm afraid of how her accent and pronunciation reflect on me.

Or maybe it is my fear that embarrasses her.

.

My father tries to teach me how to ride a bicycle. But he can't teach me, because he only lets me ride on the flat sidewalks beside our house, and he won't let go, because I beg him not to let go. So one day, while my father is at work, my mother takes me to the top of the tallest, longest hill in the neighborhood. "Just go down," she says. "Okay, but don't let go," I say. At first she clutches the seat and runs as fast as she can with me, but then she can't keep the pace of my bike rolling down the hill anymore, so she lets go. I don't panic. I don't lose balance. I ride faster and faster down the hill, and when I get to the bottom, I squeeze the brakes, then stop. I look up at her from the bottom of the hill. She is laughing and clapping. I realize that she has purposely disobeyed me, and I almost get angry. But I'm too excited. For whatever reason, my mother will always trust me more than I trust her.

.

I am seven years old. For Christmas that year, instead of visiting my grandparents in Manhattan, we have to stay in Fairport, because my father has to work. I'm mad I won't get to cross the George Washington Bridge, which is my favorite part of the trip, or see the big tree in Rockefeller Center, or eat linguini with clam sauce and struffoli. I let them know I'm mad. I know exactly what I'm doing.

My mother takes me shopping. I pick out three dresses and three Barbie dolls. Now I have forty. We wrap the gifts together, even though I already know what they are. My mother takes me shopping for my father. We pick out three ties and a wallet. On the night of Christmas Eve, I look beneath the tree at all the presents. Six for me. Four for my father. "Does Mom have any gifts?" I ask my father, as if they would magically appear, as if by Santa Claus. He shakes his head. "I didn't have time, sweetheart. We'll get her something after."

Part of me thinks that's okay, because my mother never really cared much for Christmas. Another part of me knows that's not right. I know that everyone is supposed to get something on

Christmas, not after. So I gather my crayons. I'm going to write "I love you," on a piece of pink construction paper, but somehow an ingenious idea occurs to me, and I decide I'm going to write "I love you" in Japanese. I ask my mother "How do you say 'I love you' in Japanese?" She smiles and says, "Watashi wa anata o aishiteimasu." I ask her to write the phrase on a Post-it note. I carefully copy the hiragana on a piece of pink construction paper, but the lines are all jagged, then cut out and glue a big red misshapen heart.

On Christmas morning, when we sit around the flashing tree to open our presents, I wait until the end of the very brief event to give my mother the gift. I can't decipher her face. It tenses and twists like she is about to cry. I look at the three dresses, the three Barbie dolls, the three ties, and the wallet. We should have bought her something.

Later that evening, I steal the gift, which she has tucked into the top corner of the mirror on her bureau. I tear the gift into pieces and throw the pieces into the garbage. When my mother sees what I've done, she covers her face with her hands and weeps. "Why?" she asks me. Because the gift looks bad, makes me look bad, and it belongs in the garbage. "I'm sorry, Mom. I promise I'll make you a better one"—with glitter and paint, with the lines curved correctly, with a perfectly shaped heart.

But I don't. I never will.

.

A Puerto Rican family moves around the corner from us. The mother, her sister, her two sons, two daughters, wife of the older son, and their baby all live in the same house. It is strange. It is scandalous. The younger daughter is my age. She has crooked teeth and her skin is dark, but she never makes fun of me, because her name is Dorcas. Her name sounds so much nicer in Spanish. Her brothers and sister call me Mitsubishi, but that's really the worst of it. I go to their house every day after school. The mother cooks plantains and chicken stew. Dorcas and I ride our bikes to the convenience store and spoil our appetites on Skittles. My father picks me up after work, looking sharp, wearing his three-piece suit, making the mother and her sister blush, bringing videotapes and video games, as payment for letting me come over and stay all afternoon, for welcoming me and being nice to me. As if such acts require payment.

But then Dorcas and her family have to move. Back to Puerto Rico. Suddenly, and we don't know why. She calls once in a while, but eventually she forgets how to speak English, and I forget about her.

.

I am nine years old. My father's stores have gone out of business. Now we have to move, too. He considers Manhattan, but he can't afford to live in the nice parts and send me to a fine private school, like where he went, without borrowing money from his parents, which they gladly would have loaned. My father is a man, a strong man. He's a "rugged individualist," words he spews at the talk-show hosts. He can do everything by himself. Besides, my mother and I aren't too keen on the idea, either. She has her job at the restaurant, and I have a vengeful desire to belong right here, in Fairport.

So we move into an apartment complex. Not as bad as The Pines but, still, an apartment complex. I finally make friends, though. Their names are Tiffany, Meghan, and Shannon. They're poor. "White trash," I hear people say. Their parents are divorced. But they're pretty: blond-haired, blue-eyed, fair-skinned, and freckled. And they want to hang out with me. Sometimes they call me Tinker Bell. Sometimes they call me Miss Piggy.

I am so happy about having friends that I don't care how badly they treat me. I don't care that, when we go on dates with the New Kids on the Block, I must be paired with Danny, who looks like a rat, so they say, even though Jonathan, the second ugliest, so they say, is totally available. I don't care that one time they steal three large vases of coins from my mother, coins she has saved from years of waitressing tips, and blow it all on games at a carnival. I don't care that another time they steal a diamond necklace—the diamond necklace my father bought for her, the only diamond necklace he ever bought for her—from my mother's jewelry box. Or that they steal cash from her secret wallet in the first drawer of the china cabinet.

I don't care, because I've already learned that people like me—and especially people like my mother—aren't important.

.

When I'm in fifth grade, a black kid moves to our town from Houston. Now we have three. All of our friends think we would make the cutest couple. On a Saturday, on the playground in the fields behind our school, they demand that we kiss. I close my eyes. I lunge forward, but that's a mistake, because girls are supposed to stand still. I bash his teeth with my teeth and bust his lip with my braces.

They laugh at us. He dumps me the next day.

.

In middle school, the names get worse. Sometimes they call me Chink or Gook, and when I tell them I am not Chinese or Korean, they call me Jap, as well as a more original yet terribly unclever pejorative, "Gorilla Woman," because of my flat face, pug nose, and thick eyebrows. They tear pictures of gorillas, chimpanzees, and monkeys from magazines, then shove them into my desk and locker.

This is the year 1992. This is before the obligatory people of color are exposed to mainstream America through Gap and T-Mobile ads. I guess I look strange, unfamiliar. I guess the way I look makes them uncomfortable. We are still extras, one-dimensional villains and sidekicks.

.

But I don't know if anything can account for how cruel I am to my mother.

.

I ignore her as much as I can, disregard her as much as I can. I rush off to bed just before she comes home from the restaurant. I pretend to be asleep. I don't want to eat the beautiful meals she spends all day preparing when she doesn't have to work. I mock her pronunciation behind her back. I roll my eyes and snicker to myself when she can't read the basic instructions on a shipping label at the post office.

I cut up a bunch of her clothes, dresses and kimonos she has stashed in boxes. I cut them up because they're hers. I cut them up because I need them to sew patches onto my jeans and jackets. I don't bother to ask permission. I mean, she never wears those dresses and kimonos anyway.

.

Sometimes she gets so frustrated at not knowing the words that she hits me. She slaps me across the face, or smacks me on the head repeatedly, or pulls my hair so hard that part of my scalp forms a tiny bump and throbs afterward.

Sometimes my father has to yank her off of me. I never hit her back, though—not because she is my mother and I respect her, but the exact opposite. She is weak. She is a weak woman, who talks funny, and looks strange, and cooks strange food no one else eats.

.

And she gets drunk. Mostly on her days off. She never drinks when she is alone with me. But when she starts, she can't stop.

She drinks sake and wine. And when the sake and wine run out, she switches to bourbon, which is my father's booze of choice.

Sometimes my father has to block her from the front door. She charges and crashes into his stout pillar of a body, trying to escape. Then he wrestles and restrains her, pins her to the floor, until she punches, kicks, wriggles free, and then she starts charging again. She wants to go back to Okinawa, she screams, but she is shit-faced and barefoot and wearing only a nightgown.

Sometimes he has to drag her to the bedroom by her armpits, legs kicking and flailing, screaming, and then he tosses her—gently, of course—onto the bed. She is tired but belligerent, crawling to the edge of the bed, trying to escape again. My father waits at the edge, ready to block her, ready to grab her and toss her—gently, of course—back down onto the bed. He stands guard for the rest of the night, with one foot propped on the edge of the bed and one elbow propped on his knee, assuring me with a smile that she will feel better in the morning.

We stand guard and watch her together, making sure she doesn't leave.

Because even though I don't want her to be my mother, I don't want her to leave.

We stand guard and watch her together, until she whimpers herself to sleep.

•

I wish I had crawled into bed with her, told her not to worry, told her that I am her daughter, I am home. I wish I had been on her side, as she was always on mine.

But I was a little girl then, and more than a little scared and selfish, and I didn't want to be near her.

•

Sometimes I wonder how different our lives might have been if we had lived in Manhattan, even the not-so-nice parts, even Brooklyn or Queens or the Bronx. If we had lived in Seattle or San Francisco.

Or what if I grew up now? Is the world kinder, better now? Or am I just older?

VI

THE GRAY CITY

*I*s it bad luck to rain on a baptism?" my mother asks, peering through the blinds of the window of her bedroom, the master bedroom, with the nicest bed and the biggest TV and its own bathroom. She is wrapped in a towel, her skin and hair dripping wet from a shower.

It is the middle of May. The weather is typical for this time of year in western upstate New York. Chilly. Gray. Clouds swollen with rain. Rochester is ranked fourth in the nation for cloudiest cities in America, with an average of three hundred and four cloudy days a year. Rochester is called "the Gray City," partly because of the perpetual overcast and partly because of the pervasive gloomy mood.

Rochester originated as a boomtown, a hub for the flour-milling industry, then later for the headquarters of Kodak, Xerox, and Bausch & Lomb, but these companies also fell out of favor and relevance. Growing up, before I graduated from high school, before I moved away to Boston, I sensed that Rochester was a city on the demise, a city hoping and pretending to be on the verge of some of the greatness it had once promised itself. I heard about the layoffs of thousands of employees. I heard about the factories shutting down, the local restaurants and shops shutting down, replaced by franchises and gleaming new sections of department stores at Eastview Mall. I heard about retired professionals and college graduates competing for jobs at Barnes &

Noble and Staples, barbers selling haircuts for five dollars. I saw the residents getting older and older, no more kids strutting in packs on the sidewalks, loitering under bridges, jumping from the spans of bridges into the Erie Canal. And that is how I'll always remember Fairport and the rest of Rochester, as a place of steady decline, a place of stagnation. No matter how many Trader Joes and Cheesecake Factories and boutiques and craft beer breweries open for business.

I suppose my parents still live here because I grew up here, because they want me to have a hometown, somewhere to remind me of who I was even if I was someone who felt strange, wrong, out of place, somewhere that could be a fixed marker by which to track my progress. Sometimes I wonder if I would visit more than once or twice a year if they didn't live in Rochester.

"Rain is just bad luck for weddings. Because weddings are usually outside, I guess."

My mother nods. She unwraps the towel from her frail body and folds it around her head. She stands naked, lathering lotion on her arms and legs. My mother has always stood naked and comfortable in my presence. I have always been too embarrassed about my body—compared with hers—to reciprocate. I can see her sagging breasts, the thick red gash that begins at her belly button and disappears into her pubic hair. A Cesarean scar. During labor, the umbilical cord twisted and tangled and choked my baby neck. I almost choked to death. My mother was terrified, traumatized. The reason, I am told, why she never wanted to have another child.

"What are you going to wear?" she asks, balancing on one foot, slipping the other foot through the leg hole of a beige panty.

"Wear?" I toss around the clothes in the duffel bag I packed yesterday, a few hours before my flight was scheduled to depart.

Pajamas. Shapeless cotton dresses. Worn cardigans with patches sewn over rips and tears. "Um . . . what are you going to wear?"

She shows me the dress: long, black-and-white floral-printed, silk. She slips her arms through the sleeves and pulls the dress over her head, adjusting. "This look okay?"

I haven't seen my mother wear anything except black stretch pants and a white collared T-shirt on the days she works, or jeans and a sweater on the days she doesn't work. The obvious suddenly becomes apparent to me, and I realize how important this occasion must be for her. I panic. "Fuck, fuck, fuck."

"What is it? What's the matter?"

"I'm sorry, Mom. I forgot to bring something"—I hold up a dress—"nicer to wear."

"That's okay."

"No. No, Mom, it's not. Fuck."

"Do you want to buy a new dress? You have plenty of time." She removes her wallet from her purse, then hands me a Macy's credit card and twelve coupons. "One of them is twenty percent off."

"Mom, I don't need twelve coupons." I try to hand eleven of them back to her.

"Keep them! Take them with you to New Orleans. They have Macy's there, don't they?"

And here it comes. The guilt. Deluging. Surging. For not visiting enough or calling enough. For not planning ahead and packing a nice dress. For not caring enough to plan ahead. For needing to use my mother's credit card because I can't afford to buy a nice dress on my own. For being a poor graduate student, foolishly and selfishly pursuing my dreams at the age of thirty-three, at the same age she gave birth to me. For keeping these eleven extra coupons, knowing that I will never ever use them.

I drive twenty minutes to the next town, Victor. The sky is gray from rain. The grass and trees are glowing green from rain. I park in the parking lot of Eastview Mall by the Macy's entrance. As I walk through the parking lot, I remember how my mother used to take me to this mall on the days she didn't have to work. We would walk through this mall, in and out of stores: Aeropostale, American Eagle, Express, Gap. We barely spoke. I just rifled through racks and tried on clothes while she exchanged sizes and waited outside the fitting room. She bought me everything I wanted, no matter how much it cost; if I wanted it, she bought it, hundreds of dollars she spent, all her tips from waitressing, in one spree, week after week. I barely wore half of those clothes. We barely spoke. I stop, stunned, in the parking lot. I cover my face with my hands. *This is why I only visit once or twice a year.*

Then I take a deep breath. I ask myself how I can make this right. *How can I make this right, right now?* I tell myself that today is about my mother. I have to be gracious and graceful for my mother. I have to buy a new dress. I tell myself this guilt is not her fault. I tell myself that maybe, just maybe, because this guilt is too much, maybe this guilt is not entirely my fault, either. Maybe it starts before me. Maybe it starts before my mother.

VII

BEFORE THE ENEMY TAKES JAPAN

> No prefecture contributed so little to the war and its
> prosecution . . . but none suffered as much in widespread
> misery, in loss of human lives and property, and in the
> ultimate subservience to military occupation.
>
> —George Kerr, *Okinawa: History of an Island People*

*J*ust outside our old capital of Shuri, along the banks of the Tomari River, beneath the double arches of our most impressive Izumi Bridge, kings and queens, princes and princesses, noble dignitaries and high priestesses, merchants and peasants once came together at the beginning of every fall to watch oarsmen wearing fantastic costumes, standing in boats painted purple, green, and yellow, paddling with all their might, and trying to be the first to pass through.

But that was a long time ago. Water that was clear and pure is now gray and poisoned from garbage and oil slicks that have floated down from the ships at the port in Naha. Our new capital.

.

Now one of us, a man, thirty years old, the only son of a widow, stands in the middle of the dirtied Tomari River, beneath the ancient bridge for shade, pants rolled above his knees, smoking a pipe and trying to catch a fish for breakfast. This man, one of us, will die of diarrhea and thirst in a cave crammed with fifty other sick, wounded, thirsty, hungry, reeking bodies. This river will fill with bullets and shrapnel, blood and maggots. This ancient bridge, a relic from a time when we once knew prosperity and independence, will be destroyed.

*   *   *

The enemy will be here soon. He is coming from the west, from the south, taking back lands the Emperor and His Imperial Army have conquered. We are next, the last line of defense. We feel a certain pride that our small, insignificant island bears so much responsibility. If the enemy takes us, then he will take the rest of Japan. But we have no idea how much and how horrifically he will take.

.

Our hearts sink when we see the Japanese troops arrive at the port in Naha. Only five thousand. We are concerned by how little the Emperor and His Imperial Army are preparing us. The Emperor assures us that seishin, "the National Spirit," will save us. Seishin will overcome any seeming lack of strength or provision. So we donate all of our iron, steel, copper, anything made of metal, even our sewing needles. We donate all of our crops and livestock. We donate all of our hospitals. We donate all of our schools and convert them into barracks. The children are needed in the farms and factories now. We bow low and salute each time we pass a Japanese soldier on the street.

.

We are preparing on our own. Each morning, before dawn, children who are old enough to walk, mothers and fathers, grandmothers and grandfathers, all of us march together to strengthen our bodies. We form long lines from buildings to public wells. We stand together in a line, passing buckets of imaginary water to put out imaginary fires. When one of us throws a stick on the roof and shouts "Shell!" we rush to the building with ladders and climb up the ladders with buckets. When one of us throws a large rock on the ground and shouts "Bomb!" whoever is closest pounces on it with a drenched cloth. When one of us shouts "Air raid!" we quickly lie down on the ground and cover our heads with our hands. We have never fought in a war before. We have never needed weapons. So we chop down tall sticks of bamboo and sharpen the ends. We practice fighting together with homemade spears.

·

In a village on the outskirts of Naha, three hundred and twenty-nine of us are laying the foundations for an underground shelter. We are pounding large stones into the ground with a heavy log tied to a dozen ropes hanging from a pulley. One of us, a woman, the oldest among us, sings a song. When she sings the verse, the rest of us tug the ropes and the log rises. When she sings the chorus, the rest of us join her song and let go of the ropes, and the log comes down with a loud thud. Over and over again, until each stone is settled. We sing in a language that's forbidden, a language the Japanese don't understand.

·

In a field, near a stream, a father crouches on his knees to get eye level with his youngest daughter, seven years old, whose mother died of tuberculosis two years ago. We want to show her which plants are edible and which are not. We pick a handful of herbs and shove it into our mouths. "Now you," we say. We pick a handful of herbs, shove it into our mouths, then we spit it out. "Too bitter!" we yell, drooling and spitting. We grab her face in both our hands and scold through clenched teeth: "Soon there will be no food, so you better learn to eat!" So we take another bite, and, this time, we chew.

This father will die of a stray bullet to the head. This daughter will survive.

*　　*　　*

On August 21, 1944, three ships carrying six thousand children, ages five through eleven, set sail for Japan. Most of us don't have the status or means or courage to part with our children, to leave our parents behind, but those of us who are eligible believe this might be our only chance. Everyone else who stays on the island could surely die.

Besides, who wouldn't want to see the mainland firsthand, a place we only read about in books? Who wouldn't want to see the palaces of Tokyo and Kyoto, the peak of Mount Fuji in the distance, the cherry blossoms in the spring, the leaves changing in the fall, and snow? We have never seen snow.

Our mothers sew our names onto our shirts, pack rice balls into our bundles, and kiss our foreheads, holding back sobs as we board. "It's okay, Mother," we say. "Japan promises to take good care of us."

On August 22, 1944, at two in the morning, a torpedo hits one of the ships. Eight hundred of us, merely children, drown.

*　　*　　*

On October 10, 1944, the enemy makes his first attack on the city of Naha. It starts at sunrise. The sky darkens with planes. The sirens blare. Those of us who haven't evacuated crawl into our underground shelters, our trenches, our holes. Bomb after bomb drops, and the ground shakes. We hear the screeching, the rumbling, the explosions. We hear the flames burst, then crackle. The air fills and fills with smoke. For the rest of the day, we cough and we cower, and when the blasts and shaking stop, we emerge.

Naha is a rubble of burning embers. No buildings, no trees, no grass. Just red embers and black ash.

Except for Shuri Castle. With its high parapets and massive walls of stone, built on the highest mountaintop, erected five hundred years ago. Shuri, our ancient capital, a relic from a time when we once knew prosperity and independence, withstands the enemy. And if Shuri can stand, maybe the rest of us can stand. Maybe there is hope.

When General Ushijima hears about our castle's resistance, our castle's power, he expels the Okinawan guards and replaces them with Japanese officers. They occupy Shuri as their headquarters.

.

For the next several months, many more of us evacuate. But there are no tears, no long goodbyes. We gather our portraits and framed photographs, our beads and jewels, our robes and kimonos, our incense burners and ceramics, heirlooms passed on to us through generations. We bury them in our yards.

We have stopped our morning drills. We know that our marching, our buckets of water, our drenched cloths, our homemade spears are useless.

•

The Emperor sends more troops. A total of seventy-five thousand. By now, we have seen the enemy, the destruction and devastation caused by the enemy, and some of us feel this is too little and much too late. Twenty thousand of us are conscripted. Of those, only forty-five hundred are properly trained. We are beginning to suspect that we are being sacrificed, forsaken. That the Emperor and His Imperial Army do not care if we survive. Our purpose is to show the enemy that death is not a deterrent, that the loss of human life, mostly our human life, will not lead to surrender.

•

Many of us want to surrender. Here, in Okinawa, we believe that life is precious and must be preserved at all costs. We don't believe that dying for one's country is an honor. We don't believe that dying is an honor. So the Japanese lie to us. They tell us the enemy will rape us, torture us, skin us alive, and feed us to dogs if we are captured.

•

A fleet of fifteen hundred ships surround our island. We see them on the horizon.

•

On March 29, 1945, in a village on the outskirts of Naha, three hundred and twenty-nine of us are ordered to leave our underground shelter. We are ordered to commit suicide. We are handed one grenade for every thirty of us, not nearly enough for a clean, instant death. Those of us who don't die right away slice ourselves with razors and strangle ourselves with ropes. Those of us who don't die right away beat each other to death with tree branches, stones, pipes, gardening hoes. Husbands killing wives, fathers killing sons, mothers killing daughters, older brothers and sisters killing younger brothers and sisters.

.

On March 31, 1945, late in the evening, under the cover of darkness, sixty-two of us, middle-school students, assemble in an auditorium to participate in our graduation ceremony. As each of us, one by one, walks up to the podium, we are given diplomas and infantry assignments.

We are thirteen years old. A few of us, who have late birthdays and started school early, are twelve years old.

.

On April 1, 1945, at eight o'clock in the morning, twenty thousand of the enemy invade our shores. General Ushijima waits and watches behind the castle walls. General Ushijima waits for the enemy to come closer, close enough to strike, closer to us.

*   *   *

Fifty thousand. One hundred thousand. Five hundred thousand. The enemy is everywhere. The enemy in the sky flies in menacing circles, like giant evil birds. He searches for movement, shifts of color, then dives closer to the ground, dropping bomb after bomb, shell after shell, and spraying bullets. The enemy on land throws grenades and shoots guns, aiming at the Japanese, but the Japanese retreat among us. They defend and fight among us. The enemy doesn't know or care who we are.

.

During the day, we hide. We hide in caves. We hide in tombs. We hide in shelters and tunnels. We hide in ditches and holes we dig with our bare hands. We huddle together, thirty, forty, fifty of us, crammed into our hiding places. The ground shakes and we tremble. We hear the screeching, the rumbling, the explosions. We hear the flames burst, then crackle. Sometimes we hear their strange voices outside our hiding places, and our chests pound and pound, and some of us die from fright.

.

At night, we flee to the south. We carry bags of rice, sacks of potatoes, carrots, radishes, jars of dried fish and pickled seaweed. We carry babies and small children on our backs. But soon the food will be gone. Soon our bodies will become too weak to carry even ourselves.

We stumble over bodies in the dark. Many of us lose each other. Sisters lose sisters. Brothers lose brothers. One of us, a mother, grabs the hand of a child. The child holds her hand, and we walk together for a long time. The child looks up and realizes the mother is not her mother. We keep holding hands. We keep walking.

We walk with thirst and hunger. We walk with filth and lice. We walk with wounds oozing blood and pus and infection. We walk without shoes. We walk without chunks of flesh, without eyes or ears, without limbs. One of us, a man who lost his legs, drags himself across the ground on his stomach, his hands and elbows bleeding from dragging his body. One of us, a woman, shrapnel bulging from her chest, still alive but just barely, feeds milk from her breast to her infant for the last time.

The farther south we go, the more of us there are and the fewer places there are to hide. The Japanese soldiers guard the caves and do not allow us to enter. They chase us away with their guns and swords. Sometimes they don't even bother to chase. Sometimes they shoot and swing their swords without warning. They kill mothers with babies. They kill children.

Some of us prod our heads into the mouths of caves, calling out "Mother!" or "Father!" or the names of sisters and brothers, aunts and uncles we lost. "Stop shouting! They'll hear you!" we say. Or, even worse, "Go away! There's no room for anyone else!" And it's true. There's not.

Some of us are more welcoming than others. We crawl into a cave and ask if we can stay. "Yes, please stay. You can die here with us."

*   *   *

It takes two months for the enemy on land to reach Shuri from Kadena, a distance of ten miles. The Japanese defend and fight, sniping and shooting, stabbing and slitting throats, bludgeoning with branches and rocks.

.

On May 25, 1945, after fifty-five days of blasting and firing, the walls of Shuri Castle begin to crack and crumble. Nothing is left of the ancient city.

.

Everything in Okinawa is crushed and burned. Our homes, our shops, our schools, our shrines, our temples, our farms, our gardens. All crushed. All burned. Charred black.

.

On June 21, 1945, the enemy has forced General Ushijima and his lieutenants to the high cliffs of Mabuni. General Ushijima and his lieutenants stand on the edges of the cliffs, salute to the sea in the direction of their Emperor, and quietly commit seppuku.

They have done their duty. They have delayed the enemy for eighty-two days. They have bought time. They have shown the enemy what to expect when he reaches Japan.

*   *   *

And now we, too, have reached the end, the farthest south we can go. To the high cliffs and rocky shores. To the adan bushes with their sharp branches. There is nowhere else for us to go, and we don't bother to hide anymore. We sit on rocks and let our skin burn in the sun. Some of us haven't had a sip of water for days. So some of us, who are gods, are merciful and let the sky pour rain. We sit on the rocks, look up at the sky, and let our mouths hang open.

.

We see a band of ships approaching the shore. We see the enemy, with their pale pink faces and straight white shiny teeth, standing on the decks, waving and laughing.

We are ready to die, eager to die.

We hear the enemy's voice through a loudspeaker, in broken

Japanese. "Come out of hiding! We will not hurt you! People of Okinawa, the war is over! The war is over!"

A Japanese soldier tells us not to listen, tells us it's a trick, but we don't care.

How much more harm can the enemy do?

VIII
MIKI

*W*hen I asked my father why I didn't have a Japanese name—that is, a name my mother could pronounce, which I would never dare ask—he answered that he wanted to name me "Elizabeth" after his mother, after his mother's mother, and so on. "Elizabeth" is a family name, a queen's name. My mother, of course, agreed.

But how could she have known how the name would sound to me? That the name would sound like marbles in her mouth, that the "l" and the "th" would get stuck in her cheeks?

.

My middle name, however, is "Miki," which means "tree" or "destiny" or "story" or "beautiful princess" in Japanese, depending on how it is written.

The last definition is the one they chose for me, though not the one I would have chosen for myself. I suppose that is how my parents intended to raise me, as their princess. That is the promise my father represented when he sat on a stool at the bar, in a nightclub called the Blue Diamond, wearing an officer's uniform, smiling with straight white shiny teeth and flashing a wad of crisp cash, ordering a bourbon on the rocks in a language and accent she had heard in movies and songs all her life. He must have seemed like royalty.

*　　*　　*

When I am thirteen, I decide that "Elizabeth" is a common and ordinary name. I decide that I no longer want to be common and ordinary. Or, rather, maybe it is decided for me. I insist that my friends call me by my middle name, "Miki." But the new name doesn't catch. My friends know me as "Elizabeth," as "Liz," as quiet and unassuming and eager to please.

At that age, friends don't let you change so easily.

.

It is ironic that I insist on being called by a Japanese name but I also insist on bleaching my hair blond and wearing fake thick-rimmed glasses that hide the shape of my eyes and the lack of a bridge on my nose. I beg my parents to buy me fake blue-tinted contacts. They refuse, on the grounds of expense and frivolity. They don't mention the term "internalized racism." This term doesn't exist in our vocabulary, especially not in Fairport, New York, especially not yet.

The first time my mother sees my blond hair, she covers her face with her hands and weeps. Maybe she's crying because I'm becoming more independent, more rebellious. Maybe she's crying because I look hideous. My hair is so dark and thick that when I bleach it blond it's not really blond, but more of an aggressive, gaudy orangish yellow. Or maybe bleaching my hair is another sign of rejection. Rejection of her, rejection of where she—we—come from.

I bleach my hair so many times it turns brittle and breaks off at the ends. I chop my hair short and keep bleaching it. Then I start listening to punk rock and dye my hair cherry red, violet purple, and midnight blue instead. I listen to angry punk rock and write the lyrics of angry punk rock songs on the surface of my desk in pen. One afternoon, my Spanish teacher glimpses what I'm writing and sends me to the principal's office. The principal, disturbed by the angry content of the lyrics, sends me to the school psychologist. I visit the school psychologist for four, maybe five sessions. She feeds me hot cocoa and candy. We talk, not about anything important, but when she calls my father to discuss her diagnosis, she concludes that I'm ashamed of my mother, ashamed of being half Japanese (she doesn't know what Okinawa is). My father and I both laugh. "What a hack!" he says, and I agree. I never visit the school psychologist again.

.

When I am fourteen, a boy, a cute boy, two years older than me, a drummer in a punk rock band with hair shaved in the shape of a mohawk, tells me that I would be much more attractive with my natural hair color. I take his advice as a token of kindness, as attention he has generously spared. I promptly dye my hair black. He notices. He compliments. A clear sign I have a chance. I tell my friend to tell his friend to tell him that I have a crush on him. He processes the news with immediate resourcefulness and tells his friend to tell my friend to tell me that he will let me give him a blow job.

"He'll *let* you?" is my friend's offended and appropriate response. We don't know if he's joking, just aiming to shock, a tendency among proclaimed punk rockers. But my response is different. I take his offer as a token of kindness, as attraction, and attraction equals want and want equals value. Because if he would allow my mouth to go so near and around his penis, then he must be at least a little fond of me. I do not yet know of the expression "a blow job has no face"—or a body for that matter, a body attached to a person with a humble desire to touch and be touched. I do not yet know that acts of physical intimacy are not meant to be offered, like alms to charity, like a stick of gum. They are not meant to be passively received or performed or endured.

But nothing else has ever happened to me. I have never held hands with a boy or cuddled with a boy. The last and only time someone kissed me was four years ago, on a playground—yes, on a fucking playground, when I lunged forward instead of standing still, accidentally bashing his teeth with my teeth and busting his lip with my braces. This blow job could be my start, my big break, my opportunity to woo him. I tell my friend to tell his friend to tell him I accept.

It happens in a basement. It lasts less than a minute. It is the least sensual experience of my life. We don't hold hands. We don't cuddle or kiss. He doesn't ask me for my number or ask his friend to ask my friend for my number and call the next day.

.

There really is no such thing as black hair. Only very very dark dark brown hair. Only a brown so dark and so deep it contains many other colors. Sometimes in the sunlight or firelight or lamplight, it reflects tints of yellow, red, purple, even blue, naturally.

After I dye my hair black, it doesn't look right. The color is flat. The color is dead. It takes months for me to grow my hair out, for my natural hair to grow past my ears to my chin. The cute boy who let me give him a blow job ends up dating a blonde anyway.

.

The blow-job offers don't necessarily come pouring in. There are two. I accept both. I also accept when someone offers to finger me while having sex with his girlfriend. I also accept when someone offers to let me put my hand down his pants and fondle his dick in an auditorium, surrounded by our English class, during a staged production of *Hamlet*.

And so on, and so on.

None of them asks for my number. None of them asks his friend to ask my friend for my number and calls the next day.

•

And I don't think this is because they're entitled and insensitive. I don't think this is because they have been encouraged their whole lives—some subliminally, some not—to derive a sense of status and power from exploiting and degrading those of us who are vulnerable. I don't think this is because I'm a member of a race that has been fetishized, because I'm one of the only Asians in a ninety-nine percent white town and therefore undatable. I think this is because I'm doing something wrong, uniquely wrong. I'm uniquely wrong. Just me.

•

When I am fifteen, a boy, a very cute boy, three years older than me, an avid reader and a loyal disciple of T. S. Eliot and Karl Marx, a very cute boy with brilliant red curly hair and a Black Flag tattoo covering a faint scar on his left forearm, returns to Fairport, New York, after living in Flagstaff, Arizona, with his aunt for a year. I see him in the halls of our high school. I see him sitting in the corner, reading poetry, or standing by the double doors of the cafeteria, passing out pamphlets on the proletarian uprising. One afternoon, in between lunch periods, by the rear entrance, I empty a can of pepper spray into a trash bin. Just to see what will happen. Just to get his attention. Then, not knowing what will happen, I inhale the fumes. Students passing through the halls are coughing, coughing, eyes burning and watering. One induced asthma attack. I flee and hide in the bathroom until dismissal. He's the first suspect, of course. Because of his anti-establishment attitude. Because he has a tattoo and a scar. I send myself to the principal's office and confess. I'm suspended for five days. He asks his friend to ask my friend for my number and calls to thank me.

But when we go to diners and parking lots and movies together, we don't know how to talk. His intelligence intimidates me. I try to prove my intelligence, but he retorts and insults me, and I insult him. He's a shy boy pretending not to be shy. I'm a shy girl pretending not to be shy. We're afraid to talk. We fuck it up.

Then he joins the Marines. I don't know why he joins the Marines. He doesn't know why he joins the Marines. Maybe he feels lost. Maybe he feels afraid and weak, like so many boys who join the Marines. He is sent to Camp Lejeune, North Carolina, for boot camp, and then to Guantanamo Bay, Cuba, for his first active-duty assignment. We write each other letters, a letter a week, every week, for two years. We don't hurt or insult each other in these letters. We are brave in these letters. We share sadnesses and fears and best intentions in these letters. We fall in love in these letters. But when he comes back on leave and we see each other face to face, we're still afraid to talk. We still fuck it up.

It doesn't help that while he's gone I give a hand job and a blow job to two of his best friends. It doesn't help that when he comes back on leave his best friends tell him what I gave them, and then he and his best friends call me a slut. "Bros before hos," he tells me when I ask him why he isn't angry with his best friends. It doesn't help that during his second year in the Marines, while guarding the armory, he and his patrol partner play a game of "quick-draw," a game many of the Marines play, a game to occupy long stretches of idleness and boredom, a game to normalize the constant threat of violence, except usually there isn't a bullet lodged in the barrel of the gun. He shoots his patrol partner in the throat and kills him. He's convicted of manslaughter, dishonorably discharged, and sentenced to a year in prison.

And this is a sadness and a fear he can't share with me. Not really. But we try. We keep writing letters. We keep hiding behind letters, promising we'll be there for each other, pretending to be people we're not ready to be yet for each other. My father also writes letters, which I'm not allowed to read. My father can share this sadness and fear with him. My father knows what death is, what killing is. And perhaps this connection between them is what I've always revered, what I've always coveted from this boy with a Black Flag tattoo covering a faint scar on his left forearm.

When he's released from prison, we're still afraid to talk. We still fuck it up. He becomes even more distant. He gets mad at me for no reason. Or rather, a reason that has nothing to do with me. But I believe the reason is me. I'm doing something wrong, uniquely wrong. I'm uniquely wrong. Just me.

.

When I am eighteen, I move to Boston to attend Northeastern University. It is my first time living in a big city, a real city. A city means culture and refinement, maybe even open-mindedness. I believe I'll be different and better here. My life will be different and better here. And this is somewhat true. Sometimes, when I'm walking through a park, standing at an intersection, or sitting on a train, someone, almost always a man, asks me, "Where are you from?"

"Fairport, New York," I answer.

"No, where are you really from?"

I tell him I'm half Japanese (I don't know what Okinawa is). He smiles. Intrigued, enthused, approving. He looks at me like I'm beautiful. It feels glorious. It feels like an achievement.

But I don't know how to wield this attraction. I don't know how to channel this attraction toward respect, toward care, toward love. A precedent has been set. A habit has been formed. I don't know how to make new choices. I don't want to disappoint them. I don't want to defy their expectations. Sometimes it's easier to be what's expected.

I accept when someone offers to let me lose my virginity in the backseat of his Ford Bronco during freshman orientation weekend. I accept when someone offers to pound me from behind on a towel on the floor of the laundry room of my college dormitory.

And so on, and so on.

None of them asks for my number. None of them asks his friend to ask my friend for my number and calls the next day.

.

When I am nineteen, I decide that I must use my exoticness to my advantage. I get a tattoo of my middle name in between my shoulder blades: the kanji inside of a red sun with a white crane flying toward it. The red sun is a symbol of good fortune, and the white crane is a symbol of grace. The premise of my tattoo is a bit ridiculous, because only gangsters and criminals get tattoos in Japan. And the kanji might not be correct (and for the rest of my life I will be too afraid, too ashamed to check if it is correct), because before I get the tattoo I thumb through an English-

Japanese dictionary, consulting my English-speaking American father, because my Japanese-speaking Okinawan mother couldn't possibly know the kanji for my middle name. She never went to high school. She's practically illiterate.

Throughout my life, only lovers will refer to me as "Miki." They will take it as their pet name. They will take it as intimate. Often, they will forget to ask permission. Although I love to hear the sound of it, something feels wrong, fake about it. Maybe because I am not a miki. Maybe because I used to mock my mother for not being able to pronounce my first name.

IX
WITHOUT BEING TAUGHT

I am eleven years old. I am lying on my stomach on the living room floor, too close to the television, watching an episode of *Beverly Hills, 90210*. My father summons me to the dining room table, and I can hardly hear what he says as Dylan declares his love to Brenda, or Brandon declares his love to Kelly, while leaning against a motorcycle or sitting in the backseat of a Cadillac convertible, on a cliff's edge, the city of Los Angeles twinkling below them. Somehow the stories of these characters seem so complex, so compelling, even though they're all leading generally pleasant lives and reciprocating love for each other. My father waits until the commercial, as soon as Noxzema promises to dissolve oil without overdrying. "Elizabeth?" he asks again.

"This better not take long."

I join my parents at the head of the table, with my mother and father on either side of me, with my back turned toward the television, but I can still hear what Brenda or Kelly has to say next if I stretch my ears to listen. My mother sits with her knees bent close to her chest, her nightgown pulled around her legs, her toes clutching the cushion of the chair. Her eyes are wet. My father, as usual, reveals nothing. His shoulders relaxed. His hands clasped. He gets directly to the point.

"Your mother met a man who is very nice to her . . ."

I wake up, just a little, at that moment. And a wakefulness carries through, just a little, beyond that moment. From now on,

I will pay more attention. From now on, I will watch my own life more closely. But I don't understand most of it, not for a long time.

My mother won't let my father finish. "No, stop . . . Just forget it . . . I don't want you to say anything else."

My father doesn't say anything else.

My mother wipes her eyes.

"Can I go watch TV now?"

.

His name was Sonny. And we never spoke of him again, not out in the open, with all three of us sitting together at the dining room table. I never saw him at the house again, after that conversation. I had no idea they were even talking about Sonny until many years later.

I remember his long hair and thin mustache. I remember he wore a black leather jacket, which I thought was cool. I remember he took me to Chuck E. Cheese and Ground Round for dinner, won giant stuffed animals for me, twisted balloons into silly shapes for me, bought Aerosmith and Guns N' Roses cassette tapes for me, because the music he blasted through his car stereo made me smile at the breeze out the open window and think I was cool.

But the most significant detail about him, a detail I hadn't considered as a child, had to be that he spoke Japanese. Sonny and my mother spoke Japanese. They were two of the few people who spoke Japanese in a small suburb of a small city in upstate New York, where people who spoke languages other than English were scattered across miles and surfaced only occasionally. Sonny and my mother found each other at the restaurant, where he worked as a sushi chef and she worked as a waitress.

Even now, I can't truly appreciate the immediate intimacy she must have felt—after spending the majority of her years as wife and mother fumbling for words—finally to be able to converse with someone with ease and grace, to understand and be understood on her terms. Not my father's. Not mine.

I remember that Sonny let me drive his car along the back roads near my neighborhood. The roads were straight and wide, padded by fields and farms. I sat on his lap and gripped the steering wheel. He shifted the gears and pressed his foot against the gas pedal. My mother laughed and cheered in the passenger seat. "Ki o tsukete" she said to him. Be careful.

I remember mentioning to my father what I had learned and who had taught me, perhaps trying to check for signs of jealousy, trying to boast of Sonny's playfulness and leniency.

"You're too young to drive," was all my father said.

He didn't sound jealous. In fact, my father never seemed jealous or suspicious or angry about my mother's hanging out with Sonny so much. And my mother never seemed cunning or anxious or guilty about hanging out with a man who wasn't her husband. For three years, from when I first saw him at the house until I had that conversation with my parents, she never tried to hide Sonny.

Maybe my parents had an arrangement, whether spoken or unspoken. As little as I know now, I knew even less then. I knew that they rarely kissed or held hands. I knew that they slept in separate beds. I was still quite young when I began to detect, to compare, but I knew from watching movies and sitcoms on television, and perhaps even intuitively, that married couples were supposed to kiss and hold hands. They were supposed to sleep in the same bed.

"Why don't you and Mom sleep in the same bed?" I asked my father once.

"Because I snore too loud," was all my father said.

* * *

I am twelve years old, and I have heard this before: their voices loud and bickering. His voice is stern. Her voice is a whine, a protest. He commands her to go to bed, to go to sleep. She refuses. I don't care much for *Melrose Place* anyway. I turn off the TV and walk upstairs.

I walk through the hallway and pass the bedroom. The door is open. I watch him holding her limp body, holding her steady, helping her undress and put on a nightgown. I have seen this before: my mother awake but can't move, can't speak, except in slurs, my father helping her undress and put on a nightgown. He lifts her, like in the movies, one arm cradling her back, the other arm hooked beneath her knees. He lowers her to the bed and kneels on the floor. He leans close, very close, almost as if he wants to kiss her. Instead, he applies cream to her face and wipes her makeup off with a tissue. This is my father when he is most tender, most affectionate: when he is taking care of her, when he must take care of her. My mother giggles at the touch, at the tickle of cold cream on her face. She turns her head and finds me standing in the hallway. She asks my father, "Why is she looking at me like that?"

"Well," my father says, with that same certainty he always possessed, "she's old enough to know what's happening now."

That must have been when she started telling me. She would tell me in slurs and mumbles, in fragments, in tediously repeated phrases and broken—a word I use now with apology—English.

She would tell me that she didn't really love my father, she did, but not really, not . . .

She would tell me that she and my father didn't have sex, not since they first met, and even then . . . the war, probably . . .

She would tell me that I was artificially inseminated, that having me was the reason, having me was the only reason . . .

She would tell me that she agreed to marry my father because he was American, because he was rich—at least, she thought he was rich, because he paid her rent, bought her a car, taught her how to drive, and promised to take good care of her—because she wanted to get out of Okinawa, get away from her sad poor family, especially her oldest brother, who beat her . . .

She would tell me about Sonny, how she wanted to leave my father for him, almost left my father for him, but she couldn't, because of me.

"What do you mean, 'because of me'?" I would ask.

Then she would cover her mouth with her hands. She would cry and say she was sorry, she was sorry, and that she loved me, she loved me.

She never gave me an answer.

.

I used to be angry at my mother for not knowing the answer, for lacking the words to explain herself. But now I wonder if she withheld the answer on purpose. Maybe she didn't leave my father for Sonny because she feared she would lose me. Because if she left my father for Sonny, I might prefer her absence.

.

I used to be angry at my mother for settling, for merely surviving, for not being a hero, a bold and fearless protagonist. I used to be angry at my mother for telling me stories, real stories, without offering any resolution or wisdom. Stories I was too young to comprehend fully, too young to forgive.

.

My mother told me once that shortly after she decided not to leave my father, Sonny started dating another waitress. Another married waitress. She caught them sneaking a kiss in the supply closet.

I never asked her if that shattered her perception of the past, made her doubt the sincerity of his actions, her own judgment. I never asked her about regret, or anything pertaining to who she was as a thinking, feeling, autonomous human being, who she was as a woman. And after my mother stopped drinking so much, she stopped telling me about her life with such raw and desperate openness. I should have asked more questions when I had the chance.

*   *   *

I am thirteen years old. I am lying on my purple-canopy bed, which I hate with all my heart. I am lying awake late at night, watching MTV. I almost exclusively watch MTV. *120 Minutes* is my favorite show, which she interrupts by bursting through my bedroom door with a glass of wine wobbling in her hand. Her lips and the front of her shirt are stained red. I roll my eyes.

"Not now, Mom. Please."

The walls of my bedroom are scribbled with angry lyrics in pen and marker. My parents try to ground me for it, but I just scribble more angry lyrics in pen and marker. I have eight safety pins in each ear, and a safety pin in my belly button, which I pierced myself. I have an ugly shade of orangish yellow hair, which I bleach myself, which won't get as light as I want, no matter how much I bleach, or look right against my skin tone. I am convinced, have concluded from a series of brute facts subliminally absorbed through movies and television, almost exclusively through MTV, that I will never be the lead singer of a punk rock band, I will never attract a punk rock boyfriend, and my mother is to blame. She tells me stories I've already heard, stories I will forget for the rest of my life, while I stare at the screen flickering over her shoulder, at videos I've already seen, videos I will see again tomorrow, far more interesting and important. I tolerate and ignore for about an hour or so, as long as I can, but after a while, she finds a phrase that traps me into attention and outburst.

"Your father is mean . . ." "Your father is crazy . . ." "Your father won't let me . . ." "Your father—"

"Mom, shut up! Leave me alone! Please!"

.

But who else could she tell? Who else knew him as intimately as I did? Who else knew about his quiet, slumbering rage, which occasionally arose and erupted into an explosion of temper? Because we said something ignorant. Because we said something that challenged or shocked—sometimes inadvertently, sometimes not—his staunch belief system of right and wrong, true and false. Who else knew about his persistent irrational fear that something awful would happen to us, something he alone could prevent?

I wouldn't let her say anything bad about my father. It felt like betrayal. It felt inappropriate. Because my father was the parent who took care of us, helped us, always tried to save us. He always knew what to say, and said it so well. I didn't realize then that she needed to free herself from him. That I needed to free myself from him.

.

Eventually, my mother would need to vomit. I would yell for my father. He would run upstairs the moment I yelled. He would lift her by her armpits and drag her to the bathroom, her feet dragging behind her, in between his legs. He would wrap his arms around her waist tightly as she heaved into the toilet. Wrapping his arms around her waist tightly, he informed me, helped the heaving hurt less.

Sometimes, if I didn't yell for my father in time, there would be accidents. Sometimes she puked in the sink, in the trash, on the floor, on herself. Sometimes, as she was rushing to the bathroom, she fell down the stairs. The stairs were carpeted and divided by floor sections, so she didn't have to fall too hard or too far. But sometimes she hit her head on the wall. One time, she hit her eye on the doorknob, and her whole socket turned dark purple, almost black, eyelid gorged and swollen shut, and I cry sometimes when I remember how awful her eye looked, because maybe I shouldn't have been yelling at her and begging her to leave me alone.

My father would clean up the mess. Fetching sprays and paper towels, ice packs and aspirin, sitting on the rim of the bathtub until she passed out, slumped over the toilet. Then he lifted her, like in the movies, and carried her to bed.

.

I used to be angry at my father for letting my mother get so drunk and burst through my bedroom door late at night. I suppose he needed a break. I suppose he wanted his wife and daughter to share some quality time together.

.

I used to be angry at my father for marrying a woman who wasn't good enough for him, for marrying a woman simply because he wanted to save her. I suppose the concept of "good enough" is entirely subjective, inflicted, as is the concept of "saving" or "being saved."

.

My father told me that when he started dating my mother he used to pour bottles of booze down the drain. She kept replenishing her stash, and he kept pouring.

"Are you stupid?" she asked him. "You're just wasting money!"

After that—he laughed as he told me—he stopped pouring bottles of booze down the drain.

Was this a gesture of total acceptance, refraining from judgment? Was this a gesture of unconditional love?

.

We never uttered the word "alcoholic." We never discussed her drinking. Because she didn't get drunk—certainly not *that* drunk—more than once or twice a month, definitely not more than once a week. Because her drinking was normal to us, a standard condition of our lives, and very often change is too scary even if it might be for the better. Maybe we were afraid to offend her, insult her for consoling herself the only way she knew how. She had a hard life, a sad life. Didn't that warrant some self-medication?

Or maybe our denial came from a deeper, darker place. What would happen if we removed the booze? If my mother didn't have it as a means to make herself visible to us, vulnerable to us, to divulge her secrets? If my father didn't have it as a reason to nurse and look after her? If I didn't have it as an excuse to resent and look down on her? What would happen if it were just the three of us? What would we have to face about each other, about ourselves? Maybe we were afraid to admit that none of us had the resolve or inclination to replace the booze, that my father and I weren't willing to be there for her the way she needed, to love her the way she needed, that the pain she was trying to numb was partially our fault.

*   *   *

I am fourteen years old. I am lying in the backseat of our car, pouting, giving my father the silent treatment as he drives us to the store. I can't be left at home alone, because I am grounded, banished from television. My grades are bad—flunking science, math, PE—and, furthermore, I stabbed the living room couch with a kitchen knife a bunch of times after watching the video for "Longview" by Green Day.

My father has assigned a list of books for me to read during my punishment, and despite my best adolescent efforts to rebel and set myself apart from him, I have brought one of these books, *Great Expectations*, with me. I am reading along to the rain dribbling against the windshield, and weeping at the ending.

I close the book. I don't look at him, but I can feel his pride fill the car. I know he is smiling, nodding. This is how we know we are connected.

I wait until the sobbing eases, until my voice steadies. I climb into the passenger seat and we talk. The whole way to the store. The whole way back. Through dinner. Until my mother comes home from the restaurant.

.

My father and I talked. And talked and talked. We talked about the minutiae of our daily activities, about religion, history, politics, and current events. As a child, I heeded and regurgitated all of his bold and brash opinions. That the God of the Old Testament was, in fact, the Devil. That the expanse of Western civilization was proof of its superiority. Together, we believed in the absolute democratic necessity of the Second Amendment, in the noble dignity of Richard Nixon, that O. J. Simpson was innocent. As a teenager, I dissented. I would choose an opposing side just to practice my rhetoric, but hadn't yet allowed myself to become aware of any intrinsic harm in his ideology. We argued and argued, and relished each debate, because we only disagreed on a superficial level. I still sought his pride, his approval.

We disagreed about almost everything except books. Together, we believed that books were the best teachers. That books showed us how to live with courage and compassion. My father taught me that about books. When I asked for advice, he had plenty to offer. Often accompanied by a quote:

"Grow your own legs, Ham."
—Jack London

"No legacy is so rich as honesty."
—William Shakespeare

"A mind, once stretched by an idea, can never return to its original dimensions."
—Oliver Wendell Homes, Jr.

"Whatever you do to the least of us, you do to me."
—Jesus Christ

My father and I talked and talked. Talked fast. My mother's eyes would dart back and forth, trying to keep up, trying to understand. She didn't read books, not even in Japanese. She quit school before she finished eighth grade, and for the rest of her life she worked hard with her body. No time for books. My father and I rarely had the patience to pause, to slow down, to switch to topics she might enjoy. When we sat at the dining room table together, my mother and father on either side of me, my body and gaze instinctively turned toward my father.

*　　*　　*

I am fifteen years old. I am pouring bourbon into a shot glass, all the way to the brim. I swallow it in a single gulp. I feel nothing. I pour another. I drink. Feel nothing. Pour another. Drink. Nothing. I want to feel something. I don't know that it takes longer than a few seconds to feel something. I am standing at the kitchen counter, pouring and gulping above the sink. My parents wake to the sound of me laughing and hauling the big trash bag outside to the dumpster. It is the middle of winter, and

I'm marveling at how I don't need a coat. My skin buzzes with warmth.

"Elizabeth?" my father asks, standing at the front door.

"Taking out the garbage is soooo fun!"

"She's drunk," my mother says, hunched behind my father, shivering.

I can't remember what I said or did after. Flashes of me slumped over the toilet, my father handing me aspirin and a glass of water. The next morning, I wake up with all the warmth I felt the previous night concentrated in my gut, burning hot, and an electric pain throbbing through my skull. My father cooks me a baked potato for lunch. He spares me the lecture. So does my mother.

.

I am sixteen years old, and drunk at a party. My best friend and I sit across from each other, cross-legged on a shiny tiled floor. The bodies crammed above us are just a bunch of noisy blurs. We are invisible down here, invincible down here. We share a bottle of strawberry-flavored vodka, one chug and pass, one chug and pass, until the bottle is empty. We can feel it working. Our lips and the tops of our heads tingle.

"Wanna make out?" she asks.

"Yes!"

We giggle and kiss softly with the wet part of our lips. We don't kiss because someone is watching, or because we want someone to watch. We kiss because we are new best friends having fun. But her boyfriend eventually spies us. He crouches down to the floor and shoves his face between us.

"Let's go upstairs." He grabs our hands and pulls us up.

We can't say no because he is her boyfriend. We can't say no because I already have a reputation for saying yes to anything anyone asks.

.

I am eighteen years old, and my boyfriend has called me drunk at two o'clock in the morning. I haven't heard from him in a week, not since the last time he called me drunk at two o'clock in the morning. I call a cab to his apartment. I pay for the cab myself.

We are having sex, and then, suddenly, he flips me onto my stomach and shoves his dick up my asshole. He doesn't bother to ask permission. I can't say no, because he is my boyfriend. I can't say no because we are already having sex. I already have a reputation.

This happens twice before he finally decides to break up with me.

.

I am twenty years old, and it happens again.

.

I am twenty-two years old, and I'm dating an agoraphobic. He's a fellow philosophy major at Northeastern University. He can't graduate, because he can't finish one paper to pass one required class. He writes nonsense for sixty pages. He reminds me of the character Jack from *The Shining*. He takes out the garbage once a month and collects trash bags underneath the kitchen table, and his apartment smells of rotting food scraps. He orders delivery for every meal, including two large bottles of Coca-Cola and two packs of Marlboro Reds. We eat pizza, burgers, burritos for dinner. We play video games until six o'clock in the morning.

By the time his parents drive from New Jersey to Boston to bring him home to live under their supervision, I'm nearly two hundred pounds. After he leaves, I'm relieved that I never see or hear from him again.

.

I can't remember exactly when it started. Eleven, twelve, thirteen years old. I developed an intense, frantic desire to be in love. The kind of love that exists in sitcoms and movies. The kind of love that is total acceptance and consumption of another person, a feeling of wholeness, nothing left lacking that could lead to loneliness, regret, an affair. The kind of love that could undo unhappiness, prevent me from becoming my mother: married to a man who hardly touched her, who treated her more like a daughter than a wife. The kind of love that could redeem her sacrifice, a sacrifice I always resented. I threw myself at boys, saying yes to anything any of them asked, hoping they would succumb to gratitude and throw themselves back.

.

My father was the best at consoling. At twenty-three, twenty-four, twenty-five years old, I would call him drunk and bawling in the middle of the night after every breakup, after every one-night stand, fling, delusion of possibility. He never grew tired or reluctant. He never mentioned the obvious, that I was repeating the same behaviors, again and again, and expecting a different result.

"I should have seen this coming," I would say.

"You're an optimist."

"It's humiliating."

"Don't be so hard on yourself, Elizabeth. You didn't lie. You weren't cruel. Believe me, your guard will go up naturally. Your heart will harden on its own."

That's how he talks. Like a book. He teaches me, guides me.

.

My father taught me love and kindness. For that, I am grateful. I will always be grateful. However, over the years I began to realize how dependent I was on his teaching, his love, a love that could never be matched, both a blessing and a curse. I began to realize how much easier it was for him to teach me. In his country. In his native language.

And for all the lessons he learned and taught me, why didn't he learn and teach me Japanese?

.

When I tried to talk to my mother about breakups, it took twice as long. I had to slow down, reiterate, correct details.

"Oh, come on. Why are you so upset? He doesn't like you. Just forget it."

Which is also good advice.

.

I know my father loves my mother, has always loved my mother. I know this because he brings her a cup of tea while she puts on her makeup every morning. I know this because he arrives at the restaurant to pick her up thirty minutes early and waits so she doesn't have to wait, and kisses her on the forehead while she sleeps before he goes to bed every night. I know this because he asked her to marry him, and since then he has stayed loyal, stayed devoted. He stayed. He never thought of leaving, only of letting her leave. I know my father loves my mother, has always loved my mother, but it is a complicated love, and I don't pretend to know the extent of the complication of his love for her, of anyone's love for anyone else. I know my father loves my mother, but I don't know if he truly thinks of her—or me—as equal.

We are women.

.

Now, whenever I argue with my father, his opinions no longer seem harmless and amusing. They seem dangerous and disturbing. They are the opinions of a man clinging to a power he is slowly losing, a power he won't admit to having. But I try not to get too angry. He can't help how he was raised.

Neither can my mother. Neither can I.

*   *   *

I am twenty-six years old. I am visiting for the weekend, sitting at the dining room table, my mother and father on either side of me. We have just finished a meal my mother spent hours preparing to welcome me home. My father and I delve into our typical rant-exchange, shouting over each other about capitalist warmongering and the fallacy of laissez-faire economics. We ignore my mother as her eyes dart back and forth, as she drinks two bottles of wine by herself. We ignore my mother as she slides off the chair, bends down on her hands and knees, and crawls under the table. We don't even notice. But then she starts screaming and kicking the table, kicking it up from below it, kicking it up as it crashes to the floor. Plates and silverware bounce. Glasses topple. My father reaches under the table and grabs her foot, but she kicks him in the chest. She keeps screaming and kicking. His chest, his shoulders, swatting away his arms and hands. He can't get a grip on her. He can't hold her.

I would usually retreat from these episodes. I would go upstairs, turn on the television or blast music. I would try to get as far away from her as possible. But for some reason, that evening, I stayed. For some reason, right then, I felt old enough to take care of her, take responsibility. When I looked under the table, I didn't see my mother. I saw me. I saw a woman hurting. I saw a woman fighting to be acknowledged and understood. Fighting to matter.

Sometimes, in real life, change can happen in an instant. This change, this epiphany of connection, that her trauma is my trauma, that our pain comes from the same source—this change is permanent. But sometimes, at first, it doesn't last. It goes away and comes back. Then goes away and comes back.

.

I bend down on my hands and knees. I crawl beside her. I speak with a voice low and soft.

"Shhh . . . Mom, please . . . Stop."

She curls up like a baby and hugs herself.

I curl up beside her and hug her like a baby.

"I'm sorry, Elizabeth . . . I love you."

"Shhh . . . It's okay, Mom. I'm sorry, too."

We stay under the table and cry for a long time. We cry for everything we can never be for each other. We cry because we forgive each other. Because if it's not her fault then it's not my fault. Because words are meaningless.

We stay under the table until she falls asleep. Then my father lifts her, like in the movies, and carries her upstairs.

X

MY MOTHER'S CHURCH

*T*he Rochester Japanese Christian Congregation doesn't have its own church. It doesn't have its own name on its own sign mounted to the front of its own building.

Each week, through collective donations, the congregation rents a small room from Atonement Lutheran Church. A church with a steeple and a giant wooden cross, with its own name on its own sign—own two signs—one mounted to the front and one posted on the lawn at the beginning of the driveway. Each week, the forty or so members drive twenty minutes, thirty minutes, one hour, sometimes two hours to meet in a room with a separate entrance behind the church.

The room doesn't have a high-arched ceiling and stained-glass windows, or an altar and pews, or decorative paintings and sculptures. The low ceiling has suspended foam tiles and plastic shades that cover fluorescent light bulbs. The single window overlooks the parking lot. Folding chairs are arranged in rows. The walls are bare. At the front of the room, where service is conducted, there is a podium and a microphone, a guitar and a keyboard, a laptop and a screen for projecting slide shows.

•

My father opens the door and holds it open for us as he shakes the rain from his umbrella. He wears a suit, the only suit that still fits since he retired several years ago. I follow my mother into the room, both of us carrying a tray of sushi. My mother wears a long black-and-white floral-printed silk dress. I also wear a long black-and-white floral-printed silk dress, the dress I bought from Macy's earlier. The dress feels strange because it's new, because it's not a dress I would usually wear, but today I want to look more like my mother, more like her daughter. We set the trays on a folding table, beside bowls and platters wrapped in aluminum foil. My stomach grumbles. I wish we could eat before the service begins.

The room is bright and warm, filled with faces I don't recognize and the rhythms of chatter I don't understand. A tiny woman, much shorter than my mother, much older than my mother, with gray permed hair and a protruding curved spine, gasps at the sight of me.

"Kyoko! Kyoko!" She points at me. "Musume desu ka?" *Your daughter?*

"Hai, hai," my mother says. "So desu." She nods proudly, then smiles and blushes.

The woman grabs my hand. Her hand is smooth and cool to the touch, inviting. "Honto? Kawaii desu ne." *Really? Pretty, huh?*

"Hai," my mother says and nods again. "She is very beautiful," she says for my benefit.

More women crowd around us, greet us. They bow. We shake hands, and their hands linger. The women interrogate my mother in their gentle voices.

"I didn't tell them you were coming. I wanted to surprise them," my mother explains. I know my mother didn't want to tell them I was coming until she was absolutely sure I was coming. Until I actually showed up. Until now.

The guilt. I force it down.

"We're so happy you came. She talks about you all the time.

This means so much to her. To us," says another woman, much taller than my mother, much younger than my mother, with dyed streaks of auburn hair and matching eye shadow.

"Thank you," I say, embarrassed. I mimic her bow.

Another woman, much younger than me, a transfer student from Osaka, studying hospitality and tourism management at the Rochester Institute of Technology, asks me why I don't speak Japanese. She clearly doesn't understand the laden sting of such a question.

"I don't know," I answer, as I ponder the reasons.

"You should learn," she says, as if it's that easy. As if I can purchase a Rosetta Stone tomorrow and become fluent enough to have a meaningful conversation next week. "I speak Japanese, Mandarin, and English." Then she proceeds to try to sell me some type of insurance. She gives me a business card, but I don't have a wallet or any pockets, so I hold the card awkwardly in my hand until my mother comes to my rescue with her purse.

"Don't worry about her," my mother whispers. "She's kind of . . . weird." She pronounces "weird" as "wared."

We laugh at the weird girl's expense.

.

The Rochester Japanese Christian Congregation meets once a week to worship the same religion, to worship God and Jesus Christ, but also to commemorate their shared language and culture. The congregation is made up of people who found each other in crowds, in the aisles of grocery stores, at their children's school concerts and field trips, eating or working together at Japanese restaurants. They could see right away, hear right away, that they're not from around here. That they're from the same place. The Rochester Japanese Christian Congregation has been a people long before it was officially founded by Reverend Dong Ki Kim and his wife Miki Kim in 2004.

Reverend Dong Ki Kim, also known as Sensei Kim, is from Korea, and his wife, Miki-san, is from Japan. They met in 1979, in Kumamoto, Japan, at a Lutheran church, where Sensei Kim had traveled for his mission and Miki-san attended as a member. At the time, Sensei Kim couldn't speak Japanese and Miki-san couldn't speak Korean. But they learned each other's languages together. They got married. They lived in Kumamoto, then in Okinawa, and then in Korea so that Sensei Kim could receive more training and become a pastor. They moved to the United States so he could study social work at the University of Rochester. Their plan was to move back to Korea, but they found a people and a need here. They found a way to serve God and Jesus Christ here. Now Sensei Kim and Miki-san are fluent in Korean, Japanese, and English. Together, they conduct a Korean service in the morning and a Japanese service in the afternoon. Once a month, they conduct an English service for the husbands and children.

They founded the congregation as a way of spreading the doctrine of Christianity, but also to give their congregation an opportunity to meet once a week and simply exist in a place where their shared language and culture, their collective identity, are dominant. A place that is completely theirs, even if it's just a small room rented from a big church with another name on its own sign.

It could be worse.

·

I don't know when my mother first heard about this congregation. I don't know why she decided to join eight months ago. I asked her once, and she answered that she was too old and too tired to work at the restaurant for twelve hours a day, six days a week, and she needed something else to do with her time. I'm not completely satisfied with that answer. Maybe I should try to ask her again.

But if I had to guess, and that's completely what I'm doing, guessing, maybe she joined the congregation because of her younger sister, who died of liver failure at the age of fifty-two. Maybe she joined the congregation because of her mother, who hardly drank alcohol, watched her husband die from it, watched her children suffer from it, and died at the age of ninety-nine, five years after her youngest child died. Maybe my mother joined the congregation because of the gastrointestinal illnesses she sustained as the result of extreme alcohol consumption, the two surgeries she underwent to fix the part of the inside of her body that was broken. At the age of sixty-seven, she could feel—really, really feel—her body aging and getting weaker, her body reaping the consequences of choices she made and choices she was forced to make, choices she didn't have. Maybe she finally understood that she needed to stop drinking to save her life, save the rest of her life, and she decided to live and make the best of it. To make herself at home.

Before she joined the congregation, before she stopped drinking, maybe she was resisting. Maybe she was keeping a barrier, keeping her distance, allowing herself a figment of an escape. Maybe she was drinking to numb herself but also to feel—really, really feel—her sadness, keep it close to her, keep it around her. I remember when she used to call me drunk and sobbing, used to tell me she wished she could leave my father, wished she could go back to Okinawa. Sometimes I used to say, "Mom, I just want you to be happy," and I hoped that I was giving her my blessing, hoped that she would take a leap of faith, a leap of change, and explode her life wide open. I remember I used to be disappointed in her for not having the guts to pull out the pin. I didn't know how it felt to be trapped in my life, trapped in the choices I made and was forced to make, choices I didn't have. After her younger sister and mother died, there was no reason to go back to Okinawa. She was alone in the world. Except for her husband. Except for her daughter. Except for her co-workers at the restaurant, the restaurant where she worked as a waitress, hostess, bartender, substitute line cook, substitute sushi chef, and, ultimately, a manager. Except for her friends who joined the congregation. She took control. She made herself at home, made herself happy. And maybe that's when her husband and daughter finally welcomed her.

.

Shortly after my mother recovered from her illness, her surgeries, my father arranged to have a special satellite dish installed so that every television in the house received NHK, Japan's national public-broadcasting network. She turns on the channel the moment she wakes. She watches the channel while she does her stretches and exercises, while she cooks and folds laundry, for an hour or two in the afternoon between shifts at the restaurant, for an hour or two before she falls asleep for the night. News, talk shows, game shows, food shows, concerts, soap operas, sumo wrestling. Japanese filling the room. My father watches, too. Sometimes they watch together. Sometimes they watch the same shows in different rooms.

.

The Rochester Japanese Christian Congregation is almost all women, all middle-aged or older. More than half of these women are married to white American husbands. When the white American husbands attend the service in English once a month, they hover in the corners and stand along the wall, keeping to themselves, nodding and smiling at their wives, happy for them. They usually have a lot to say to each other, comparing stories from their younger days as soldiers, marines, sailors. All of these white American husbands served in the military and were stationed in Japan and Okinawa.

Business thrived in the war economy of such towns as Koza and Kin. "Those days we really raked it in," the owner of a nightclub in Kin recalled nostalgically when I interviewed him in 1996. Located just across the highway from Gate Two of the Marines' Camp Hansen, the amusement area remains there on a much smaller scale today. But during the Vietnam War, Kin was a town that never slept, where the lights burned brightly all night, crowded with soldiers on their way to Vietnam or on leave from the war for two-week "R&R" (military slang for rest and recuperation). At his club, which employed twenty hostesses, soldiers spent money like water, throwing so many dollars around there was no time to count them. "We stuffed them into buckets, but they still overflowed, so we had to stomp the piles down with our feet," he said. "Some months we made $1000. Dollars rained on us."

—Etsuko Takushi Crissey, *Okinawa's GI Brides*

*O*ur mother and older sister disappeared in flame, then smoke. Grandmother lost her sight, and Grandfather lost his limbs. Grandmother and Grandfather tell us to leave them behind. We beg them to let us stay. We don't want to be alone.

"We will fetch water for you. We will scratch your backs, pick off maggots, and squeeze the pus out of your wounds for you. Please let us stay here and die with you."

We beg and weep for two whole days, but they still refuse.

"You're too young to die just yet. You can't give up. You must go."

So we obey. We find a hole in the ground. We leave them in the hole with the rest of the food, not much, just a jar of miso paste and some dried squid. We cover the hole with branches. We cover the branches with dirt. We place stones in the shape of a circle on top of the dirt. We call to them through the dirt and branches, saying goodbye one last time, promising to return when the war ends and bring their bones to our ancestral tomb. They do not answer us.

We hope they die calm, sleeping beside each other. We hope they breathe their last breaths in silence, after the bombing and shooting finally stop.

When the war ends, we return to the hole, but the hole is gone. The Americans have built a road over it. We search for scattered bones along the side of the road, but the road keeps widening. The Americans build roads over tombs and graves, marked or unmarked. The Americans build roads through smoldering fields, through embers and ashes of homes. The Americans build roads in between stations and camps, clusters of tents expanding and spreading so fast we can barely recognize our island from one day to the next.

The Americans can build in a day what takes us months to build.

The Americans can destroy in a day what we will never forget.

We will never forgive ourselves for leaving Grandmother and Grandfather behind.

We will never forgive the Americans.

.

Inside the camps, we stand in long lines so soldiers can feed us. They feed us food stuffed into tin cans that doesn't resemble any food we have ever eaten before. They feed us popcorn and candy. If we are suspected of saying or doing anything un-American, our rations are withheld. Inside the camp, doctors and nurses tend to our sicknesses and wounds better than we ever could. If one of us asks for water, they bring us water. We used to tell ourselves that drinking water would make us sicker, because we didn't have enough. Inside the camp, we live in tents. We sleep on the ground, and when it rains, we sleep in mud. Inside the camp, we wear discarded uniforms. Our children run around in shirts five sizes too big, and sometimes we sew clothes from torn parachutes.

Outside the camp, we are afraid to walk alone.

.

A crowd of us has gathered on the road beside a field. We are watching as one of them, a young man, twenty years old, drags one of us, a young girl, sixteen years old, from a tent across the camp, and then across the road into the field. Her mother, one of us, clings to his leg, begging, wailing, making awful animal noises that force us to watch. He kicks the mother off his leg and drags the girl farther into the field. He rips off her clothes and pulls down his pants. We watch because we want to bear witness. We watch because bearing witness is the only power left within us. We watch because the horror doesn't frighten or madden us anymore.

We watch until he is done with us, until our mother crawls to us, then wraps a blanket around our stunned and trembling body. We watch, and those of us who can bear it look him directly in the eyes. We want to make sure he sees us. We want to make sure he knows we are watching. We don't scold or attack him. We don't seek revenge. We just keep walking. Because that is the only power left within us. We don't want to fight. We are done with this war.

.

Outside the camp, we shove poles into the ground and hang large bells from the poles. When we see one of them approaching, we ring the bells to warn each other, then run away and hide.

Between the years 1945 and 1949, one thousand of us, those of us who are counted, those of us who allow ourselves to be counted, are raped.

.

Those of us who give ourselves willingly to the Americans, those of us who get paid to give ourselves, are called pan-pan. We are called whores. Some of us are widows. Some of us are young girls who still live with our mothers. It doesn't matter what they call us, or what we call each other. At least something is being done. At least we are getting paid. After all, our island is covered in ash and dust, filled with stench and rot. There isn't anything for them—or us—to do except drink until we are numb, and fuck. Some of them would rather pay us than rape us, and for that some of us are grateful.

They come stumbling out of the bases, through the barbed-wire fences, through our villages. They shout and slur our names. We invite them into our homes. Sometimes our mothers and fathers, sisters and brothers, and children sleep—or pretend to sleep—on the other side of the walls. Some of the neighbors complain that we are dishonoring our families, defiling the children. Some of the neighbors try to banish prostitution, but when we ask how else to feed our families, our children, the neighbors have no answer, so we come up with a better solution. We move to the outskirts of the villages. Our homes become brothels, and our brothels become districts.

By 1967, ten thousand of us have become prostitutes.

*   *   *

We are done with this war. But they're not. They have a war to fight in Korea, and then a war to fight in Vietnam. "As long as communism is a threat," Vice President Richard Nixon announces during his visit in 1953, "[the United States] will hold Okinawa." They must use our land to build a fortress to protect the "Free World." A world in which we are not included. They must use our land to launch ships that carry tanks and guns, to launch planes that drop bombs. We shudder with each sound as ship after ship departs, as plane after plane takes off, remembering the damage and devastation, the slaughter those ships and planes have caused. They must use our land to store missiles and poisonous gases. We feel guilty, complicit, even though we have no choice.

Forests and fields that have just begun to heal are bulldozed and replaced with concrete. Farms that once grew pineapple and sugarcane, crops that sustained our meager economy, are bulldozed and replaced with concrete. Family-owned plots that have been passed down for generations are confiscated, often at gunpoint, and residents are evicted. Homes are bulldozed and burned and replaced with concrete. By what becomes known as the "bayonets and bulldozers" campaign, over fifty thousand of us lose titles to our land. In 1956, as part of mass demonstrations and protests, as part of our "All Island Land Struggle," one hundred thousand of us assemble at their headquarters in Naha, and they agree to pay us for the land they already stole.

But it is not enough. Not nearly enough.

So we become labor. We are hired to build bases. We are hired to build barracks, armories, loading docks, landing strips, fences, gates, more roads. We are hired to serve food in their cafeterias and clean their houses. The prettiest of us, those of us who have curves and speak the best English, get to work at the post office and fancy restaurants like McDonald's. Cities form around these bases, with bright neon signs in English, advertising to them, welcoming them. With bars and clubs where soldiers can yell and laugh, fight and flirt, and spend money like it's their last day on Earth, because, well, who knows, their last day could be very soon. They are fighting a war, and they pay us to help them forget.

But we remember. We will always remember.

.

Some of us fall in love with them. Is that so strange? Because they are tall and strong and polite. Taller and stronger and more polite than many of our men, since most of our men are gone. Because they carry heavy bags and boxes for us. They open doors for us, and let us enter or exit in front of them. They pull out chairs for us. They offer us their seats and stand for us. Because they drive us home in their cars and trucks, so we don't have to walk home by ourselves at night. Because they are rich. They make more in a day than we make in a month. They smell like soap when we can only rinse our faces and armpits with water from buckets or soak in a public bathhouse once a week. They leave us big tips and buy us gifts. Perfume, makeup, silk stockings, chocolate, chewing gum, bottles of liquor, and cartons of cigarettes that they bring from their bases and we sell to each other for cheaper than we can get anywhere else on the island. Because they let us watch movies on their televisions and wash clothes in their washing machines, so we don't have to wash clothes in the river. Because sometimes they buy us our own televisions and washing machines. Sometimes they pay our rent.

Because some of them are gentle and genuine, warm and kind, foolish and impetuous, and very young. Just like us.

Some of them fall in love with us. Is that so bad? Because we are tiny and shy and vulnerable. Tinier and shyer and more vulnerable than many of their women, who are far far away. Because we blush and we giggle. We lower our heads and avert our eyes. We don't speak much English, so they can't understand us. They don't know us. So they look at our faces and imagine who we are, see who they want to see. They look at our faces and see themselves as they want to be seen. We can't understand them, either. We don't know them, either. So we imagine that they are brave and good, will protect us and take care of us, never hurt us. Because we are grateful for everything they do for us. We are not angry, not like those of us who are older. Not like the men, who hate them because they are taller and stronger and richer. We are not used to men approaching us and treating us like beautiful delicate creatures meant to be cherished. We are not used to men lying to us in such a way that we have to believe them, lying to us in such a way that they have to believe themselves.

"Don't confuse sympathy for love," one of their mothers writes back to one of them.

*   *   *

The first "international marriage" in Okinawa is recorded on August 1, 1947, in the *Uruma Shimpo,* a weekly newspaper written by Okinawans yet supervised by American military officers to inform the public about policies and directives, as well as local news. The marriage is between one of them, Frank Anderson, a twenty-three-year-old soldier from Ohio, and one of us, Higa Hatsuko, a nineteen-year-old seamstress from Ginowan. The couple receives a certificate from a civilian governor. The marriage is annulled by a commanding officer one month later.

According to the War Bride Act of 1945, spouses and children of armed-forces personnel are allowed to enter and reside in the United States—"if admissible." However, according to the Immigration Act of 1924, otherwise known as the Asian Exclusion Act, marriage between Americans and Asians is considered illegal. Upon hearing this shameful news, Frank Anderson turns to his now ex-wife and says, "Then we'll hold hands, and by the time we get to America, I believe Congress will have changed the law."

And Congress does, eventually, in 1952, with the passage of the McCarran-Walter Act.

Before 1952, there are a few exceptions, temporary reprieves of maximum Asian immigrant quotas. In 1948, during a monthlong lifting of the ban, eight hundred twenty-five marriages between U.S. servicemen and Japanese citizens, including Okinawans, are recorded. The *Uruma Shimpo* notes that an "extremely high proportion" of these marriages have occurred in Okinawa compared with the rest of Japan. So much so that, later in 1948, the U.S. military issues a special executive order prohibiting marriages between servicemen and Okinawans, referring to an overall best practice of "nonfraternization" in occupied areas.

From 1952 to 1975, sixty-six thousand Japanese women immigrate to the United States as wives of U.S. servicemen. More than half of the total Japanese immigrant population. It is difficult to determine precisely how many of those Japanese women are actually from Okinawa. Between 1952 and 1972, Okinawa is a territory of the United States. We aren't acknowledged as Japanese citizens, yet certainly not as U.S. citizens. However, since seventy percent of U.S. military bases in Japan are located in Okinawa, it seems safe to assume, as the *Uruma Shimpo* notes, that an "extremely high proportion" of these marriages from 1952 to 1975 have also occurred in Okinawa. Plus, there is significant anecdotal evidence. Just ask any of us.

*   *   *

For many years, it is forbidden. For many more years, it is ridiculed. We are called pan-pan. We are called traitors. We are called Yankee-lovers and gold diggers. We meet them in secret. In hotels. In the backseats of cars. And when it comes time to tell our families, some of us are told we are no longer daughters. No longer sisters.

Our families warn us not to leave with them. "If you go to America, you will be lonely. If you go to America, your children will be tormented. They will call you Jap. They won't accept you." Some of us refuse to listen. Some of us listen but refuse to believe what our families tell us. Some of us believe, but decide to leave with them anyway.

.

Some of us leave by ships bound for San Francisco, crammed with a thousand or more passengers. Soldiers, sailors, marines, and a few dozen of us, their new wives. We sit together on the dock and stare at the ocean. Talking, dreaming, admiring our new husbands, promising to visit each other all the time. At night, they show movies and host parties. We drink and dance with them, except those of us who are already getting sick in the morning. The voyage takes fifteen days, and each day reminds us how far we are away from home.

Some of us arrive by planes, in New York and Los Angeles. We look around the airport and don't see anyone else who looks like us, and we realize we made a big mistake. "Is it too late to go back?" we ask, looking up at our husbands. Our husbands look down at us and nod, their faces confused and sad.

Some of us have to sit in a car while our husbands drive for two days, four days, six days, across this vast and magnificent country. We have never seen mountains so high and terrifying, deserts so dry and engulfing. We have never seen roads so wide and smooth. We had no idea. Not even an inkling. We feel even smaller now, humbled. "How much longer?" we ask, looking up at our husbands. Our husbands look down at us and smile. "Just a couple more days."

.

Some of us find out that our husbands already have wives. They hide us, put us in a trailer on the edge of town overlooking a field of corn. They visit us once a week to drop off groceries. They watch TV and drink six cans of beer while we sit beside them. Sometimes they let us sit on their laps. After they leave, we are afraid to go outside. We are afraid to answer the phone. Sometimes we wish we were dead, and some of us swallow pills or slit our wrists and crawl into bathtubs.

One of their wives comes over and beats us. One of their wives comes over and tells us it is not our fault and asks if we need help getting back home. But we can't go back home and bring more shame to our families, more shame to ourselves. So some of us stay and raise children by ourselves.

Some of our husbands turn cruel, call us "ugly" and "stupid" in front of our own children. Some of our husbands remain sweet and bring home puppies or kittens and promise to give us more children to cheer us up.

Some of our husbands' mothers hate us. Some of their mothers are the only reason we can bear this strange and lonely place. Some of our neighbors ignore us. Some of our neighbors notice our isolation and take us out for walks or shopping at the mall.

.

When we see each other by chance, in passing, we follow each other until we get close enough, until we muster the nerve to ask, "Nihonjin desu ka?" *Are you Japanese?*

"Hai, hai! Nihonjin desu. Okinawa shusshin desu." *Yes! Yes! I am Japanese. I am from Okinawa.*

"Watashimo!" *Me too!*

Then we bow and cry and hug and become friends forever. Because it is easier to miss a place when we are together.

XII

TOO YOUNG, TOO OLD

*W*hen I ask my mother why she decided to marry my father, she says because he was very handsome and polite and left big tips. She says because he was different from the other soldiers. He didn't swear. He didn't start fights. He didn't tease or grab. He didn't take without asking. He always ate whatever Obaa cooked for him. He always knelt at the tatami table even after his knees got sore and his feet tingled. She says my father bought her a car and taught her how to drive. She says she wanted to get off that sad poor island. Get away from her sad poor family.

When I ask my mother if she was in love with my father, she says, "Well . . . *now* I am."

"Well, what about back then?"

"Probably not," she says and laughs. "Maybe. I guess I don't really know."

I guess that's fair. How many of us really know?

.

When I ask my father why he decided to marry my mother, he says because she was very beautiful and clean and loved music. He says because she was different from the other cocktail waitresses. She didn't giggle. She didn't flatter. She was serious and sincere. She always took good care of her mother and younger sister, and that impressed him a great deal. He also says—without reluctance or reflection—that while serving his tours of duty in Vietnam, he formed an image in his mind of the woman he wanted to marry, the woman he wanted to bring with him back to the United States, and my mother fit that image perfectly. He says that when he went away to Korea, after being stationed in Okinawa, after meeting my mother and dating her for six months, he couldn't stop thinking about her. He missed her more than he thought he would, more than he had ever missed anyone in his life. That's how he knew.

When I ask my father if he was in love with my mother, he says, "Of course."

.

When I ask my mother if she was afraid to move to America, she says, "No, I was very excited. I never flew on a plane before. I never saw so many big buildings and cars before. I always wanted to go to Disneyland. I didn't know how hard it was going to be. I was too young."

I ask her if she ever wishes she had stayed in Okinawa.

"I used to."

"What about now?"

"No. Not now. I'm too old."

XIII
WHO IS KYOKO MAKIYA?

*M*y mother's name is Kyoko, which means "respectful" or "apricot" or "echo" or "from heaven" in Japanese, depending on how it's written. "Kyoko" is a common and ordinary name. Very popular in Japan. The name of famous singers, actresses, and anime characters. Perhaps Obaa gave my mother a common and ordinary name, a popular Japanese name, because Okinawan names had long been disparaged, because the year was 1948, and my mother was the second child born since the war, another mouth to feed, and Okinawa's fate was still uncertain, and maybe this plain name would make everything normal, would give my mother a fighting chance.

.

Here, in the United States, when she introduces herself, very often she must repeat her name. "Kyoko . . . Kyoko . . . Kyooh-kooh." The "o" sound is long. And the "k" and "y" sounds are blended. Some people say "Kyo-ko" too quickly and some people say "Ki-yo-ko" with a question mark at the end. Very often, she allows her name to be mispronounced. I'm sure I've mispronounced her name many times, not lingering on each syllable the right amount, not having the right intonation. But I have the luxury of calling her "Mom," which is an English word. The Japanese word for "Mom" is "Okaasan," or "kaasa," which I never bothered to learn until recently.

•

I try to imagine my mother as a young girl. Not as my mother but as *Kyoko,* an autonomous being, distinct from me and her relation to me, navigating the world.

My mind goes blank.

I don't know who she is. I don't know how to be her.

•

My mother before me is a story. A story she can't tell me in her own language. A story, she claims, she barely remembers. Or maybe she doesn't want to remember. Or maybe she can't remember because she was never taught how to remember. Because she was never told her life is important enough to remember.

•

I am trying to tell her now that her life is important enough to remember.

XIV
THE FASTEST RUNNER

I see a room. I see four walls made of wood, sanded and scrubbed. I see four windows, a window carved into each wall and covered with nets. A slow breeze drifts through the room. A few lizards scurry up the wall and hide in corners, waiting for trespassers. I see a portable gas stove, a kettle, a pot, a bucket of water, a large sack of potatoes, nine bowls and nine cups stacked neatly on the floor against the wall. The floor is held up from the ground by cinder blocks, so it sags at some parts, especially in the middle.

I see nine bodies sleeping on mats, sleeping in a row, across the floor, sliding toward the middle. They wear white undergarments and hold white sheets close to their chins. The breeze is cool in the morning.

My mother sleeps on her side. Her body is frail, bone frail, but her skin is soft and new, her face is smooth. Her mouth is slightly open, but it doesn't tighten or turn down. Her hair is kept short, trimmed around the ears and at the base of her long skinny neck, because she is still a young girl and doesn't care about having long hair yet. Maybe she is seven years old.

My mother sleeps next to her younger sister, Setsu, which means "loyal." Setsu is five years younger than my mother. After my mother moves to the United States, Setsu will be the only sister who sends brightly colored, carefully wrapped packages of video and cassette tapes, recordings of my mother's favorite television shows and songs. Setsu will be the only sister who comes to visit. She will visit twice. My mother will pay for the flight twice. The first time she comes to visit, I will be nine years old, and I will braid her long pretty hair and count her beauty marks. The second time she comes to visit, I will be fourteen years old and too self-conscious and self-absorbed to show her any regard. She will marry a man, a very kind man, a man with tattoos of dragons on his neck, chest, and arms, tattoos he earned while serving sentences in prison. He will adore Setsu, even after she divorces him and marries another man, a very mean man, a successful real estate broker, who gambles and steals from her, beats her. Setsu will die of liver failure when she is fifty-two years old.

My mother is holding Setsu while they sleep, protecting her from the chill of the air, from the rest of her life, from what hasn't happened yet. For as long as she can. Until she marries my father and will have to leave her.

Sleeping next to my mother is her oldest sister Kikuko, which means "precious." Kikuko is ten years older than my mother. Kikuko, the first child, the first daughter, who survived the Battle of Okinawa, will die of pneumonia when she is seventeen years old.

Sleeping next to Kikuko is my mother's second oldest sister, Chieko, which means "wisdom." Chieko is eight years older than my mother. She works at the cafeteria on the base. She will have a daughter with a man who dies young. She will have a son with a man, a U.S. soldier, who leaves her and never wants to see her again. She will work at a nightclub, and eventually own that nightclub, the Blue Diamond, where my mother will also work, where my mother will meet my father. Chieko will be suspicious. At first, she will try to keep them apart and chaperone them on dates. But eventually, she will understand that not all people and lives turn out the same. She will die of cancer when she is forty-five years old.

Sleeping next to Chieko is my mother's third oldest sister, Yoshi, which means "good." Yoshi is six years older than my mother. She will also work at the cafeteria on the base. She will also work at the Blue Diamond. She will never marry or have children, but she will adopt a son. She will have a stroke at the age of fifty-eight, and for the rest of her life she will slur, and walk with a limp and have to use a cane. Years later, when we come to visit, she will hobble behind me at the market in downtown Naha and offer to buy me whatever catches my interest. I will relent and let her buy me an assortment of gourmet seaweed pastes, which I will take back with me to the United States. I will have no idea how much it costs. At the end of the day, she will give me the rest of her money, ten thousand yen, the equivalent of one hundred dollars, in a bright-red envelope.

Sleeping next to Yoshi is Obaa. Her name is Mega, an Okinawan name, so I can't look up what it means. She has bruises from my grandfather's beatings, but her sleep is deep because her daughters are near.

Next to Obaa is my grandfather, Genko, another Okinawan name. He snores loudly, sickly, because he has passed out drunk the night before and the night before and the night before.

Next to Genko is my mother's first older brother, Gensho, named after his father. Gensho is seven years older than my mother. He is a construction worker. He helps build bases and fast-food restaurants. Because his father is too drunk and too sick, because he is the older boy, Gensho becomes the "man of the house." But he doesn't learn from his father's mistakes. He beats his younger sisters. He hurts them in other ways my mother will only tell me about once, when she is very drunk. Years later, when we come to visit, he will keep his head down and his eyes averted. He will not look at us. My mother will hug him to show him she forgives him, a gesture, perhaps, she will have learned from her new religion, from living so long in the United States. He will not hug her back. But his jaw and shoulders will soften.

Next to Gensho is her second older brother, Genshin, also named after his father. Genshin is two years older than my mother. He is also a construction worker. He also helps build bases and neon McDonald's signs. He works seven days a week. When we come to visit, he will be seventy-four years old, with a happy face and a strong body—happier and stronger than his sisters, perhaps because his life will not treat him as harshly. Before we go back to the United States, he will give me one hundred thousand yen, the equivalent of one thousand dollars, in a bright red envelope.

They sleep like this, all together, wearing white undergarments and sliding toward the middle. They never complain, never learned how, except maybe in their dreams.

.

Obaa wakes first. She stands and yawns and stretches her arms up to the ceiling, almost touching it, exposing her bony hips and ribs. Then she bends down and lets her arms hang, lets the blood rush to her head. She stretches and bends, stretches and bends, until her blood is warm, until it doesn't hurt to move anymore. She rolls up her mat and leans it against the wall. She ties an apron around her waist and a rag around her head. She kneels on the floor in the corner where the portable gas stove and cooking utensils are kept. She pours water from a bucket into the pot and puts the pot on the stove. She turns the knob, waits for the click, and lights the burner with a match. Then she starts chopping potatoes.

Gensho, Genshin, Chieko, and Yoshi wake next. They roll up their mats and lean them against the wall. They go outside and kneel in front of a metal bin beside the cinderblock fence. They splash their faces, then scrub their hands, armpits, and crevices with a rag.

They don't hide their bodies from each other. Privacy of bodies is a luxury for people who are raised to believe their bodies are special, have value, and should therefore be guarded and pampered.

Now my mother nudges Setsu awake. "Setsu-chan . . . Setsu-chan . . . okite kudasai," she whispers. *Please wake up.* Setsu groans. My mother pinches Setsu behind each knee, each elbow, pinches her earlobes. Setsu's groans turn to giggles. They roll up their mats and lean them against the wall. They push the tatami table across the room and place it upright on the floor, careful not to wake their father, who still snores. My mother and Setsu go outside and kneel in front of the metal bin beside the cinderblock fence. "Yokkorasho," my mother says, which is what she will say to me whenever she has to lift me or other heavy objects. Then she lifts Setsu and lowers her into the metal bin. "Banzai," my mother says, which is what she will say to me whenever she wants me to raise my arms so that she can wash underneath them. Then Setsu raises her arms. When my mother and Setsu finish washing, my mother carries the metal bin to the street and dumps out the dirty water.

.

The Makiya family kneel together at the tatami table for breakfast, even Genko. They sip hot tea, slurp miso broth, and chew boiled potatoes. This is what they eat for breakfast and dinner. For every breakfast and dinner. For lunch, they're on their own. On special occasions, like New Year's Day (Shogatsu) or the Festival of Souls (Obon), they eat rice with chopsticks. Sometimes the sons bring home packages of dried noodles. Sometimes the older daughters bring home cakes and chocolates, gifts from soldiers or sailors or marines.

In the mornings, while they eat breakfast, I imagine there is mostly silence. They have a long day ahead of them. Obaa goes to work. Gensho and eventually Genshin, when he is old enough, go to work. Kikuko, before she dies, Chieko, and Yoshi go to work. Sometimes Genko goes to work and sometimes he goes back to the mat on the floor. My mother and eventually Setsu, when she is old enough, walk two miles to school.

At school, they're lucky if they learn. The children are too hungry. The teachers are too tired. If the children complain or disobey, they have to sit on their legs on their desks with their hands clasped behind their backs for half a day, or get spanked with a stick.

After school, they walk a mile to the public well and carry home buckets of water. If the water in the well is low, they tie the edges of a palm leaf together and tie the stem to a string, and then lower the makeshift bowl instead of a bucket, so that the bucket doesn't stir the mud at the bottom. Palm trees are planted near wells for just this purpose.

After their daily chore, they wander the fields. They pick berries and dig for snails to eat. Sometimes my mother steals from the market downtown. She steals pieces of bread, cookies, and candy.

She steals because she's hungry, because her sister's hungry. She steals because she's young, and still possesses that noble stupidity we often need in order to act against injustice. But my mother gets caught. An officer brings her home, and Obaa has to pay for the stolen food. When Gensho finds out, he dunks my mother's head in a bucket of water. He holds her head under the water, while Obaa and Setsu scream and beg for him to stop, while my mother gags and chokes. My mother will never steal again.

.

I ask my mother for a happy memory. She can't tell me one.

.

Except for playing kakurenbo, "hide and seek," and ishi o keru, "kick the stone." Because Kyoko Makiya is the fastest runner in the whole neighborhood. Boy or girl.

.

In the evenings, while they eat dinner, I can't imagine what they're talking about, because I don't understand what they're saying. Maybe they don't have much to say to each other now, but years later, when we come to visit, they will share ten bottles of sake and chain-smoke cigarettes, and not a moment of silence will pass between them. Their bodies will remember how they used to be so close and naked around each other. There will be no awkwardness. Or shame.

*M*y father's name is Arthur, which means "bear" or "warrior" or "king" in Celtic. From an early age, my father knew the meaning of his name, intended to become the meaning of his name. He read the legends of King Arthur and the Knights of the Round Table, studied and absorbed their code of chivalry: to serve the church, protect the weak, defend thy country, speak the truth, and keep thy word, devote thyself to the causes of the Right and the Good against Injustice and Evil, etc., etc. He read about boys who became men. He read about men who became heroes. He read all day, burrowed on top of the heater vent by the window of the living room, overlooking Seventy-second Street and Broadway. He read all night, under the covers with a flashlight. He read so much because he loved to read, but also because my grandfather lost his temper one evening and bashed the television to a pulp with a baseball bat.

"Why'd he do that?" I ask, after the tenth time of hearing about this formative event.

"Your uncle Philip got smart with him, wouldn't listen, wouldn't stop watching the damn TV. He wouldn't join the rest of the family at the dining room table for dinner." My father chuckles as he recollects, with a tone of accusation, with a sentiment of *he had it coming, we had it coming.*

"Quite a reaction," I say, years later, after the twentieth time, when I'm no longer inclined to agree with my father that bashing a television to a pulp with a baseball bat is particularly funny.

"Your grandfather was harsh yet effective. While the other kids my age were hooked on *Leave It to Beaver*, I was reading Rudyard Kipling." Then he straightens, lifts his chin.

He also tells me about the worst discipline he can remember. My grandfather beat him with a long wooden shoe horn. My father couldn't walk or go to school the next day.

"Why'd he do that?" I ask.

"I was a fat boy. He caught me in the kitchen in the middle of the night, fixing myself a snack," my father says.

"That's abuse," I say.

My father shrugs and laughs when he says, "Things were a lot different back then."

.

The last books my father read were the Bible, cover to cover, and the Quran, cover to cover. That was maybe fifteen years ago, shortly after 9/11. He wanted to understand the origins of these feuding religions. Now he only reads the latest news from the Internet, right-leaning websites such as Zero Hedge and Drudge Report. He reads all day, in between naps, hunched at his desk, staring at the computer, the television turned on and turned up behind him. He reads all night, screens shining and flickering, commentators reporting and discoursing and blathering. He complains that he doesn't sleep enough. He reads so much because he loves to read, but also because he needs—that's his word, "needs"—to stay informed.

"Why?" I ask. "What good does it do you?"

"It's my duty as a citizen."

"Yeah, but it's making you depressed."

Same answer.

"You should move around more. Go for a walk," my mother tells him.

"You're brainwashing yourself. Read a book," I tell him.

*   *   *

My father was an altar boy and a Boy Scout. He obeyed the priests and the catechism. He earned badges, escorted the elderly across the street or up and down staircases. In school, he was the first in his class, read every assigned textbook cover to cover over Labor Day Weekend. Not popular, but respected, because he could recite the longest and most difficult passages in Latin, and defended himself, his fellow chubby peers, his smaller scrawny peers, against bullies by swinging his big bag of books at them. He applied to Princeton University just to show my grandfather the acceptance letter, but enrolled in Fordham University, where he received a full scholarship, because my grandfather had two other children to put through college.

The Vietnam War had already begun. My father had already planned to enlist, to fight. He joined the ROTC in 1967, just as the Fordham chapter of Students for a Democratic Society first organized campus protests. Joining the ROTC meant that he could serve in the army immediately as an officer, as a lieutenant instead of a private. My father believed that if he could lead men he could lead them to honor. He could prevent them from committing crimes, from exploiting and harassing civilians, from tainting the efforts of those who possessed noble intentions, from being the exceptions, the scandals blown out of proportion by misguided pundits and naïve pacifists, the bad apples that spoiled the rest of the bunch. He could prove himself and his love of his country, his devotion to the causes of the Right and the Good.

As part of his personal program to prepare his body, he also joined the rowing team, which met each morning for practices and races on the Hudson River. He exercised. He trained. He ran a mile, then two miles, then six miles a day. He didn't care about grades. For the first time in his life, he got straight C's. By the end of his junior year, he felt invincible. He ran through secluded paths of Central Park in the dark to conjure the rush of danger, to test his strength if warranted. One evening, on the subway, on the way home from Fordham's Rosemont campus in the Bronx, he tackled and subdued a man who pulled out a knife. The nuns who were riding in the same car thanked him and blessed him. This was what he had been waiting for his whole life: to become a hero.

A week after graduation, in the spring of 1969, he shook my grandfather's hand, kissed my grandmother's cheek goodbye, and left for Fort Indiantown Gap Military Reservation, Pennsylvania, for boot camp. He loved boot camp. He loved having to wake up before dawn, having to shave and do jumping jacks and run for miles. He loved the punishment of push-ups. He loved getting called "city slicker," "rich boy," and "Park Avenue," getting teased for his aristocratic prep-school accent. He loved sharing quarters with "rednecks" and "Negroes," getting them to trust him. He loved the meritocracy. He believed that in the army everyone was equal, everyone could prove himself. He believed that if everyone joined the army, or any form of the military, then we could build a nation of citizens, not just subjects.

After boot camp, my father signed on for four years of combat in exchange for one year of Special Forces training in Fort Benning, Georgia, then Monterey, California, then Fort Gulick,

Canal Zone, Panama. He loved driving south, the swamps, the shantytowns, the churches and graveyards, the statues of Confederate soldiers, the way of life most Northerners never saw or considered. He loved driving west, through the plains, the deserts, the mountains, to the coast. Most of all, he loved driving deep, deep south, across the border, through Mexico, then Guatemala, then El Salvador, the torn-up highways and dirt roads, the shoot-outs over soccer games, the day he spent detained at a police checkpoint, the night he spent trapped inside his jeep with a pack of wild dogs barking and jumping at the windows, the waves and cheers of residents as his jeep sputtered and rattled to the top of a steep hill into town, the mechanic kind enough to fix the engine for nearly all the money my father still had left, which didn't cover the total cost. My father mailed him cash weeks later. When my father reached Fort Gulick, he was a celebrity, the only one of the ten Special Forces officers who finished the trip on ground. Nine had to be rescued, had to be flown. Even the battalion commander greeted him at the gate.

My father became an Airborne Ranger, then a Green Beret, then a captain. He was ready for the jungle, ready for Vietnam, Cambodia, Korea, ready for war, ready to realize his destiny.

My father served for six years, then quit, devastated and disheartened by what he deemed to be the cowardly abandonment of the South Vietnamese army. He fought, and he fought, ultimately, for nothing. And he carried this sense of defeat with him for the rest of his life.

Long after the war, he yearned and searched for opportunities to confront Injustice and Evil. At work, on daily errands, his antennae raised, scanning the premises for commonplace crisis, charging toward it without reservation or concern for consequences. When he worked at Merrill Lynch, he gathered evidence and testified on behalf of his client, a widower, an old man, too senile to notice that his former stockbroker, my father's colleague, had been skimming extra commission. My father got fired. Late one night, when we were driving my friend to her dorm at Nazareth College, we passed a herd of drunken frat boys, stamping knee-deep in the snow, chasing another frat boy, a few feet ahead, frightened, naked except for a pair of boxer shorts. My father swerved onto the lawn in front of them, leapt out of the car, honked the horn, and started raving like a lunatic. The frat boys halted, astounded. Then they laughed and ran back inside the dorm.

"Dad, you could've gotten hurt. There were twenty of them and one of you."

"I had to do something, Elizabeth."

He always has to do something.

An irate customer unleashing on a young cashier. A fender-bender hit-and-run in the parking lot. A car on the side of the road buried under snow. I remember a big scene at the post office, my father lecturing the poor clerk behind the counter, quoting the creed: "Neither snow nor rain nor heat nor gloom of night stays these couriers from the swift completion of their rounds!"

Recently, I texted my father from the backseat of a taxi at LaGuardia Airport to complain about a possible swindle. He called the company headquarters, verified its legitimacy, inquired about the rates, then implored the dispatcher to call the driver directly, so he could reproach him for his "bum-rush" tactic. The driver said that in his twenty years of driving a taxi that was the first time he was ever yelled at by a passenger's dad. My father is always willing to fight, especially for the safety and well-being of his only daughter.

*　　*　　*

When I was growing up, my father was always there, always within eyesight or earshot or looming in the back of my mind. His physical presence certainly commanded attention: five feet nine inches tall, technically obese at two-hundred and twenty pounds, but solid, perfect posture; if he widened his stance, no single grown man could knock him down. He wore thick bifocal glasses and all black—black cotton collared shirt, black slacks or black sweatpants, and a black nylon jacket—for the extra pockets—no matter how high the temperature. And his voice, his voice was what really impressed people: projecting, booming, unapologetic, with a tone of urgency, of authority, diction heightened and exceedingly formal. For instance, when I asked if I could be home at seven o'clock instead of six, rather than a simple "maybe" he would say, "That's within the realm of possibility." Or, when I left the house to hang out with friends, he would say, "Keep me abreast of your whereabouts," and "Please notify me as soon as you're safely ensconced." He would talk for minutes without pause, impromptu meandering orations detailed and dense with obscure facts and statistics.

"Dad, please, I just need a short answer right now."

"Ask me the time and I'll give you the history of watchmaking."

.

When I was six, seven, eight years old, I would play on the playground behind our house, and he would pace on the grass, sit on the balcony, or at the dining room table with all the curtains and windows open. He would watch me play, just in case any trouble arose—a slip off the swing, a tumble off the slide, a scraped knee, a concussion, a kidnapper, anything at all—just in case I needed him. If I wandered into the woods to build forts, or onto the street to ride my bicycle down the hill, my father would yell, "Elizabeth!" and I would yell, "Yeah, Dad!" and he would yell, "As long as I can hear you!" And if I didn't yell back right away, he would yell and yell again until I answered. I had a keen sense of where that boundary lay, the farthest I could venture and still be able to hear his voice. If I drifted too far, if I couldn't hear, didn't answer, he would find me. Sometimes, if the place wasn't obvious or posed too much of a risk, like the side of a busy road or a construction site, he would scold, and scold loudly, his face red and twisted, the temper he inherited from my grandfather, which terrified me. More often, he would nod and wave, then watch and wait. As a child, I didn't mind. I relished his protection.

As I got older, no longer content with the playground, the patch of woods, the parameters of the neighborhood, my father would drive me and my friends to the movie theater, the mall, the local amusement park. He would pay for our tickets, our snacks at the food court, our games at the arcade. He would sit at the end of our row, watching movies with us, pace while we perused shops or rode roller coasters. As I got older, craved more independence, he would walk me and my friends to the entrance, then return to his car, and wait for hours in the parking lot. If we didn't get back to the car in time, he would find us, and he would scold, and scold loudly, no inhibition, no mitigation for the innocent bystanders just trying to enjoy their Saturday afternoon, which was now interrupted by a big man wearing all black and roaring at a group of young girls. The ride home would be silent. My friends would snicker and tease me, but they also understood that none of their parents were volunteering to drive us around, wherever we wanted to go, and pay for our admission and snacks.

Perhaps his generosity felt a bit like bribery, compensation for tagging along. Perhaps it wasn't coincidence that most of my friends were raised by single mothers, working or going on dates with their boyfriends during the weekends. Perhaps they, too, my friends and their mothers, relished his protection.

When I was thirteen, fourteen, fifteen years old, the repertoire of hangout spots expanded to diners, the bowling alley, the pavilion at Perinton Park, parties in basements, bands playing at vacant warehouses. Even then, he would wait for hours in the parking lot. His car, a dark green Nissan Pathfinder, might have remained inconspicuous, might have evaded scrutiny, if the dome light hadn't been beaming onto his face, stern with concentration, as he listened to the radio and read a newspaper spread over the steering wheel.

"Oh my God, who is that man?" A new acquaintance, not yet aware of this omnipresent guardian force in my life. "Is he spying on us?"

"That's just my dad," I would say, no longer embarrassed.

"Um, that's creepy."

"Yeah, I know."

Some of them, more curious and less disturbed, would tap on the window. "So you're Liz's dad?" Or "What's your deal?" Or "What're you reading?"

Forbes. He was delighted to engage, to offer a recap of news events, a political analysis, a history lesson. One of them asked me if I was sure, absolutely sure, that my father wasn't medicated.

"Trust me. He doesn't take drugs."

"He's so freaking cheerful."

A few of them told me they wished they had fathers who cared so much, and that made me feel special. I was shy, and my father helped break the ice.

At the end of the night, many of them would gather around his car for rides home. He always welcomed them, driving around for an hour, to each of their houses, with me squished on the center console, two in the passenger seat, and four, five, six in the backseat. He heard all the gossip. He chimed in, gave advice and pep talks. We would actively seek his approval, eager for a nod, a grin, for him to say, "That's a good point," or "I think you're right." He was undeniably the adult, the patriarch, but also, in a way, our friend.

And, yes, I might have protested, whined, begged him to let me go alone. And sometimes, if a place became familiar, in regular rotation, he would drop me off and pick me up—early, of course. But even when he wasn't there, he was still there. Like a holy spirit, a moral conscious—a Jiminy Cricket, as he referred to himself—nagging in my ear, guiding my choices.

.

His protection wasn't just confined to waiting in parking lots. Throughout middle school and high school, on weekdays, my curfew was four o'clock, plenty of time for after-school extracurricular activities, which I skipped, opting to roam the village of Fairport, stroll on the paths by the canal, loiter on docks and under bridges, walk the two miles to my house, savoring a brief stretch of precious freedom. My mother left for the restaurant at three o'clock every day except Wednesday, which was our designated mother-daughter bonding day, which we spent shopping at the mall for CDs and brand-new wardrobes for me, one of her only ways of showing love, which I counteracted with bitter silence. In order to guarantee that I was home at precisely the hour I should have been home, my father would call the house. If I didn't answer, he would call the house again and again, every ten minutes. I had about a half-hour leeway. After that, he would target his list of contacts: the secretary at the attendance office; the managers of Riki's, Friendly's, Tom Wahl's, and Salvatore's Pizzeria; the parents of my friends, but they didn't keep as close tabs on their children. More than a few times, he persuaded local law enforcement to get involved. Nothing was more chiding than being stopped on the street by a police officer and the exasperation in his voice when he asked, "Are you Elizabeth?"

Yes. Unfortunately.

"Please go home and call your father."

On weekends, my curfew was ten o'clock. However, my weekends were abridged by two hours every Saturday and four hours every Sunday, which had to be dedicated to "mind enrichment." He assigned articles from *The Wall Street Journal* or *The Economist* to read, highlight, and annotate. I could watch the news, a documentary that was suitably academic, or I could read a book. *A Tree Grows in Brooklyn* by Betty Smith, *I Never Promised You a Rose Garden* by Hannah Green, and *The Heart Is a Lonely Hunter* by Carson McCullers were three of my favorites, but my father advocated for Dickens and Orwell, Hemingway and Fitzgerald, more titles from the canon. If my friends called the house, he would say, "Elizabeth can't come to the phone right now," or "Elizabeth is busy at the moment," or "She's tied up," and I could hear my friends snicker, picturing me actually tied up and bound to a chair.

Sometimes I cried. Sometimes I threw tantrums. One time I tore apart his collection of *National Geographic* magazines. Sometimes I lay on my bed and stared at the ceiling and did nothing, watched nothing, read nothing. "Well, you can bring a horse to water . . ." my father would say.

By the end of my junior year, I was in full rebellion mode. I would skip electives like PE and choir, classes more lenient about tracking the roster. During lunch and study periods, I would sneak past security, which wasn't too difficult, since security consisted of four middle-aged women, two of them named Nancy and two of them named Carol, then escape the school grounds to smoke cigarettes and marijuana. One afternoon, hubris—i.e., marijuana—clouded my judgment, and I convinced myself that the teacher wouldn't notice if I wasn't in class for a chemistry test in sixth period, and the secretary at the attendance office, in deep cahoots with my father, called him at work to alert him of my sudden midday absence. He found me at Lyndon Bridge, an abandoned rusted bridge, a notorious haven for delinquents, my feet dangling off the edge, my hand caressing a boy's bare chest. I remember seeing the car, the door swinging open, and his face, the temper, the rage aiming at me from the other end of the bridge, from the other side of the chained gate. I remember the panic. I considered jumping into the canal thirty feet below and swimming home. He drove me back to school, but he didn't drop me off. He escorted me to my next scheduled class, yelling, roaring, his huge voice reverberating through the halls. Teachers poked their heads out of their classrooms to glance at me with sympathy and quickly shut their doors.

"Dad, please, come on," I whispered. "You're embarrassing me."

"Public humiliation is part of your punishment!"

And this punishment seemed fair. I disappointed him. I worried him.

.

My loophole was the basement. My father couldn't hear any noise, smell any odors coming from the basement. There was a window near the corner, and if I pushed the couch against the wall, I could lean out and smoke cigarettes. I could crawl out in the middle of the night and swing on the swings in the playground by myself. I could crawl out in the middle of the night and meet my friends in the patch of woods, at Lyndon Bridge, at parties of older friends, bringing bottles of booze I had stolen from the liquor cabinet and stashed in the closet. My friends joked that Mr. Brina was probably following me, probably hiding behind the trees, spying on us. Until I put enough alcohol in my bloodstream, my chest pounded. I feared his wrath, yes, but I feared his fear even more. What if he went downstairs to the basement? I knew his mind would jump to the worst possible conclusion. Abducted. Bleeding to death in a ditch. I knew I would feel guilty for worrying him.

I never stole the bourbon, not since the first time I got drunk and so sick I swore I would never drink again. I never stole the wine, too faithfully monitored, too easily detected. I stole the vodka, gin, and rum. Then the Goldschläger, triple sec, and crème de menthe. One night I puked on the futon. Tiny gold flakes. Orange and green syrup. The next day, my father caught me trying to drag the futon to the dumpster.

I couldn't lie, not to my father. He raised me to be honest. He raised me to uphold my actions, to admit my mistakes. I confessed everything. The window. The woods. Lyndon Bridge. The parties of older friends.

He didn't scold. He didn't forbid. He thought it was natural for me to experiment. Instead, he struck a bargain: My father would provide the booze if I promised to stay home, to drink under his supervision and instruction, to let him keep me safe. I could even invite my friends.

I remember my father pushing a shopping cart loaded with

six-packs of Zima, Hooch, Mike's Hard Lemonade, wine coolers, vodka, and mixers. I remember how my friends and I—six,
seven, eight of us—giggled and bounced with glee to the check-
out lane. I remember the blatant debauchery at our house. Minors
pouring stiff cocktails and drinking in the kitchen, drinking
in the dining room, drinking in the living room, drinking and
chain-smoking on the balcony, ashing and throwing butts into
empty bottles. At first, his sanctuary for underage drinking was
strictly for girls, but getting drunk without an added incentive
to get drunk lost its appeal. So we would invite boys to meet us
on the playground, share our booze with them. And since they
were drinking on my father's watch, they were compelled to enter
his sphere of protection. All of us would sleep on the floor of the
basement, bodies in a row, wall to wall, some of us passed out,
some of us kissing and groping each other. My father would sleep
on the living room couch, ears peeled for the potential squeaking
sounds of the window.

He did his best to contain us, but we got our fix and our fill.

Were we safe? Were we better off?

If my father hadn't provided the booze and the place, we
would have secured an alternate source, an alternate location, like
most kids our age. None of us died of alcohol poisoning or in a
fatal car crash. None of us got seriously ill or injured. But I wonder how much of his bargain to keep us close was about safety and
how much of it was about control, and if there's a difference in his
mind. I wonder if his enabling, his normalizing and condoning,
skewed our perceptions of binge drinking in general. I know I
still struggle with binge drinking.

My mother would come home from a twelve-hour shift at
the restaurant to a mob of teenagers cackling, stumbling, leaving behind a trail of spills and stains throughout her otherwise

pristine house. Sometimes my mother would shake her head, gripe about the mess, and go upstairs to her bedroom. Sometimes she would pour herself a glass of wine, or two, or three, or a whole bottle. Sometimes she would drink by herself in her bedroom, and sometimes she would drink with us in the dining room. When she drank with us in the dining room, my father and I would hover around her, making sure she didn't drink too much. This was how he protected her. This was how I protected myself. From embarrassment. From admitting the glitch in my adolescent logic, the fine-line reason why my mother getting drunk with my friends was so much more mortifying than my father surveilling my friends getting drunk.

My mother could do wrong. My mother wasn't my hero.

*   *   *

I am thirteen years old. I idolize Courtney Love, and my favorite band is Hole. I revere her bleached blond hair. I wear baby barrettes, baby-doll dresses, Mary Janes, and bright red lipstick. I practice singing and screaming to every song on the album *Live Through This* in the mirror, emulating and perfecting the dips and rasps and cracks in her voice. I learn how to play "Doll Parts" on the guitar. This year, 1994, the year Kurt Cobain commits suicide, Hole is touring. Hole is playing the Horizontal Boogie Bar in downtown Rochester. All ages show.

I ask my father if I can go to a concert. A rock-and-roll concert. Rock and roll, like the Rolling Stones, Led Zeppelin, and AC/DC. I don't tell my father that the music of Hole is a bit heavier, a bit cruder, a bit of a departure from his preferred genre. Besides, didn't he once nod his head and sing along to Black Sabbath on the radio? I don't tell my father that Courtney Love is the same woman in the photograph that I cut out of a magazine and taped to a discreet section of my bedroom wall, the photograph of her crowd surfing and playing guitar while wearing a very short dress and a thong, flashing a buttock and the left labia of her hairy vagina, the photograph my father detected, then ripped from the wall and crumpled as he called her a whore. I don't tell my father that many of the members of the audience attending this concert might presumably be just as "unladylike." I just want to see Courtney Love and my favorite band. But I am thirteen years old.

He drives me and my two best friends to the venue, a large brick warehouse with metal bars on the windows. "Horizontal Boogie Bar," he says. "Cute name." He walks me and my two best friends to the entrance. He buys me and my two best friends and himself tickets. My two best friends bolt to the front. "Sit back here," I say to my father, pointing to a bench tucked in a corner, the farthest from the stage. I join my friends at the front, and when I turn around, my father is standing six rows behind us. His face, stern and disapproving, his crew cut, his bifocal glasses, so abrasive, so obvious amid the bleached blond hair, the leather, the fishnets. But if I don't look at him, maybe no one will notice that he is looking at me.

The opener is Maggie Estep, a feminist spoken-word artist with a surprisingly mellow, funky accompaniment of upright bass, horns, and keyboard. I turn around to see my father nodding and swaying to the music and smiling at the clever lyrics. He gives me an okay sign. I ignore him, but I think to myself, *Huh, maybe my dad's sort of cool.* But now it's time for Hole.

There she is: perfect tangled hair, black lace bra exposed beneath a white lace slip. She lifts her leg and rests a high-heeled Mary Jane on the amp, and I can see her black lace underwear. She smacks her guitar. She screams. I can feel the erratic pulse of the crowd, bouncing, bumping, pushing forward, and releasing. In a moment of empathy, I check to see how my father is doing, and then I realize I have neglected to warn him about the mosh pit. Bodies jumping, flailing, slamming into each other. He isn't nodding and swaying and smiling anymore. He is slamming into the bodies—but for real—punching and kicking, grabbing collars and wrists and ankles, tossing them and yanking them to the floor. He is beating the crap out of them.

"Dad, stop it! Stop it! What are you doing?"

He whips his head around to look at me. Jaw clenched and teeth gritted. Crazed and furious. "Elizabeth, what's happening?"

"Dad, it's okay. They're dancing. They're having fun." I point. The jumping and slamming in rhythm. The smiles and laughter.

He tells me that I have to stand with him or we're leaving. I tell him that I will stay away from the mosh pit. I tell him that I will stand in the front with my two best friends. I tell him that I just want to see Courtney Love and my favorite band up close. Before he responds, I bolt to the front, weaving between bodies. I get to the front, to my two best friends, just in time for the second song.

"Elizabeth!" I can hear his voice, even over the screams and distortion. I can see in his face that he isn't angry, he's terrified. He grabs my arm. Hard.

"You don't have to go anywhere with this man!" A husky woman with a septum piercing and a shaved head puts her hand on my shoulder.

"He's my dad," I mutter.

"So?"

I don't want to stand with my father. I don't want to leave and ruin the chance to see Courtney Love and Hole for my two best friends. My father and I compromise. We sit in the car and wait for hours in the parking lot.

I can hear every song through the brick, and it hurts. I'm angry. I'm humiliated. But for some reason, I don't blame my father. I don't think of the situation as his fault, as a situation he alone caused. I feel pity. I feel guilt.

*   *   *

My father never talked about the war. Not the fighting and killing and death. Not the terror and panic and confusion. Not the remorse and regret.

But he loved to talk about jumping out of airplanes, and how the mountains glowed purple in the moonlight. He loved to talk about wading through sludge and tying himself to a tree so he could sleep without slipping into the water and drowning. He loved to talk about the time he shined a flashlight on a spider the size of his head hanging from a tree inches from his face, and how he jumped backward and upward so high he did a backflip and a belly flop, and how he and his buddies laughed, squeezing their mouths shut tight with their hands, not wanting any Viet Cong to hear, all of them crying and shaking together from laughter. He loved to talk about the time he earned a buffalo nickel, a prized token of bravery, by dropping the coin into a full bottle of Cognac, lighting the rim on fire, chugging the whole bottle, catching the coin between his teeth with his last gulp, then standing on a stool while ringing a bell and shouting, "Truth and courage!" He loved to talk about the friendship and solidarity, the special bond that is forged. He loved to talk about strategies, leading attacks and defenses, about his relevance and importance.

But now, as he gets older, after several glasses of bourbon, more and more of the war leaks out of him. He talks about running for his life through dark thickets of jungle, through black swamps, throwing grenades to clear escape routes, the guts of snakes splattering, as the Viet Cong unloaded rounds of gunfire. He talks about positioning a man on his side or facedown so that the blood drains to the ground rather than floods to his lungs after his throat is slit, so that the man bleeds without choking on his blood, which is more merciful. He talks about uniforms and medals of men who died, men who were killed, uniforms and medals given to him to give to their families. When my father remembers and mentions the names of lives that were lost, names of lives he couldn't save, his eyes water, and tears stream down his cheeks. These are the only times I have seen my father cry. Not when he dislocated his knee. Not when his foot swelled from gout. Not when his stores went out of business. Not when he got fired from his jobs. Not when his father died. Not when his mother died. Only these times.

My father tells me about ghosts.

He tells me about guarding his camp, lying on his stomach in a trench and falling asleep, and how he heard the voice of his friend, a friend who had just died, had just been killed. His friend yelled, "Brina, look out!" My father woke up and looked out, in the direction of the voice of his friend, just as a bullet whizzed past him, grazing his left ear. When I sat on his lap as a child, I used to trace the small dent in the cartilage with my finger.

He tells me about a lieutenant nicknamed Jelly Bean, who went MIA, hadn't returned or contacted the camp for weeks, who appeared beside my father's bed one night, held his hand, and whispered, "See, Art? Don't worry, I'm okay." My father felt a rush of relief and calm, hadn't felt such relief and calm for weeks. "Oh, thank God, Jelly Bean. Thank God, you're okay." The next morning, my father received news that Jelly Bean was dead.

He tells me that many friends who died, who were killed, approached him in dreams to let him know they were okay. He tells me these friends used to visit him often, many years later, long after the war ended. He tells me that his friends mostly just wanted to talk, to rehash memories, but sometimes they wanted him to fight with them, to go back to the places where they fought, to finish what they had started, to embark on new missions. Then, one night, for reasons he can't explain, my father didn't want to fight with them anymore.

"Stop coming to me, damnit!" he reenacts, slamming his fist on the dining room table. "I'm too old! I'm too fat! I can't help you!" Then my father cries when he tells me that he hasn't seen them again, not since. "I miss them," he says.

.

Growing up, I didn't understand PTSD. I thought PTSD was suicide and schizophrenia. I thought PTSD was a homeless person holding a cardboard sign. I thought I was lucky because my father was a veteran but he didn't have PTSD. He wouldn't let me watch *Platoon* or *Full Metal Jacket*, because those movies were pinko-commie-liberal propaganda, but not because those stories and images were real to him. My father didn't have PTSD.

His PTSD didn't dawn on me, didn't become apparent to me, until I was thirty-four years old. My parents were visiting for the weekend, for Thanksgiving. My mother was sleeping on my bed in my bedroom. My father and I were sitting on an air mattress on the floor of my living room in my new apartment in New Orleans. I had recently moved from a place where I was living with someone to a place where I was living alone, and hadn't acquired the proper furniture to entertain guests yet. My father and I shared a whole bottle of bourbon. We talked about the civil rights movement. He kept referring to "Negroes," and I kept correcting him. We talked about Guantanamo Bay. He kept referring to "Bradley" Manning and I kept correcting him. Somehow we wandered to the topic. He told me that a doctor at the VA clinic had diagnosed him and suggested he file for government assistance.

"Why didn't you?" I asked.

"Because that would have been dishonorable."

"But, Dad," I said, brave on liquor, brave on learning for the first time that a doctor saw it, a doctor knew it years ago. The loud nightmares. The loud cursing at himself in his sleep, while taking a shower, while washing the dishes. "You *do* have PTSD."

"I know I do, Elizabeth," my father said, also brave on liquor. "But I survived. My friends died in that war. What right do I have to complain about PTSD, to collect a few hundred dollars a month, when my friends died in that war?"

Then my father cried. Thick, hiccupping sobs.

I didn't think about how that money might have helped us, helped my mother, might have tempted her to take an extra day off from working at the restaurant. I didn't think about how his obsession with honor was inflicted, internalized, hindered his own healing. I just thought about his pain and what he was hoping to accomplish with his pain. I wrapped my arms around his neck and kissed the top of his head.

"You're a good man, Dad."

"Thank you, Elizabeth."

My father believes that letting emotional trauma interfere with duty is "goldbricking," a term used by General George S. Patton when he rebuked a young soldier who was suffering from shellshock. He believes that priests should replace all therapists. My father misses the world before the war, before he tried to save the world and was thwarted, before he tried to save the world and was defeated. He misses the world he read about in books, the world of heroes, of men, of strong men who protect the weak. He misses the old order of the world, before the rest of the world confronted and challenged the order: *We don't want your protection. We don't concede to your noble intention.*

And I feel pity. I feel guilt. For no longer wanting his protection.

Now I feel I must protect him. From rejection, from the pain of being cast aside, invisible, irrelevant. I know that pain.

*   *   *

After I moved to distant cities, to Boston, Missoula, Oakland, Kansas City, New Orleans, places far away, too far away for him to follow me, for him to wait for hours in the parking lot, he still called every morning and every night. If I didn't answer or return his calls within a couple hours, he would leave a dozen messages. If I didn't answer or return his calls within four hours, he would call my friends. More than a few times, he called a man I had only met at a bar the night before.

"Um . . . Liz?" the near-perfect stranger would say. "Your father called? Wants to know if you're okay?"

"Jesus Christ, I'm sorry. I'm so, so sorry," I would say, hung over, just waking up at one o'clock in the afternoon.

"*Are* you okay?"

"I'm fine. Really. My father's crazy."

"I just want to . . . Can I ask . . . uh . . . how did he get my number?"

"He looks up my cell-phone records."

"Wow."

"Yeah, I know."

One time a forest ranger parked his truck outside my tent at the Myers Flat Campground, in the redwood forest of northern California. "Are you Elizabeth? . . . Call your father." One time two deputies of the Oakland Police Department buzzed my apartment from the gate at midnight on a Saturday. "Are you Elizabeth? . . . Call your father." Both times, I was twenty-seven years old.

When I called my father, I remember the register of sheer relief, of thanking God, in his voice. As if I had been brought back to life.

But I also remember the countless times I needed those phone calls. How his voice gave me strength, motivation to "carpe diem." How his voice gave me comfort, reassurance that my mistakes weren't so bad or consequential. I remember the countless times I called him sobbing, anxious, on the verge of panic, at one, two, three o'clock in the morning. He always answered.

As I got older—thirty, thirty-one, thirty-two years old— I weaned him to one phone call a day, then one phone call every other day, and then, finally, to one text a day and one phone call a week. Except sometimes, he cheats. I try not to let myself get too upset or annoyed.

I think about how, after my father's gone, I won't get those phone calls anymore.

The thought fills me with dread.

I'll miss them.

XVI

BAMBOO

I am twenty-seven years old. I have just parked my car, a rusted Nissan Pathfinder, outside my new residence, a one-bedroom apartment in an orange 1970s motel-style two-story building of twenty identical units. There are palm trees and birds-of-paradise planted in the courtyard. I can't bring myself to start unloading the trunk yet. I have driven for four days, camping overnight, by myself, taking two-lane highways from Missoula, Montana, through Idaho to Washington through Oregon to Oakland, California, and now I need an adult beverage.

Or six.

I walk down my new street, down a huge hill that makes my shins ache. At the end of the street, there is an estuary: ugly, puny, compared with the splendid lakes of Montana and the ocean vistas along the coast. This is Lake Merritt, with shores of gravel and chipped sidewalks and overflowing trash cans. In a few years, it will transform into a dazzling gem of the Bay Area, completely renovated, with shores of landscaped lawns and terraces and pretty trinket lights strung from lamppost to lamppost. But now it's rather creepy, ominous. I look to my right, toward the hills, toward the houses stacked on the hills; the giant marquee sign of a movie theater towers and flashes above an overpass. I look to my left, toward the setting sun, toward downtown, the buildings blackening in the coming darkness. I turn right.

This is the year 2008. Just before Oakland became the new

Brooklyn. Just before the rich dot-com and start-up transplants saturated San Francisco and spilled across the bay, before the rent scaled impossibly high, impossible for anyone earning anything close to an average income to afford. Just before the peak of gentrification. I guess I'm part of that initial wave.

I walk around Lake Merritt; around the Grand Lake movie theater, the size of a city block. I walk by the empty restaurants, the padlocked stores, and then, yes, thank God, I spot a neon red sign for Kingman's Lucky Lounge. From inside the bar, through the open door, I hear Marvin Gaye's voice crooning, beckoning. A good omen.

"Hi!" I blurt to the bouncer, a handsome man with thick sideburns, wearing a hooded sweatshirt under a leather jacket, even though the temperature is well above sixty degrees. "Tonight is my first night in Oakland! I moved here from Missoula, Montana!"

I haven't interacted with many humans in the past four days. Only multiple phone calls from my father, brief conversations with gas-station attendants, campsite hosts, and cashiers at fast-food restaurants.

"Welcome," the bouncer says, and smiles as he hands me back my ID. "New York, huh?"

"Yup, I grew up in Fairport, and then I moved to Boston, and then I moved to Missoula, Montana, and now here!" I nod, pleased with myself.

"Okay," the bouncer says, and smiles again. "Come in and get yourself a drink."

The inside of the bar is dim and red. Red lights, red walls, red velvet cushioned couches and chairs. I notice right away that the bartender is black and the DJ is Asian. I tend to notice right away, when I enter a new place, who is there and not there, who else is another not-white person, especially another Asian. Maybe this is because of where I grew up. Maybe this is part of a defense mechanism. This is how I try to gauge my strangeness, my foreignness, whether someone is likely to ask me where I'm from, why I look the way I look, if someone might try to guess. *Arab? Egyptian? . . . Not Chinese, not Korean . . . Filipino!* When I enter a new place, I'm hyperaware, and sometimes I feel a preemptive urge to explain myself before I'm explicitly asked to explain myself. Sometimes I want to tell the truth, and sometimes I want to tell a lie.

I'm too impatient to wait for an opportune moment to tell the two women sitting next to me that I'm Native American, Blackfoot tribe, that I was born and raised on a reservation, and that tonight is my first night in town. I tell them this because I want attention and sympathy. I tell them this because I'm alone and scared in a new place and I want someone to welcome me. I tell them this because when I lived in Missoula, people would often ask me, "Are you Indian?" I tell them this because I think being Native American is more interesting than being half Okinawan.

The two women buy me a drink. So does the man sitting next to the two women. They ask questions, but not about my fake heritage. They ask about the length of the drive, the scenery. They ask what brings me to Oakland. I answer their questions, downing the shots of bourbon on ice with a splash of soda. I look around the bar, notice more of the staff and clientele. A fairly evenly blended mix of black, white, Asian, Latinx. I'm not in Missoula, Montana, anymore. And I'm not quite sure exactly what I'm seeing quite yet, because I've never seen anything like it. Not even in Boston, in my homogenized neighborhoods, in my various social groups consisting of college kids who either smoked a lot of cigarettes and listened to Belle and Sebastian or smoked a lot of pot and listened to Phish. I regret the lie I told. Stupid.

I'm alone and scared in a new place. I want to call my father. But I won't, I refrain, because this is my first night in Oakland and I can't waste my first night in Oakland talking on the phone to my father. I drink a third, fourth, then fifth shot. I go outside to smoke a cigarette. I chat with the bouncer. He is originally from Argentina, has been living in Oakland for twelve years, and moved here with his cousin; his mother died ten months ago. He is sweet, disarming, the only person in a thousand miles who knows my name, knows where I'm really from, so I decide to confess to him about the lie. He shakes his head, blowing the smoke of his cigarette through his lips in staccato puffs. He laughs from amusement, not ridicule. I am grateful.

"Don't worry about it," he says.

"Is it safe to walk home?" I ask. Because this is Oakland, and every square inch of Oakland is extremely dangerous.

"Where do you live?"

"On Hanover."

"You'll be fine."

"Okay." But my eyes stay wide.

"Give me your number. I'll call you in thirty minutes, make sure you get home okay."

I like the sound of that. I like the idea of someone besides my father, someone who lives in the same city as me, calling me to make sure I get home okay.

The bouncer and I will date for a month. He will be very sweet, very kind to me. But I will fixate on his bad breath, his crooked teeth, and the small circle of baldness on the back of his head. I will dump him for another white guy, who dumps me. Old habits are hard to break.

*   *   *

Oakland is the first place where I experience diversity. Real diversity. Not an abstraction, a theory, a proposed agenda. But concrete, in practice, people being it and doing it every day. They're mowing lawns, pushing strollers, designing clothes, instructing yoga, kneading dough in bakeries, braiding hair in salons. People of color. People of many colors. To prove I'm not exaggerating: in 2010, the population of Oakland was twenty-seven percent black, twenty-six percent white, twenty-five percent Latino, eighteen percent Asian, and a whopping three-point-six percent multiracial. I can see them. Seeing them is a revelation.

I can also talk to them. And they talk to me as one of them, a person of color. They hint at some sort of insider knowledge, something like *Yeah, you get it.* At first, I'm surprised, taken aback. Because being part Asian, half Okinawan, is something I used to consider intensely private, used to try to keep hidden. I didn't know how to talk about race casually, as a matter of fact. I didn't know how to talk about race seriously, as a matter of importance. But we talk. And I get better. And I do get it. *Oh yeah, that's right, I am a person of color.*

Just their mere presence puts me at ease, and I realize that before I came to this place I wasn't at ease. I realize that a lot of the time, whether consciously or unconsciously, I felt like an oddity, a curiosity. I felt distinct and disconnected. Oakland is the first place where I experience the power of visibility, of majority. Where I feel seen, rather than exposed.

*　　*　　*

But before I moved to Oakland, I moved to Missoula, Montana. Missoula, Montana. It sounded romantic, wild, outlandish.

I wanted to be able to say to people after it happened: "I moved to Missoula, Montana . . . I lived in Missoula, Montana." I was twenty-five years old and hadn't done anything with my life except barely graduate from Northeastern University after thirteen semesters, earning a bachelor's degree in English and philosophy as well as a transcript blotted with a series of F's, withdrawals, and incompletes. After barely graduating from Northeastern University I worked as a cashier at Barnes & Noble, and quit after a month. I worked as a waitress at Pizzeria Uno, and quit after a month. I worked as a hostess at a swanky restaurant on Newbury Street, and quit after the head chef got me drunk on rum, then offered me a hundred dollars to have sex with him. I worked as a hostess at another swanky restaurant on Newbury Street, and got fired after a customer invited me to sit at his table and convinced me to let him feed me chocolate mousse with a spoon. I served beer at a brewery, and quit after two months. I bagged groceries at a supermarket, and quit after one day. After I had ended an unhealthy numbing relationship with an agoraphobic and gained twenty-five pounds, I ended an unhealthy draining relationship with a manic-depressive and lost twenty-five pounds. I was sick of Boston. I was sick of myself in Boston. I wanted to be somewhere and to be someone drastically different. I lied on my résumé and applied to be an AmeriCorps VISTA (Volunteers in Service to America, like the Peace Corps but domestic). Alaska was on the list. So were Wyoming, Idaho, Washington, and Oregon. I chose Missoula, Montana, just because it sounded the best.

My father gave me his rusted Nissan Pathfinder and stocked the trunk with a ten-day supply of bottled water and nonperishable food items—just in case. My mother cashed three large jars of coins that she had collected from years of waitressing tips and gave me seven hundred eighty-nine dollars. In a straight route on

Interstate 90, I drove through Ohio, Indiana, Illinois, Wisconsin, Minnesota, and South Dakota, two thousand two hundred and one miles west, to the Rocky Mountains, in the middle of January. Too scared to explore, but I loved to gaze out the windshield at the openness, the vastness, feeling like it was cleansing me. I was alone.

.

When I arrived in Missoula, snow covered the mountains and chunks of ice floated on the rivers. I rented a room in a house owned by a forest ranger from Alaska who kept the thermostat at fifty-five degrees. I bought a space heater, a mattress, a wool blanket, and a down comforter. My assigned position as an AmeriCorps VISTA was to work at the YWCA. I answered phones, directed calls. I compiled intake forms and typed information into spreadsheets. Once a week, I drove to high schools, sometimes thirty, forty, fifty miles away, to deliver PowerPoint presentations on the warning signs and strategies for prevention of domestic violence. Twice a week, I worked at the women's shelter as a child advocate, which is a glorified term for "babysitter." I watched the kids play with toys and video games while their mothers ran errands, such as obtaining documents for employment and searching for permanent homes.

At the shelter, I stood by the wall in the back of the room, letting my co-advocate do most of the supervising. I didn't know how to take care of children. I felt inept and, at the same time, above it. As if my minimal yet nevertheless invaluable skills were not being utilized properly. I feigned interest in their stories, forced abrupt answers to their abundant questions. But some of them still latched on to me, wanted me to sit with them, play games with them. Were they that starved for affection?

Maybe because my skin was a shade darker and my eyes were slightly less round. Maybe because we gravitate toward people who look like us. Many of the women and children who stayed at the shelter were Native American and Mexican migrant workers.

Maybe the gravitation is nurtured, but maybe it is also hardwired. *You look like me, you are family, you will keep me safe, you are home.*

I kept the job for one year and one month.

.

While I lived in Missoula, my best friend, perhaps my only friend, was a fellow AmeriCorps VISTA I met at a mandatory conference. She grew up in Kalispell, a town a few miles southwest of Glacier National Park. She impressed me with her humor and spontaneous dances, how she jumped up and knelt on a stool and waved her arms and shouted the name of a bartender to get a drink faster. I moved out of the house where I was living with the forest ranger from Alaska and moved into an apartment with her. We chased dumb boys around town together. We never really discussed our ethnicities, our experiences of our ethnicities, and I would have been her friend no matter what her background, but maybe we became so close, at least at first, without realizing why, because she was adopted as a baby from an unwed mother from Mexico, because her skin was a shade darker and her eyes were slightly less round.

.

I couldn't have lasted too long in Missoula, Montana. I didn't know how to ski, snowboard, or fly-fish. The center of town was a grid of six main streets, and I had burned through nearly all of the eligible bachelors who frequented the five hip bars. I was restless. It was time to move again.

Oakland Unified School District was basically hiring warm bodies with college degrees who could also spare two months on an unpaid training program. My parents loaned me money to cover living expenses until the first paycheck, as did most of the parents of the other members of the cohort. Most of the members of the cohort were from suburbs of Des Moines, Milwaukee, St. Louis, etc., with dreams of doing good in the world, doing good while living near San Francisco, doing good while alleviating a good portion of their student loan debt. Seventy-four out of eighty-eight members were white. Most of the students we would teach were not white.

Again, I lied on my résumé, adding amplified phrases like "at-risk youth outreach" and "crisis counseling." The mental health coordinator of the Special Education Department requested an interview for the position of "Special Day Class High School Teacher" at a "separate school facility." During the interview, the mental health coordinator, also serving as acting principal of this separate school facility, asked me what I knew about emotional disturbance. I didn't know anything. I gave her a completely wrong answer. She recited the definition as if reading from a piece of paper and then hired me.

I learned later that the separate school facility wasn't a school, not a school like any I had ever seen, but a conjoining of six portable trailers: three for classrooms, one for a bathroom, one for an office, one for an intervention room, where the students were taken for a "time out." No library, no computer lab, no cafeteria. A parking lot with a basketball hoop for a gymnasium. Each classroom was assigned a teacher, a social worker, and a behavior interventionist per ten students, ninth through twelfth grade. The teacher taught these ten students, ninth through twelfth grade, English, math, social studies, and science. No breaks.

I also learned later that the definition of "emotional disturbance," according to the IDEA (Individuals with Disabilities Education Act), didn't adequately prepare me for the behavior I encountered. Behavior such as constant shouting, cursing, threatening, and sexual harassment. They rapped and roasted each other throughout lessons. One student told me to shut the fuck up or he would slap his dick on my forehead. Some of the students couldn't sit still and paced around the classroom, walked out and back in and back out and back into the classroom every two minutes. Some of the students couldn't stay awake and slept at their desks, or at my desk, or directly on top of my desk, or on the floor. Some of the students threw chairs, threw desks, punched holes into walls and ceiling tiles. One student punched the door so hard he broke his hand and had to wear a cast for three weeks. One student ripped apart a young tree, branch by branch. One student caught a mouse, dropped the poor creature inside a jar, closed the lid, then shook the jar until blood smeared on the glass. The fights were terrifying, not because the students were especially violent—most of them weren't—but because there was no control; nothing could be done except try to grab them and hold them and talk to them in low soft voices, or call the police and wait.

Some of the students had lost their mothers, fathers, sisters, brothers to gun violence or incarceration. Some of the students were being raised by grandmothers, grandfathers, or great-aunts. Some of the students lived in foster or group homes. Some of the students were born addicted. Some of the students didn't have food in their refrigerators. These students were in tremendous pain, and when they expressed their pain, they were expelled and sent to this separate school facility.

It wasn't all bad, though. The first several months, I cried every day, multiple times a day. The first several months, they were quick to point out my failures, weaknesses, and insecurities with vicious, ingenious precision. But each new day was like a brick in the wall of trust for them, for me, and eventually we warmed up to each other. "Stupid bitch" turned into "Miss B, you're a really nice person, but you're not very smart." "Ugly bitch" turned into "Miss B, if you just knew how to dress yourself, you'd have hella n**gas hollerin' at you." "White bitch" turned into "What are you, anyway? Puerto Rican?" Most of the students were charismatic and funny. I laughed with them every day. Most of the students were perceptive and empathetic. "Miss B, you look like you ran through a forest," and they brushed and braided my hair for me. "Miss B, you look like you goin' through it. Do you need a nap?," and they played basketball while I napped on the hood of my car. I was in awe of them. Some of the students couldn't memorize their multiplication tables or read beyond a second-grade level, but I knew they knew more than me, were immeasurably smarter and wiser than me. They had already witnessed more than I ever would. They had already survived more than I ever would.

It was irresponsible of me to teach at this school. It was irresponsible of the mental health coordinator (who, also as acting principal, visited the school once a year) to hire me. I suppose neither of us had a choice. I needed a job; the school needed a teacher. Most of the teachers didn't last long. Some of the teachers quit after three weeks. Some of the teachers quit after three days. No teacher lasted longer than a year except the teacher who started with me, who taught the students math and history and poetry and photography, who volunteered at refugee centers, who grew up in Oakland, the greatest teacher in all of Oakland, the real deal, in my humble opinion. No teacher lasted longer than a year except him and me.

I made countless grievous errors. I wasted hours and hours of instructional time planning half-assed haphazard lessons, then sulking and resenting the students when they revolted and mocked me for my bare-minimum effort. I reacted to their insults with passive aggressiveness and grudges. I called a student an asshole. I pushed a student. I made the rookie mistake of saying to a student, "If you have to pee so bad, then pee in the trash can," and he peed in the trash can. I let verbal altercations escalate into full-blown physical brawls because I was too afraid or too lazy to discipline. But we read a biography of Muhammad Ali and watched footage of every single one of his fights and the documentary *When We Were Kings* together. We planted sunflowers and morning glories along the chain-link fence together. We went to Country Town Buffet and Jack in the Box together. We went to parks, the beach, the zoo, and the Monterey Bay Aquarium together. I lasted four years. I lasted four years until the district transferred me without notice. A few months later, the school closed.

I'm not trying to boast or claim I did anything for these students that changed their lives for the better. But they definitely changed mine for the better. They taught me how to care, and I cared about them, though not as much as they needed or deserved. I learned so much from them, much much more than they learned from me. I am sorry. I am grateful.

I know I lasted those four years because of my father. Because he called me every morning to pep-talk me, then called me every afternoon to console me. "This is your Vietnam," he would say. "This is not your fault," he would say. I know I lasted those four years because of my mother, even though I couldn't recognize her influence back then. Because of my mother, her upbringing, her history, because of how her life and past shaped the way I inhabited the world, the way the world inhabited me, maybe I could understand more, just a little bit more, what it was like to be them. Because of my mother, maybe when they looked at me they didn't see the type of face that represented everything that was stolen and withheld from them. Because of my mother, maybe we were more, just a little bit more, the same. I am grateful.

*　　*　　*

I didn't want to leave Oakland. I left Oakland because I fell in love, because someone fell in love with me, and I followed him to his hometown of Prairie Village, a suburb of Kansas City, Kansas.

I met Kendall at a bar, a sports bar hosting University of Kansas alumni to watch the Jayhawks play in the Final Four Championship. I didn't give a damn about the Jayhawks or the Final Four Championship. My friend, also from Kansas, lured me to the bar with the promise of free beer and nachos.

Kendall wore a KU T-shirt and a KU jersey, but he also had a beard, and those thick dark-rimmed glasses, which indicated to me that he was probably well rounded, probably into hiking and crossword puzzles. Yes, he chugged a whole pint of beer with one press of glass to his lips, but he also ranted about the prison-industrial complex, the murder of Trayvon Martin, the new movie by Paul Thomas Anderson, and the new album by

Japandroids—during commercials. I ironically yelled "Rock Chalk!" each time the Jayhawks scored, because I was drinking a lot of free beer and feeling flirtatious. We shouted at each other over the blaring flat-screen televisions. After the Jayhawks lost, we staggered to a karaoke bar across the street, holding hands, but exchanged numbers and went home, both of us to our separate homes, before it was our turn to sing "Islands in the Stream."

Before Kendall, there was nothing. Nothing important. A slew of flings and one-night stands. Before Kendall, I took a ten-month hiatus from sex because the last time I had sex was with a stranger in a hotel room in Missoula, where I stopped overnight on my drive from Oakland to Lewistown, Montana, for a wedding. I spent the day of the wedding at a clinic because I couldn't pee, and when I could pee it was sudden and uncontrollable, squatting behind a bush or on the shoulder of the interstate or peeing directly onto my car seat. I was thirty years old and one of the bridesmaids, and the bride was not particularly pleased with my condition.

"Was he cute?"

"Nope."

"Was he smart?"

"Nope."

"Was he nice, at least?"

"Well, he paid for my tab at the bar and didn't murder me in my sleep."

"Hmmm."

I realized I had told so many of these stories throughout my twenties. I realized that in my twenties such behavior might be regarded as wild and adventurous, if a bit reckless. But in my thirties such behavior seemed heedless and pathetic.

My friend told me to aim high, to keep a strict standard of respect and admiration, to hold out until someone achieved that standard. To be patient. Ten months later, I met Kendall.

We didn't have sex the first time we hung out. We didn't have sex the second time we hung out. Or the third or the fourth. He called after each time, and we hung out.

The morning after the first time he spent the night, I woke to him sitting on the edge of my bed, fully dressed.

"You're leaving?" I asked.

He must have heard the trace of panic in my voice, because he laughed a little and replied, "Well, I'm not leaving you, darling. I'm just going to work." Then he bent down and touched his forehead against mine.

Two months later, he told me. We sat on a bench to rest and kiss one evening after a stroll through Golden Gate Park. I straddled him to make our bodies closer, streetlamps buzzing and flickering around us. I was thirty-one years old and had never heard those words whispered in my ear before. And yes, of course, waited my whole life to hear those words whispered in my ear. Haven't we all?

.

Being in love felt awful. For the most part. After those initial surges of relief and fullness and warmth. I couldn't handle it. I squirmed under the weight and pressure of it. I accused him of having crushes. I imagined he was cheating on me, convinced myself he was cheating on me, if he didn't return my texts or calls within a couple of hours. I snooped through his texts and emails and Facebook messages. Despite the perpetual anxiety and suspicion, I was still so afraid of losing it, this love, this thing I'd wanted so desperately for so long, afraid of losing him, afraid he was too good to be true. I needed endless reassurance. In the beginning, Kendall complied, but I soon exhausted his stamina. I don't blame him. I wasn't ready to be in love.

.

Kendall and I had known each other for nine months, and had been living together for two months, when he asked me to move with him to Kansas City. Maybe another one of his attempts to prove his commitment. Maybe a bluff. Someone who is happy where he is, with the person he's with, doesn't ask that person to move with him to Kansas City so he could try to start a business, open a delicatessen, with his sister, without any capital or experience working in a restaurant. I couldn't communicate these concerns. I couldn't be argumentative, contrarian. I wept for a day and answered no, then I wept for a day and answered yes, then I wept for a day and answered no, then I wept while I packed. He touched his forehead against mine, hummed the song "As Long As We Got Each Other." *This is sacrifice. This is love.*

On the morning we left Oakland, we fought. As we drove to Kansas City, we fought. I suspected him of texting his exgirlfriend, the one from Kansas City. I doubted and secondguessed, wanted to turn around, go back, but my stuff was packed in boxes, in a truck. Within hours of parking in the driveway, greeting his mother and sister, lugging our suitcases to the guest bedroom of his mother's house, borrowing an iron to smooth my wrinkled dress, we were rushed to attend his father's seventieth-birthday party. I was surrounded. His father, stepmother, stepbrothers, aunts and uncles, step-aunts and step-uncles, cousins, step-cousins, friends from childhood. The bartender of the restaurant was his ex-girlfriend's brother. All born and raised in Kansas City. All tall, fair-skinned, light-haired, corn-fed. There I was again: an outsider, an anomaly.

After one week, Kendall got a job as a cook. I rode my bicycle to the restaurant with him, then rode my bicycle to a coffee shop and sat by a window to read, then rode my bicycle to the restaurant and sat at the bar until his shift ended. When he wasn't working, we cooked and ate dinner with his mother, played board games with his sister, and hung out with his friends.

After three weeks, I broke out into hives. Oozing, red, itchy splotches on my face, neck, stomach, back, arms, and legs, that kept me hiding in the guest bedroom during the day, kept me awake at night. I lay in bed, skin on fire, seething with anger at Kendall's deep-sleep snores. Kendall diagnosed the cause as extreme change of climate and prescribed patience as my body adjusted. The doctor at the emergency room diagnosed the cause as stress and prescribed a steroid ointment.

"My family loves you. My friends love you. You're fitting in just fine," Kendall would tell me. But that wasn't the problem, that wasn't what I wanted to hear. I tried to explain. I felt completely reliant on him, like I was someone only in relation to him. I felt I was losing myself and being replaced by him. I felt like . . . my mother.

For the first time in my life, I wanted my mother.

I knew she would understand.

.

I didn't have to ask. They could hear it in my voice. They drove from Rochester to Kansas City in two days. When I opened the door to greet them, my mother was cradling a cylinder vase containing six spiraling stalks of bamboo and their nest of roots.

"This is from your room at home." My mother kept a vase of bamboo in every room of the house. She kept the vases full of fresh water, kept them green and growing, rubbed their leaves with her fingertips, and wiped the dust off with a cloth. She handed me the vase as we kissed and hugged hello.

"Your mother carried that vase in her lap for the whole trip," my father told me.

"Your father is crazy. He drive too fast."

I cradled the vase and smiled at her. I didn't have to ask. She didn't have to explain.

.

While I lived in Oakland, my one-bedroom apartment rented for eight hundred fifty dollars a month. Right after I moved, the apartment rented for thirteen hundred dollars a month. That was one of the reasons I couldn't go back.

We moved to Kansas City in July. By November, I started contemplating how to move again, how to get out. During the months of winter, Kendall rode his bicycle to work alone. I stayed indoors and wrote. I wrote poems. I wrote essays. I wrote a screenplay about a romantically dysfunctional alcoholic named Izzy. Kendall always read and loved what I wrote, and I will always be grateful. I applied to four M.F.A. programs, one in New York City, one in Nashville, one in Los Angeles, and one in New Orleans. I got accepted to the one in New Orleans. I didn't know what he was going to say. I didn't know what I wanted him to say.

We decided to try New Orleans together, to try to be new to each other again. We drove south. We camped for a night on the banks of the Buffalo River in Arkansas. We rented a canoe and hiked to a waterfall. We sat on a boulder at the edge of the waterfall. Kendall pulled a ziplock bag out of his pocket, pulled a diamond ring out of the ziplock bag, and proposed. I couldn't stop laughing, from joy, mostly from shock. I couldn't look at him, couldn't look into his eyes as I kissed him. I looked at the couples and their children wading and swimming, seeming so happy and sure of themselves, belonging to themselves. Could I do that with him? Could I do that with him for the rest of my life? I remember feeling a wave of panic, which I ignored. *He chooses me. He loves me.*

.

Sometimes I wonder if Kendall proposed because he thought being engaged would calm me. I thought being engaged would calm me, too. It didn't. It still felt awful, and worse and worse, and so bad one night that, after hours of trembling in the dark, seething with anger at Kendall's deep-sleep snores, I tiptoed to the kitchen, stood over the sink, and put the point of a knife to my wrist. I couldn't bring myself to puncture the skin, so I just tiptoed back to bed, then snooped through Kendall's texts and emails and Facebook messages.

We were engaged for one year. We canceled the wedding.

*   *   *

I am thirty-four years old. I have just parked my car, a rusted Nissan Sentra (the Pathfinder expired in California), outside my new apartment, half of a shotgun. Magnolia and live oak line the street. I have loaded and unloaded the trunk of my car several times. I have saved the potted plants for last. On my lap, I carry a cylinder vase containing six spiraling stalks of bamboo and their nest of roots.

This bamboo survived a year in Kansas City. It survived the backseat of a car for eight-hundred sixty-four miles. It survived a year in New Orleans, including a breakup, two apartments, and once, for two weeks, I abandoned it, left it on the porch in the sun in the sweltering merciless heat of a Louisianan August.

Sometimes I let the water go stale, let the roots go dry. Sometimes I forget to rub their leaves with my fingertips and wipe the dust off with a cloth. Some of the stalks turn yellow and soft, but new stalks grow, and I cut them off and place them in jars.

XVII
MY MOTHER'S BAPTISM

Every service begins with music. The reverend's wife, Miki-san, plays acoustic guitar. Her sister plays keyboard. A member of the congregation holds the microphone and sings. The whole congregation sings along in Japanese to the melody of "Amazing Grace." The lyrics of the hymn are written in Japanese and projected onto a blank white wall.

My mother told me she used to practice English by singing karaoke. Maybe I should practice Japanese by singing karaoke.

After a few hymns, Sensei Kim stands at the podium and reads from the Bible. After a few passages, he looks up from the page, looks at his congregation, then translates and explains the words in Japanese. He lowers his head and leads a prayer.

They close their eyes as they listen.

I sit between my mother and father in the front row. I look at my mother. Her eyes are closed. I look at my father. His eyes are open. My father and I don't understand, so we must keep our eyes open, look and guess to understand. *It's our turn now.*

I look at the aging earnest faces of the congregation, eyes closed and listening. They understand. *How blessed they are to have a place like this, how blessed they are to be here.* And then I think *No, no, it's not a blessing, it shouldn't be a blessing.* And then I think, *Why has it taken so long?*

I wish my mother could have come here sooner.

I wish all of them could have come here sooner.

·

Sensei Kim closes the Bible. His voice tightens and elevates to the tone of announcement. The congregation rise from their chairs. They move toward the door, shaking hands, bowing to each other, saying "Konnichiwa . . . Konnichiwa," instead of "Peace be with you." My father and I rise slowly, looking and guessing. Sensei Kim smiles and tells us in English that the congregation is going to the chapel of the church for the baptism.

He stands at the door, smiling, shaking hands, bowing. My father and I follow and mimic, as each member of the congregation shakes his hand and bows to him.

·

I follow my mother into the restroom. She washes her hands and brushes her teeth. I wash my hands and borrow her toothbrush to brush my teeth. We both brush our teeth obsessively, after every meal, before leaving the house, whenever our mouths feel stale, whenever anticipating close proximity to someone else. I think this is a personal quirk I adopted solely from my mother, but later this year, when I travel Japan, I will see other women brushing their teeth in public restrooms.

She digs into her purse and retrieves a bottle of lotion. She dabs a little onto her palm, a little onto my palm. We rub our hands.

"I'm nervous," she says to me.

"Why?" I ask, wondering if my mother is getting cold feet.

"I never been inside the real church before. Just that room."

"Don't worry, Mom." I try to think of what to say to reassure her. "You belong here. You're a Christian."

But even if she weren't.

.

The chapel is expansive, with a high-arched ceiling and stained-glass windows, with an altar and pews, with decorative paintings and sculptures. The ritual is brief. A few movements. My mother kneels on the floor beside Sensei Kim, who stands beside a stone basin of holy water. Sensei Kim dips his hand into the basin and drizzles holy water on the top of my mother's bowed head. Her eyes are closed. A few movements, and she is saved. Sensei Kim holds both of her hands, braces her as she stands. He rests both of his hands on both of her shoulders, beams at her like a proud father.

The congregation rise from the pews. They clap and cheer, their voices echo. They aim the cameras on their phones and press buttons. Sensei Kim gestures for me and my father to join. My mother stands in the middle. We smile at the flashes of the cameras.

.

Every service ends with food. Lids are removed, cellophane and aluminum peeled off, revealing pots and platters of stir-fried rice, stir-fried noodles, beef curry, kimchi, seaweed salad, potato salad, macaroni salad, gyoza, shumai, teriyaki chicken wings, bean dip and tortilla chips, cheesecake, and chocolate-chip cookies. And the sushi my mother made this morning, which is the centerpiece of the spread. Miki-san and her sister pour hot green tea from a kettle into Styrofoam cups. Some of the members rearrange folding chairs around tables. Some of the members set plates, silverware, and a cup of tea at each chair.

When everyone in the congregation has a plate of food, they

all press their palms together, bow at their food, and say, "Itada-kimasu!" *Let's eat!*

I sit next to my mother and across from my father. My father and I don't speak. We eat in silence and listen. We look and guess to understand.

They notice our silence and say, "Sorry for speaking Japanese," with their hands covering their mouths.

"Oh, please, don't be sorry," my father says. "There's nothing to be sorry about."

We eat until we're full, then load plates to take home. Some of the members wash dishes in the kitchen. Some of the members wipe tables and put the folding chairs back into rows. My father and I follow my mother, mimic my mother, as she bows and thanks her friends for coming.

·

Later that night, we sit around the coffee table in the living room for cocktails, for an assortment of cheeses and roasted almonds. My father and I drink Maker's Mark Manhattans. My mother drinks a glass of wine. She allows herself two glasses of wine, the second glass mixed with water. I ask her what Sensei Kim preached during his sermon.

She pauses and tries to remember. "He told us that God is perfect."

I wait for her to continue. She doesn't.

"Why is God perfect?" I ask.

My mother pauses and blinks. "Because he's God."

"Yes, but . . . did Sensei Kim tell you how God is perfect? What does God do that makes him perfect?"

My mother pauses and blinks again. My father leans back

on the couch with his hands clasped behind his head. "Not all Christians are philosophers like the Jesuits, Elizabeth. You see, the Jesuits—"

"Not now, Dad."

My mother repeats. "God is perfect . . . because he's God."

.

And maybe that is the best answer. Maybe God is perfect simply because he exists. Because he is the only one who exists.

And by God, I guess I mean life—this life, every life, this history, every history, every intricate unfolding of time. The only ones we'll ever live. The only ones we'll ever know.

Just like our own mothers, I think. *The only ones we'll ever know.*

XVIII

THE FIRST AMERICANS IN OKINAWA

The most prominent race-characteristic of the Luchuans is
not a physical but a moral one . . . their gentleness of spirit
and manner, their yielding and submissive disposition, their
hospitality and kindness, their aversion to violence and
crime.
—Basil Hall, British Royal Navy captain, in a letter to
Napoleon Bonaparte, 1816

The President agrees with you in thinking that you are
most likely to succeed in your objective on the Lew Chew
Islands. They are, from their position, well-adapted to the
purpose; and the friendly and peaceful character of the
natives encourages the hope that your visit will be welcomed
by them.
—Edward Everett, U.S. secretary of state, in a letter to
Commodore Matthew Perry, 1852

*W*e must solve this Japan problem. Their isolation. Their
foolish, stubborn resistance. We must open their country, open
their ports. We must help them understand the benefit of trade
and commerce, the benefit of advanced technology and superior
weaponry. We must help them understand the benefit of us.

We must compete with the Russians, the Dutch, the French,

and especially the British. How can the rest of the world take us seriously if we don't extend our influence?

We tried diplomacy. We tried persuasion. But the Japanese are so rude, so impudent. And even, that one time, *violent*. A few months ago, the former commodore directed one of our ships into Edo Bay and attempted to board a Japanese craft, intending only to engage in polite conversation, in informal negotiation, but a Japanese soldier pushed him, struck him, with two flat palms to his chest. It was an outrage, a humiliation. A regular Japanese soldier dared to attack such a highly ranked American officer— without provocation! We retreated. Or rather, he, the former commodore, retreated. Back to his vessel and back out of Edo Bay. We can still hear them snickering, spreading the news: The Americans are weak. The Americans are afraid of a little shove. We must convince them to be civilized, to be reasonable. And next time, if they insult us again, threaten us again, we retaliate. We must use force if necessary.

Now our leader is the fearless and dignified Commodore Matthew Calbraith Perry, "father of the steam navy," who oversaw the entire conversion of our ships from wind power to steam power. He fought bravely in the War of 1812 and Mexican-American War, capturing cities and acquiring many disputed yet much-deserved territories. He is competent, ruthless, strict— deeply regrets the recent ban of flogging. Commodore Perry will solve this Japan problem.

Once promoted, the Commodore reads every book, every article, every dispatch concerning Japan. He reads about the islands of Lew Chew, how these islands are claimed as dependencies of both Japan and China, how the people of these islands have been disarmed and are therefore defenseless, therefore in need of protection. The Commodore resolves that we must establish a reputation for strength, for unwavering firmness, on these islands of Lew Chew before we proceed to Japan.

We set sail with a list of demands. We must have free access to ports. We must have coal depots for our new steam engines. We must have permanent stations to seek refuge and resources. We must have guaranteed safety and comfort. We must be welcomed.

On the morning of May 26, 1853, we drop anchor offshore the largest island. We stand on deck and observe the red cliffs jutting out of the water, the golden hills rolling inland, the green forests draping the slopes and crests. Farther inland and north, on the highest hill, we see the gray stone walls of a castle. Rays of sunshine slant through the clouds, and a drizzle brightens the colors. Perhaps some of us forget why we came here, why we traveled so far uninvited. Perhaps some of us, for a moment, are humbled.

A small boat approaches our flagship. Four men row the boat, the first Lew Chewans to greet us, and they are a strange sight to behold. They have long beards, and long hair tied in knots on top of their heads, held in place with copper pins. They wear long robes with sashes tied around their waists, and sandals on their feet. As soon as they step onto the deck, all four of them bow profusely, excessively. One of them bows almost prostrate to the floor, then raises a card, a folded piece of delicate paper, above his head. We stand and watch, not knowing what to do. Finally, one of the mess boys the Commodore hired and brought from China steps forward, accepts the card, and speaks to the Lew Chewans in their language. The messboy brings the card to the Commodore, then promptly returns with the card, informing the Lew Chewans that the Commodore has reviewed their credentials and they are much too low of rank to be allowed appointment to see the Commodore. The mess boy sends them away. The Lew

Chewans comply and seem a bit embarrassed. Perhaps some of us feel a bit embarrassed for them, too—after that whole production of bows and curtsies. But we're not here to make friends. We must be stern.

An hour later, another small boat approaches. One man rows the boat and one man holds an umbrella. The man who holds the umbrella is fair-skinned, wearing the clothes of a missionary. As he climbs aboard, he can't contain himself, shaking hands and grinning. We are the first of his kind to grace these waters in two years. He tells us his name is Dr. Bernard Jean Bettelheim, born in Hungary, now a loyal subject to Great Britain, doing God's work across heathen Asia. He arrived from Hong Kong with his wife and two infant children. Since the local port master forbade him or any missionary from disembarking, he bribed the crew members to smuggle his family and possessions ashore. By the time he, his wife, and their children reached land, it was very dark, and a couple of Buddhist priests took pity and granted him, as a fellow man of the cloth, shelter in their temple, though only for the night. The Buddhist priests even slept elsewhere, so his wife could have privacy. The next morning, Dr. Bettelheim refused to leave. That was seven years ago. And he won't leave Lew Chew, he brags, until he saves them, every last inhabitant of the island. He burns objects of idolatry. He disrupts worship in private homes and public halls to preach the Gospel. Victory for Christianity and Great Britain. Except, contrary to previous opinions, the Lew Chewans are a cruel, savage people with no interest in ennobling themselves. The Commodore is happy to meet with Dr. Bettelheim, and together they agree that we must correct and guide these Lew Chewans. That the Lew Chewans are not to be trusted.

The next day, more boats approach. The boats carry chickens, pigs, goats, eggs, and vegetables. By order of the Commodore, the gifts are rejected. The Lew Chewans seem very confused, and, yes, some of us are quite baffled, too. We suppose we have to keep our guard up. We can't be swayed by gifts, by tokens of goodwill. The next day, the Commodore sends his lieutenant and interpreter to invite a principal dignitary, not these lowly officials, to dine with him in his cabin.

On the evening of May 28, the prince regent and his two aides answer the call, and to us, at least, they appear more worthy. The regent wears a red robe and sash made of fine silk. His long beard is white. His long hair is tied in a knot on top of his head, held in place with a *silver* pin. His aides wear blue robes, and their long hair is tucked beneath yellow caps. They wait on deck for close to an hour until the Commodore is ready to receive them. Perhaps some of us wish we could offer them chairs, but that might give the wrong impression.

On the way to the cabin, we point to special features of the ship. We show them the engine. We show them the arsenal. They stare at these feats of science for a long time, their faces full of intense wonder and grave alarm. Like they have encountered an absolute limit, a boundary they can't fathom beyond. Like they know they've already lost. Most of us are proud, like we've earned their admiration. Perhaps some of us, even just a few of us, feel a twinge of guilt, of sorrow. This isn't a fair fight, even if it's for a righteous cause.

Inside the cabin, the Commodore, having donned his dress uniform, presides over an elaborate meal of tenderloin steaks, mutton chops, veal chops, pork chops, salmon, boiled potatoes, brown bread, pudding, and chalices of wine. He is joined by his chief interpreter, who speaks Chinese. The regent and his aides find their seats at the table, and when they begin to eat, they fumble with the forks and knives. The Commodore doesn't mind. No more than a few bites into the meal, he announces, magnanimously, that on June 6 he will visit the royal palace to meet with the king and queen, and that he expects a proper reception for his title. The Lew Chewans drop their forks and knives onto their plates. There is a grim silence as they glance back and forth at each other. They explain that foreigners have never set foot on palace grounds, that foreigners are forbidden by law, and, besides, the king is a boy, ten years old, and the queen dowager is very ill. They plead with the Commodore to abandon his plan, to honor the regent for a banquet at his home, a short distance from the castle. The Commodore slams his fist on the table. He mocks their silly custom and declares that this is a new era, and he is not just any foreigner but the Commodore of the Navy of the United States of America. The Lew Chewans are dismissed.

The day after this dinner, the Commodore sends a squadron of us, fully armed, ashore, to go anywhere we please. Some guards follow us, but they have no weapons. The rest of the Lew Chewans ignore us, and try to resume their daily activities. Some of their eyes spark with curiosity. Some of their eyes flash with fear and anger.

We wander around until dark, until it is too late to row back to the ship, which is part of the Commodore's plan. We choose the town hall at the base of the road leading to the castle. The gates are locked from the outside, so one of us climbs over the wall. The gates are locked from the inside, so one of us breaks the gates. Within minutes, guards and officials surround us, begging us to leave. Our interpreter says we'll only stay for the night. The Lew Chewans explain that foreigners are forbidden by law, even if only for a night, and that if we stay they'll be punished. Our interpreter asks who will punish them. The Lew Chewans look to the ground and have no answer. Must be one of their lies—another trick. We unpack our bags. Then, to our tremendous surprise, one of the officials says: "Gentlemen! Doo Choo man very small, American man not very small. I have read of America in books, of Washington—very good man, very good. Doo Choo good friend American. Doo Choo man give American all provision he wants. American can have no house onshore." Hearing these words in English puts us in a predicament. Do we defy these Lew Chewans, who have no weapons, who have told us plainly and simply and rather kindly that we aren't welcome? Or do we defy the Commodore?

The next day, the Commodore sends more of us, including a sick officer, to the building we borrowed. The Lew Chewans don't beg or protest. Instead, they bring fruit to the sick officer.

For several days, several efforts are made to dissuade the Commodore from his plan to visit the castle. Officials come to the ship, delivering letters and gifts, which, once again, by order of the Commodore, are rejected. The regent himself comes to the ship to appeal to the Commodore in person. Once again, he is dismissed.

On June 6, the Commodore does exactly as he promised.

"It was a matter of policy to make a show of it," the Commodore will later attest in his *Narrative of the Expedition of an American Squadron to the China Seas and Japan*. "Hence some extra pains were taken to offer an imposing spectacle."

Indeed, an imposing spectacle. First, Dr. Bettelheim and the interpreters. Second, captains and lieutenants in ceremonial uniforms. Behind them, two sets of sailors dragging field guns. Followed by a band of horns and drums. Followed by a company of armed marines. Followed by the Commodore, decorated with all his ribbons and medals, perched in a sedan chair, which was carved and fashioned specifically for this occasion, painted gold, adorned with red, white, and blue curtains. Four Chinese mess boys carry him in his chair. Four more march alongside, as substitute bearers. Followed by four more, for personal attendance to the Commodore. Another two carry gifts for the royal household. Followed by another company of armed marines. A total of two hundred men.

We march through the town of Naha, up the road leading to Shuri Castle. We pass huts of bamboo, clay, and coral. We pass garden patches of sweet potato, corn, and melon. We pass chicken coops, farms of pigs, goats, and cattle. We pass palm trees, banana trees, and citrus trees. Crowds gather. Some of them cover their mouths and gasp. Some of them run away and hide. Some of them point and laugh. Some of the children cry. Some of the children frolic at the commotion. We look straight ahead. The band plays on. When we reach the outer walls of the castle, the regent is waiting. He waves his arms and pleads with the Commodore. The Commodore waves him off. We march forward to the inner walls, but the gates are locked. And though these gates could surely withstand the gunfire we have now, the regent has seen the engine and arsenal of our ship. He can see the Commodore now, screaming and slamming his fist on the arm of his sedan chair. He can see the crowds of his people now, exposed and utterly defenseless. He unlocks the gates. We march forward to the tune of "Hail, Columbia," and enter the palace grounds. We are the first foreigners to set foot on the palace grounds.

We are Americans.

But the courtyard is empty. No sign of the king or queen dowager. No sign of any preparation for our arrival. Just the breeze whistling. The three palace buildings, made of wood and orange tile, are mansions compared with the dwellings in town, but modest compared with the palaces in China. No shining ornament. No towering pillars or pagodas. The Commodore motions to the largest of the three buildings; then he and his closest counsel, and those of us who are able to fit, march single-file into the reception chamber. Also empty.

The regent and his aides hasten through the side screen doors, assembling across from us. They bow stiffly, insincerely. We mimic. Neither side broaches any topic for discussion. We stand and shift our weight, our weapons and instruments getting heavy. After much time passes, more of their men enter the chamber, offering cups of barely steeped tea. The regent, as if for the very first time, invites the Commodore to his home, where a proper feast is ready to be served. The Commodore concedes and follows the regent. The Commodore walks.

And yes, there is a proper feast. Plenty for all of us. Platters of baked fish and fried pork, bowls of steamed rice and vegetables, eggs, fresh fruit, porcelain pots of sake. Some of us think about the march through town, passing their homes, their gardens, their farms, and wonder how much this meal might have cost the Lew Chewans, how many went without and will go without for weeks to come. But we try not to think about that for too long. The Commodore and the regent converse through their interpreters, who both speak Chinese. The regent's interpreter admits that he knows a little English, and that he has read Japanese texts on the geography and history of the United States, as well as the biography of George Washington. The Commodore is delighted. He raises his glass. He toasts to the regent, to the king and queen dowager, to the people of Lew Chew. "Prosperity to the Lew Chewans! May they and the Americans always be friends!" Then he stands to excuse himself and when the regent tells him that there is still more food and drink to be served, the Commodore tells the regent that he is done eating and drinking, and decides to end the banquet honoring him before it is finished.

The day after the march to Shuri Castle, we begin military drills. Seventeen ships, wielding cannons and rifles, flaunting and blasting along the coast for all the Lew Chewans to see and hear. We borrow more buildings for barracks, for infirmaries, for a photographer's laboratory. We use one of their ancient temples as a stable for our cattle. When a more brazen official suggests that a building other than a temple could be used for a stable, the Commodore replies that they have gods enough to worship in other places.

On July 2, 1853, the Commodore and four of his finest, most formidable ships set sail for Edo Bay. And those of us who are left behind discover the truth about the Lew Chewans. From the stares and jeers and taunts. From the rocks they throw. Two of us are beaten in the streets. One of us is pushed off a cliff. They accuse us of stealing. They accuse us of raping their daughters. This is not how civilized nations deal with crimes allegedly committed. The Lew Chewans are not the gentle, peaceful people that so many who came here before us have claimed.

After a year of negotiations, of summoning more ships, more men with guns, Japan is open for business. The expedition, a complete success. Lew Chew has fulfilled its purpose. Those of us who are left behind will leave soon and gladly. But first we must secure our legacy. We must have a treaty.

The Lew Chew Compact, otherwise known as "the Friendship Treaty" or "the Amity Treaty," states, "Whenever citizens of the United States come to Lew Chew, they shall be treated with great courtesy and friendship," and that Lew Chewans are responsible for safe anchorage of our ships, and that supplies shall be purchased at fixed prices, and that "whenever persons from ships of the United States come ashore in Lew Chew they shall be at liberty to ramble where they please, without hindrance, or having officials sent to follow them, or to spy what they do; but if violently go into houses, or trifle with women, or force people to sell them things, they shall be arrested by the local officers but not maltreated, and shall be reported to the captain of the ship to which they belong, for punishment by him." Our demands will remain in practice for centuries. Anniversaries will be celebrated, monuments will be erected, a ward in Naha will be named after Commodore Matthew Calbraith Perry. Future generations will understand his impact and importance.

The Lew Chewans do not agree to sign at first. They insist that the compact indicate in writing, in bold print, that they signed under compulsion. But that would be ridiculous. That would negate the whole concept of a treaty.

On July 11, 1854, the day the treaty is signed, the Commodore visits the regent with a company of armed marines and two howitzers at his side.

This is how we solved the Japan problem.

We are Americans.

I remember reading about Commodore Matthew Perry and his success, about the end of isolation and the opening of Japan, in my ninth-grade social-studies textbook. I remember feeling proud, victorious. I remember thinking it was for the best. For them as much as for us. Why wouldn't they want steam engines and guns? Why wouldn't they want better, more modern stuff? There was no mention of his visit to Okinawa and the Lew Chew Compact in my ninth-grade social-studies textbook. There was no mention of Okinawa in any textbook. Maybe a sentence, maybe a paragraph, maybe a picture and a caption, in the unit on World War II.

I remember reading about pilgrims, settlers, pioneers, about Andrew Jackson and the Trail of Tears, about James K. Polk and Manifest Destiny. I remember feeling vindication. I remember thinking, thinking without words, *No, this isn't fair, but yes, this is inevitable, we are bigger and stronger, we are the future, better not to fight, better not to resist, better just to accept what must be, to become one of us.* I remember reading about the Middle Passage and seeing a photograph of a painting of a slave ship, the bodies crammed belowdecks, suffocating, defecating, the chains, the torture. I remember feeling pity, but not remorse, not guilt. I remember thinking, *That's not me, I would never do that, and that happened so so long ago.* I suppose the textbooks were written to make me think that way. But before I even read those textbooks, I was already taught to think that way.

Growing up, I thought America was a melting pot, should be a melting pot. America should welcome anyone from anywhere, as long as we knew our place and fulfilled our duty to assimilate. As long as we knew that White was on top—and though I didn't think the word "White" I understood what it signified. As long as we fell into line, and the closer we got to White the better, and if we couldn't get very close for whatever reason, well, then, tough luck. When I was growing up, White was always what I strived to be, and White always felt just beyond reach. Except that I was already White. White was how I viewed the world, looked out at the world, no matter what the world saw when it looked back at me.

Later, as an adult, as I began to comprehend the systems of White supremacy, the systems of America, I tried to renounce White. *No, that's not me, I would never do that, I'm not the perpetrator, I'm the victim.* I thought I couldn't be held responsible. I thought I couldn't be racist. How could I? I'm not white, I'm half Asian.

But I must admit who half of me is, where half of me comes from: the long-standing tradition of conquest and absolution. Half of me was born with a sense of entitlement, a sense of the right to pursue happiness, to control and improve my life while taking for granted the resources and methods to do so, the mindset that if it doesn't work out it's not tough luck, it's a raw deal. Half of me is offended by the label of privilege, by the notion that there is no such thing as clean wealth, as pure good fortune. Half of me is afraid of accusation, of culpability, of guilt. Half of me uses the other half to maintain innocence.

I believe we inherit sin as much as we inherit trauma. I believe inherited sin is its own form of trauma. But maybe we have a chance at redemption. By being aware, being honest. By giving up power. By letting the world change. By changing ourselves.

By apologizing.

By forgiving?

What would atonement and forgiveness look like?

Within a person, a family, a nation?

I am twelve years old. I have not yet bleached my hair an ugly shade of orangish yellow, then cherry red, then violet purple, then midnight blue, or started wearing fake thick-rimmed glasses that hide the shape of my eyes and the lack of a bridge on my nose. This will happen very soon.

It is the summer between seventh and eighth grade, and all I want to do is hang out with my two new best friends. I want to chase them, run after them on the sidewalk as they ride their skateboards down the street. I want to sit on a curb in the parking lot and watch them as they practice ollies and kickflips. They are the only girls in Fairport who ride skateboards, and they are so cool. They ask me why I won't ride a skateboard, and I tell them I can't ride a skateboard because I'm too clumsy, but I was a gymnast for five years, before I quit this year, because gymnastics is for kids and surely Kurt Cobain wouldn't approve. I don't know the real reason why I won't ride a skateboard. Maybe because I'm still too afraid to be different. Maybe because I'm already different.

It is the summer between seventh and eighth grade, and all I want to do is hang out with my two new best friends and all the boys who want to hang out with my two new best friends—my two new best friends, who are so cool because they ride skateboards, because they have fair skin and freckles, hazel eyes and blue eyes, light brown hair that gets even lighter, almost blond, in the sun. I want to go to pool parties and slumber parties. I want to go to the mall and the movies. I want to invite my two new best friends, and all the boys who want to hang out with my two new best friends, over to my house to hang out in my basement while my parents are at work, so all of us can sit on the couch in front of the television and watch MTV and Comedy Central, arm touching arm, thigh touching thigh, under a blanket in the cool dimness, wishing for and waiting for and dreading an unmistakable grope.

But instead I have to go to Okinawa with my mother.

I haven't been to Okinawa since I was three years old. My mother hasn't been to Okinawa since I was three years old. My mother misses her homeland, her family. She misses her daughter, the daughter who is the small child in the photographs, who used to want to be held, used to coo and giggle at her mother's touch, used to hide her face in the curve of her mother's neck, listen to her mother without averting her gaze, point to the things she wanted and ask for these things in Japanese. But none of that matters to me. All that matters to me is my two new best friends and the boys who want to hang out with my two new best friends. My mother doesn't ask me if I want to visit her homeland, her native country, the place we call Okinawa, a place that is imageless in my mind, meaningless in my mind, in my American mind, a place I can't remember. My mother doesn't ask me if I want to see her family again, especially my grandmother, the grandmother who is the old woman in the photographs, who used to feed me, used to potty-train me, carry me on her back, and teach me words in Japanese, the grandmother who is the strange voice I hear when my mother shoves the phone at me and tells me to say, "Obaa, genki desu ka?" *Grandma, are you well?* and then the strange voice weeps and asks me if I'm well, asks me a bunch of questions in Japanese, and of course I don't know what to say, so I look at my mother, who smiles at me expectantly, and I feel so stupid and helpless and angry, so I shove the phone back at her, shaking my head, whispering, "No, no, here, I don't want it." My mother doesn't ask me if I want to remember. She doesn't prepare me. Even my father, who always foresees, always warns, who will stay behind, stay here, like he did nine years ago, who will let us go alone to have some quality mother-daughter bonding time together, doesn't prepare me. Both my mother and my father don't know. What it's like to be American and a girl and twelve years old. They think it will be fun. They think it will be good for me.

.

On the plane, I sit by the window and my mother sits in the middle. I stare out the window and daydream. Not wondering about my grandmother, my aunts and uncles, my cousins, not wondering about immersing myself in a culture, a culture that is connected to me, a culture that could belong to me if I chose to accept it, not wondering about learning more about my mother, this woman sitting next to me with her eyes closed, not wondering what she's thinking, what she's excited to see, scared to see. Instead, I worry about getting too tan, and if my bangs will grow out by the end of the summer, and if an entire summer is how long it takes for my two new best friends and the boys who want to hang out with my two new best friends to forget me.

We arrive at the San Francisco International Airport. Our connecting flight to Tokyo has been canceled. We follow the other disgruntled passengers and stand in line, and as we shuffle closer and closer to the agent behind the counter, my heart beats faster. *Does she know what to say?* I've never flown on a plane with just my mother before. I've never navigated an airport with just my mother before. My father has always done the talking, the planning, the problem solving. He always told us where to go and we obeyed. *What if she doesn't understand? What if I can't explain?* Right now, twelve years old seems so young, too young to be flying on a plane and navigating an airport. I'm frightened and embarrassed, yet relieved that at least I'm not alone, at least I'm with my mother, even though she's just as confused and helpless as me, according to me. Luckily, though, we don't have to talk. The agent gives my mother two new tickets and a voucher for a hotel, then directs us to the shuttle bus.

.

"San Francisco!" I shout, bouncing up and down on the king-sized bed. San Francisco is not imageless, not meaningless. San Francisco is a very cool, very brag-worthy place. My mother has been to San Francisco once, on her way to New York City with my father, when she first immigrated to the United States. But that was way before I was born, so I don't know and I don't care to know.

"Do you want to go somewhere?" my mother asks, leaning close to the mirror, freshening her eyeliner, mascara, and lipstick.

"Yes!"

We take the shiny gold elevator to the lobby and exit through the gleaming glass doors. Outside, we are shocked by a chill and a hard gust of wind. I shiver, look up at the palm trees, odd and ominous, then scan the row of taxis, smug and uninviting. I've never taken a taxi with just my mother before. I've never explored a city with just my mother before.

"Where should we go?" I ask.

"Let's go to Chinatown," my mother answers.

And suddenly I'm so cold, too cold, to go anywhere.

.

So many of them. Round, dark, wrinkled faces. I can't remember. "This is your aunt . . . This is your uncle . . ." After they smile and hug and squeeze my face between their hands, they lift our luggage off the baggage-claim conveyor belt for us, carry our luggage through the airport for us, and lead us to the parking lot, and then it hits me: a wall of hot heavy air like nothing I've ever felt. *I want to go home. I want to go home.* There's hardly enough room for all of us plus our luggage in their rusty, noisy, un-air-conditioned van. My aunt sits on her husband's lap. Her plump arm slides and slips against mine. *Why did they all have to come to pick us up?*

They drive us to a restaurant, a fancy restaurant, but I can't tell that it's fancy, because the restaurant doesn't have any chairs, only straw mats on the wooden floor, and we have to leave our shoes at the entrance. We sit cross-legged on the straw mats around a huge table. Now Obaa is here, but I sit far away from her. Now more cousins and second cousins are here, but they don't speak English and I don't speak Japanese. So many of them. Round, dark, wrinkled faces. Sweaty faces. I can't remember. They ask me a bunch of questions in Japanese. I can't answer. So they stop asking me and start asking my mother.

"What are they saying about me?" I ask her.

"They want to know why you don't speak Japanese."

They look at me and smile. I look down. I don't know, and I don't care to know.

Waitresses wearing stiff kimonos kneel at the table, arms balancing wide platters of glittery fish. They put a platter right in front of me, and I gasp, appalled that the fish is still alive. Fins flapping. Mouths opening and closing. Gills expanding and contracting. Bulging eyes. The flesh of the fish peeled and sliced, served on their bones while still alive. *Who are these monsters? These barbarians?* I can't move. I can't eat. I look at my mother. She looks at me and sighs. She picks at the poor fish with her chopsticks. The rest of my family jabs at the fish, digs into the fish, the fish that are dying but still alive. They slurp whole pieces and chew happily. This meal is a luxury, a delicacy. They eat like this when a loved one, someone they want to welcome, want to honor, comes to visit. But I don't know that. I try to nibble on some rice smothered in soy sauce, but I don't have much of an appetite.

One of my aunts nudges my mother with her elbow and points at me with her chin. *Is she okay? Why isn't she eating?*

My mother shrugs. *She's American.*

A few minutes later, a waitress brings me a platter of grilled chicken on a skewer.

.

For two months, I spend the bulk of my days sprawled on the futon in the only air-conditioned room of my aunt's house. I watch the American channel on television for hours. *Saved by the Bell, Growing Pains,* and even shows like *M*A*S*H* and *The Jeffersons,* which I wouldn't watch back home. I listen to cassette tapes on my Walkman for hours—Nirvana, Pearl Jam, Green Day—until the cassette tapes wear out and the voices sound slow. I talk to my two best friends—who actually remember me—on the phone, racking up a bill of eight hundred dollars. When my father gets the bill, he says he understands, says it's okay. I pluck my eyebrows off, both eyebrows, one hair at a time. I pierce my ears, each ear six times with a safety pin. I pierce my belly button and the skin between my index finger and thumb with a safety pin. This makes my mother cry, and when she asks why, I tell her I'm bored.

I venture out of the air-conditioned room to the kitchen for lunch and dinner. My uncle feels bad for me, and sometimes he brings me hot dogs and hamburgers on his way home from work. And even though my palate is so American, I like to eat the thick noodles with pink pickled ginger and pork ribs in broth. I like to eat the stir-fry of tofu, bitter melon, and Spam. Maybe the daughter who is the small child in the photographs remembers what she used to eat, used to love to eat.

One day, my uncle drives us around the perimeter of the island. I sit in the backseat and stare out the open window at turquoise water, white sand, lush hills, trees with roots that rise above the ground, orchids that grow from the branches, bushes of hibiscus, fields of tall pampas grass, sugarcane and pineapple farms, but the beauty doesn't inspire me. I must be determined to hate this island. I see the long stretches of concrete and barbed wire, the military bases, and I blame Okinawa. One day, we ride to another island on a glass-bottomed boat—below me, gardens of red coral reef, silver fish, purple urchin, a bright green eel, and a pale blue sting ray—and I lose myself, get rid of myself, almost have a nice time. One day, we go to a museum, the site of a mass suicide. I see the photographs of soldiers, some of them boys my age, some of them boys who look much younger than me, dressed in torn and frayed uniforms, dressed in rags, holding rifles in their limp arms, these boys, so young, and I succumb to an incredible sadness that turns into guilt that turns into anger, like *Why did they bring me here?* One day, I go to a karaoke bar with my youngest cousin, who is four years older than me. She buys us a platter of french fries. I eat the whole platter by myself while she sings by herself. She speaks only Japanese. Everyone here speaks only Japanese. I don't realize, don't empathize, don't make the connection that everyone in the United States speaks only English, and maybe this is how my mother feels over there, but now my mother is here. Instead, I just feel very lonely and angry, and I hate her for bringing me here.

.

One day, we visit Obaa at her house, the house where my mother grew up, the house my grandfather built, made of wood and scraps of metal. I see the house and I think, *poor.* I see the carts filled with garbage, the piles of garbage scattered in the yard, and I think, *poor.* I see Obaa, withering and rickety, wearing rags, standing under the rusted tin roof, and I think, *she is not me, I don't want her to be me.* She is ninety years old, the oldest person I know, the oldest person I've ever met, from a time in history that is more foreign to me than Okinawa. When she hugs me, she smells strange. Like stale sweat and garbage. When she holds me at arm's length to have a good look at me, when she looks at me and weeps, I try to say, "Obaa, genki desu ka?" with sincerity but I don't mean it. I'm afraid of her. I sit on the floor and wait while my mother kneels and prays at the shrine to her father, who died of alcoholism at the age of sixty-two, and her oldest sister, who died of pneumonia at the age of seventeen. I sit on the floor and wait while my mother and Obaa talk and talk and point at me with their chins. When they say goodbye, they hold each other tight and weep. I just want to leave.

.

That was the last time my mother saw her mother.

.

Obaa, I am sorry. I am sorry for being so American. I am sorry for being afraid of you, ashamed of you. You, who survived the Battle of Okinawa, which wasn't your fault. You, who survived poverty, which wasn't your fault. You loved and took care of your children. You loved and took care of my mother. You gave her your blessing when she married an American and moved far away from you. You are dead now, but if I ever were to see you again, I hope I would have the courage to hold you tight, hold both your hands in mine, and say, Gomen nasai. *I am sorry.*

.

For two months, I spend the bulk of my days sprawled on the bed in the only air-conditioned room in the house, and my mother spends the bulk of her nights sitting on the floor around a table under oscillating fans with her two sisters, her brother, and her oldest niece. They drink awamori and sake and beer for hours. They play cards for hours. They drink, smoke cigarettes, play cards, talk, catch up on nine years.

Late at night, my mother crawls into bed with me. She is drunk, and I can feel her heartache and disappointment in me, and I hate her even more for it. One morning, she tells me that she wants to stay in Okinawa, that she doesn't want to go back with me to the United States, that I will go back by myself. I'm not surprised. At first, I'm relieved. At first, I think that if she stayed everything would be easier, my life would be easier, my life would make more sense, but then I think I should probably put up a fight, perform a bit of an objection, and then I remember the airport. *Oh, wait, no, I don't know how to go back by myself.* And as soon as I think this thought, the very moment I think this thought, my mother says, "Don't worry, you figure it out."

"Figure what out?"

"How to go back by yourself."

I don't ask her how she knows. I don't want to admit my thought.

And for this brief uncanny moment, my mother and I are close. I realize that she knows me, really knows me, understands me, even though I don't know and understand her. Maybe we should be together. Maybe she is more my mother and I am more her daughter than I am willing to admit. But I don't want to admit my thought.

.

Mom, I am sorry. I am sorry I hurt you so much that you wanted to stay in Okinawa. I am sorry Okinawa has always welcomed you more than the United States, even though you have lived in the United States longer. But I'm glad you didn't stay in Okinawa. I'm glad you came back to the United States with me, that you lived far away from your mother so you could live close to me. Because even though I hurt you, you always knew what was best for me, and did what was best for me. I am grateful. I am sorry.

.

And there is more, so much more. How do I account for all of it? How do I apologize for all of it?

XXI

SECOND HONEYMOON IN JAPAN: A TRAVELOGUE

Itsumademo aruto omouna oya to kane.

Your money and your parents won't last forever.

—Inscribed on a plaque outside a shrine in the Yanaka district of Tokyo

BEFORE
2015

I am thirty-four years old. I am sitting on a couch in a stranger's living room in a stranger's apartment, an Airbnb in Ålesund, Norway. Kendall is lying on a bed in another room, on the other side of the wall. I can't see him, but I know he's listening. I am sitting on a couch with a phone in my hand. I don't want to make this call.

Kendall and I are scheduled to meet my parents in Tokyo in three days. Kendall and I are in Norway because, after extensive Google searches, Kendall determined that the absolute cheapest route from New Orleans to Tokyo was through different airlines, through New York City, Berlin, Oslo, and Istanbul. A little less than six hundred dollars. He's kind of brilliant and tenacious when it comes to bargain-priced flights and economical—though extremely complicated and stressful—travel. Kendall had been to Germany and Turkey before, but not Norway. I would have gone to Germany and Turkey, but especially Norway. With the money we saved, we treated ourselves to ten days of hopping ferries from fjord to fjord, buses from hostel to hostel, riding bicycles up and down dirt roads, along the bases of mountains and ridges of valleys, waterfalls so close we could feel their spray, creeks so pure we could drink from them. Yesterday, after seven days of arguing about where to eat, what to eat, the order of sights to see, if it's too cold and rainy to rent a canoe or not, after six nights of sharing twin beds without kissing or cuddling or fucking at all, as we soaked in a hot tub at the Juvet Landscape Hotel, surrounded by pine forest and clear streams and jagged snowcapped peaks, Kendall and I broke up. We decided to cancel the wedding that is supposed to take place in three months, after I booked the venue and paid the deposit, after I mailed the invitations and bought a dress, and now I'm sitting on a couch with a phone in my hand. I don't want to make this call. I don't want to tell my father that Kendall won't be coming with me to Tokyo, or the rest of Japan, to Nikko, Hakone, and Kyoto, places my parents visited on their honeymoon forty years ago, that Kendall won't be coming with me to Okinawa, to meet my mother's family, to be with me as I reunite with my mother's family.

"I'm sorry," I tell my father over the phone, trying to muffle the noises coming out of me as I bawl. I know Kendall can hear. I know he's listening.

"Sorry? You shouldn't be sorry. Why are you sorry, sweetheart?"

Because I'm thirty-four years old and I'm still crying to my daddy on the phone over a breakup. Because I'm ruined, my whole plan is ruined. Because this trip was supposed to be a celebration, a homecoming, a welcoming, a chance to redeem myself for the brat I was twenty-two years ago, except now I'm ruined, heartbroken, and everyone will have to *deal* with me. Because my father has been planning and preparing for this trip for months, promising this trip for years, ever since the last trip, when my mother and I went without him, when he couldn't be there to guide us, to mediate between us. Because he has taken care of his mother and his aunt for the last nine years, more years than he originally expected, changing diapers and bathing, answering wails in the middle of the night. Because he has splurged a huge chunk of his inheritance to pay for this trip.

"If you cancel Kendall's reservations, will you get a refund?"

"Elizabeth, I'm not worried about that right now. I'm worried about you."

"I'm fine." My voice disintegrates.

After a long pause, my father says, "You live an interesting life, my dear," and I actually chuckle. "One day, you'll write a great story about this and it'll all be worth it." He always knows what to say, how I cope. "Would you like to speak to your mother?"

It has been two months since my mother's baptism, since I began to perceive her, reckon with her, with more generosity. And even though I've been doing better, doing my best to call her, answer her calls, to remain patient through the fragments, the repetitions, the small-talk, I still feel the effort, the strain, the performance. Right now, I don't have the energy to take the extra time to answer her questions, the extra time to explain, to take care of myself and my mother. So I choose to use the breakup as an excuse to regress. "No. I'll wait."

1974

Ten months after my father met my mother, he was stationed in Korea. For six months, they wrote each other letters. My father wrote his letters in English. My mother wrote her letters in Japanese. They asked friends or paid professionals to translate. My father proposed in a letter. My mother accepted his proposal in a letter. They needed friends or paid professionals to translate. They already knew, when he proposed, when she accepted, that they would move to the United States. He would bring home a wife, a symbol that he had returned home from war a man, an honorable man, a good man, a man who would go to war and marry a woman. She would leave her home with a husband, a symbol that she had achieved status, that she was special and worthy, since she was willing to take such a risk on a man, since a man was willing to take such a risk on her.

There were no parties, no send-offs, no long goodbyes. My father resigned from the army. He shook hands, clinked glasses, and sipped whiskey. My mother gave her younger sister, Setsu, her car and her furniture. She tried to give Obaa a big wad of cash, but Obaa clenched her fists behind her back. So my mother tucked the money between her sleeping mat and pillow.

They were married on December 12, 1974. Three weeks later, they left for their honeymoon in Japan.

THE FLIGHT
2015

At the Istanbul Atatürk International Airport, I purchase a chicken sandwich. A pre-grilled, pre-assembled, plastic-wrapped, cold and dry chicken sandwich. I have just been fed on the flight from Oslo, and I will surely be fed on the flight to Tokyo, and my layover is only ninety minutes, but I've never let an extended period of idle time pass without at least a snack. Kendall knows this, and he laughs at me as I approach him in the waiting area, already peeling off the cellophane. He is waiting at my gate because his flight leaves six hours later. His flight leaves for New Orleans, where he will pack his belongings and move out of our apartment before I return from my trip.

"Are you going to eat that whole sandwich by yourself?" he asks.

"Yes," I say, collapsing onto the seat next to him. I take a bite and shove the sandwich in his direction.

As we take turns taking bites, I dwell on the fact that this is our last meal together. My eyes start to sting and blur, and I toss the crusty round end of the chicken sandwich onto his lap. He looks at me, and I see that his eyes are also blurry. He rips the crusty round end of the chicken sandwich in half, then hands me one of the halves. I stuff the cold dry bread into my mouth, chewing with my mouth open because I can't breathe through my nostrils.

"I don't want to go alone," I say, mouth full and sobbing.

"You'll be fine," he says, mouth full and sobbing.

"I wish you could come with me."

"It's too late."

"I know it's too late, but I still wish you could."

The attendant announces that my flight is boarding. I unplug my cell phone and give Kendall the adapter for my charger.

"You don't have to stand in line yet. It takes a while."

"Let's just get it over with." He follows me to the line of passengers. "Okay, listen," I say sternly. "We're just going to hug and say goodbye really fast, and then you're just going to walk away." He nods.

We hug, and I try to let go of him, but he won't let go of me, which I knew would happen, so I hold him tighter and bawl without restraint into his neck. His body feels warm and open and vulnerable. His body hasn't felt like that to me for a very long time.

"I love you," I say.

"I love you, too," he says.

We kiss each other. A soft, forgiving kiss. I turn away and stare at the floor, and I don't look up until the attendant checks my boarding pass.

On the plane, before it departs, I download three Japanese-language instructional audio books to my phone. I believe I'll be able to learn a language in thirteen hours. I believe I have an advantage, that the Japanese I understood and spoke as a child will immediately activate, and I'll step off the plane in Tokyo practically fluent. I listen to lessons while I sleep, while I dream, while I stare out the window and cry. "Kuruma-ga arimasu . . . Aoi Kuruma-ga arimasu . . ." *There is a car . . . There is a blue car . . .* I listen to the same lessons again and again. I can't remember the word for "car" or "blue." I can't remember words from previous lessons. And now I'm furious at myself for not practicing sooner, for going to Norway with Kendall, for wasting the past few days, weeks, months arguing and pleading with Kendall, instead of studying Japanese. I have wasted so much time. I have betrayed my mother.

When I land in Tokyo, all I hear is Japanese. All I hear is nonsense. When I find a sign with my name on it, the driver of the shuttle to the hotel greets me in English and chats with me in English, and as soon as there is a lull in the conversation, I insert my headphones and listen to another lesson. When I look out the window, all I see is the harsh mass of tall gray buildings and neon billboards. All I see is my new empty future. All I see is my aloneness.

Tokyo's ugly.

1975

My mother had never been on a plane before. She had never left Okinawa before. For years, since she was sixteen years old, she served drinks to men in suits and uniforms, saw them come and go, stay for a few days, weeks, months, and then leave for the United States, for the rest of the world. What did the United States, the rest of the world, feel like to someone who grew up on an island, an island that was never what it used to be, an island that was owned by and existed for the purposes of other nations? Did it feel like escape? Did it feel like progress?

She carried new luggage. She wore a new dress. Two attendants stood at the gate, two more stood at the entrance of the plane, so deferential as they checked tickets, as they gestured to the rows of cushioned chairs. She walked beside my father, slightly behind my father, holding his hand. He was retired, wearing civilian clothes, but his short hair, strong build, and straight posture gave him away. A former soldier. A former officer. Her new husband. Could she detect a flicker of envy from the other passengers? Did they approve? Were they happy for her? She sat by the window. She smoothed her dress over her knees. My father helped her buckle her seat belt. He held her hand. She looked at the line of people walking down the aisle. Well-dressed people. Dignified people. She was there, among them. As the engine roared and the cabin rumbled, she was too excited to be scared. On a plane, in the air, the destination was close, the closest it had ever been, yet still a perfect dream. Her new husband was next to her. Her life was ahead of her.

When my mother landed in Tokyo, all she heard was Japanese, real Japanese, not the Japanese she grew up speaking. All the signs were written in kanji. My mother couldn't read kanji. Inside the airport—painfully bright and glossy—Tokyo felt huge, uninviting, and unnavigable. People walked so fast. Dressed so nice. If she spoke to them, they would know where she came from, they would know she didn't belong. She hurried to walk beside and slightly behind my father, who was walking so fast, pulling her hand and staring at the signs.

"Can you ask someone how to get to Ginza Station?" he asked my mother.

She stared at the floor.

TOKYO
2015

The hotel is nice, too nice. The lobby is too bright. The walls are gilded, sculpted into the shape and texture of woven reeds. Fresh flowers adorn every glass table. I'm wearing the same gross clothes, including underwear and socks, that I've been wearing for the past thirty-six hours. My father paces. My mother sits very still with her eyes closed. They both pounce as soon as they see me.

"How are you, my dear?" My father kisses the top of my head.

"Hi, baby." My mother pats my belly.

I do feel like a baby. It almost feels good. "I need a nap."

"Okay, sweetheart. Let's get you checked in." My father grabs my heavy, filthy REI-branded backpack and sets it on the floor in front of the reception desk. "Excuse me . . . Keiko?" He reads her name tag.

"How can I help you, sir?" Keiko says.

"This is my daughter, Elizabeth, and she needs to be checked in." His voice projects, startles, as if I will faint in the lobby if I don't get to my room and get a nap right away.

"Last name?"

"Brina. B as in 'boy,' R, I, N, A."

"Yes, two rooms. One for Arthur and Kyoko, and one for Elizabeth and Ken—"

"He won't be joining us," my father scolds, as if she should know. I roll my eyes at Keiko, as if she should know. I turn around so she can't see my face clench and lips quiver.

"I'm sorry," my mother says.

"Please, Mom. Not now." I'm crying.

"I'm so sorry."

"Stop."

Keiko shows me to my room. My eyes are daggers as she removes one of the robes and pairs of slippers. She fucking knows.

I know my parents will wait in their room while I nap. I know they will call the room before I wake from my nap, and then they will ask me in a frantic tone if I need ice or coffee or tea, if I have enough shampoo and toothpaste, where I want to go, what I want to do first, or if I want to stay at the hotel and order room service, and this is not just because I broke up with my fiancé three days ago. This is my life. They hover and appeal and appease. They love and love and love. This is the reason I wanted my fiancé to come with me. This is the reason I wanted to get married. Because I need a buffer. Because sometimes I feel I'm all they have and I'm not enough. How can one child, an only child, be enough for two people who love her so much?

When I wake from my nap, I'm famished. Our hotel is in the middle of Ginza, and we don't have to walk even ten steps to find a sushi bar. We're the only customers, because it's five o'clock in the evening and apparently no one in Tokyo is hungry at five o'clock in the evening. My father and I point to different items on the menu and say "kudasai," *please give me,* to the sushi chef, a man with silver hair and a smooth face, wearing a round cap and a kimono jacket. My mother leans close to my father and whispers to him.

"Mom, what are you doing? Why don't you order for yourself?"

"She's embarrassed, because of her accent," my father answers for her.

"What? No. Are you really?"

"Exactly the same on our honeymoon," my father continues. "I thought she was going to be my interpreter, but she made me do all the talking."

"Why?"

"She's a country gal," he says, putting his arm on the back of her chair. "In the big city."

My mother nods. She stares into her cup of green tea.

I examine the chef's reactions to check for comprehension. He appears to be concentrating on slicing maguro.

"How do you say 'water' in Japanese?" I ask my mother.

"Mizu," my mother answers. Her voice is quiet but certain.

"Mizu kudasai," I ask the chef.

"Omizu o kudasai," my mother corrects.

"Wait. So 'water' is 'omizu o'?"

"No. 'Water' is 'mizu,' but when you ask for it you should say 'omizu o.'"

I shrug. Later that year, I will learn that adding "o" to the beginning of a word makes a request more polite, and that the "o" at the end of a word is a particle that indicates the direct object of a verb. For instance, "Osushi o kudasai."

The chef reaches over the bar and lowers our platters. He speaks to me and my father in English. He speaks to my mother in Japanese. My mother replies in Japanese. Her reply is terse, and her posture shrinks a little under his gaze. Why is this happening here, in Japan, my mother's native country?

"What did he say?"

"He just asked me where I'm from."

I'm proud. We're not tourists. My mother is Japanese.

Later that year, I will learn about the history of Okinawa, the culture of Okinawa, how Okinawa is separate and distinct from Japan. How her accent is a signifier for "conquered," for "oppressed," for "forsaken." Maybe that's not true anymore. Maybe not now, after forty years. But for my mother, time is condensed. For my mother, forty years ago is the distance between two ends of a fold.

1975

She didn't know what he kept asking, why he kept asking. Pointing to places on a map. Places he'd read about in books. Places that were unknown and meaningless to her. "Can you ask someone where to find . . ." and the names of the places he said in Japanese sounded more foreign to her than the words he said in English. She couldn't ask. Who was she supposed to ask? Everyone talked so fast, walked so fast, dressed so nice. All the people with their fashionable scarves, with their fancy coats and boots, holding umbrellas against the wind and snow. They moved in unison, with the same steady assertive rhythm. She didn't want to interrupt. She couldn't interrupt. Better for my father, the gaijin, the foreigner, the foreigner who looks foreign, to interrupt.

She pushed the map away, shaking her head. "You ask."

2015

"Kendall not right for you," my mother says to me, abruptly, as we stop at an intersection. My mother and I are wandering Ginza, shopping for sneakers, like the ones all the people in Tokyo are wearing, flashy and sleek, but these sneakers are not my style and I won't wear these sneakers ever again after I leave Japan. My father is back at the hotel, watching the news and investigating the latest stock prices. My mother and I are together without my father for the first time since I arrived.

"It doesn't matter if he's right for me or not, Mom," I say, annoyed at her for explicitly stating what I've been obsessively mulling since before Kendall and I even broke up.

"He kind of selfish, don't you think? And . . ." She pauses, trying to think of the right word. "Bossy."

I laugh at her bluntness. I laugh because I agree. I laugh because my mother knows exactly what I need: to indulge in the sheer banal pleasure of bashing an ex-boyfriend. I bash him for two more intersections. I bash him inside the stores as we peruse sneakers.

1975

My father inferred her trepidation. *A country gal in the big city.* He knew big cities. He was born and raised in one of the biggest cities in the world. He wouldn't ask her to ask questions anymore. He would ask the questions. He would figure out the answers. He would show her Japan, her history, her culture. My mother preferred this arrangement. She felt safer when he took control.

My father took my mother to Rikugi-en, the Garden of the Six Principles of Poetry, to see the famous bonsai trees. He took her to Ueno Koen, to see the famous lotus and sakura. He took her to the Meiji Shrine, to see the giant torii gates, as high as the ancient cedars, and the magnificent ornate structures, built to honor the emperor in 1920, built again to honor him again in 1958 after the air raids destroyed the shrine during the war. This was the capital. This was what the capital of a nation could build and rebuild. He took her to the Yanaka district, the oldest and most traditional district in Tokyo, the district the air raids didn't destroy. Cemeteries and shrines along every street, around every corner. The graves marked by thin stone slabs, fields of stone slabs, like grass, white with a froth of snow. My mother was cold, but she kept walking, kept following.

He took her to the finest restaurants he could afford. They ate sashimi, kobe beef, and white rice, so white it glowed.

"From now on, I will eat rice every day," my mother said.

"We both will," my father said.

2015

We go to Rikugi-en. We go to Ueno Koen. We go to the Meiji Shrine and the Yanaka district. I walk slowly. I walk behind them. I follow them. I'm in so many places at once. I'm in Japan, with them, in awe of the spectacle of this magnificent civilization. I'm in Norway, with Kendall, replaying scenes, scrutinizing and analyzing a stored reel of hours and hours of arguments and discussions, letting snippets cut me and confuse me again and again. I'm in Oakland, Kansas City, New Orleans, tracing the lineage of what went wrong. I come back to Japan, and my parents are looking at me with such worry, such sympathy, with expressions so tender and loving, I feel worshipped and unworthy. Not just now, but whenever I'm with them, I'm in so many places at once, so many places without them, feeling like my life is on hold, like I'm stuck on a distant orbit and everywhere else time is passing, everywhere else life is happening.

We stand in line for an elevator to the top of the Skytree, the tallest building in Tokyo. As we stand in line, I email the owner of the bed-and-breakfast that Kendall and I selected, that I reserved for our wedding. I tell the owner the wedding is canceled. I apologize for any inconvenience. I pretend that sending this email will bring me some closure, some peace of mind, so I can be in one place.

We stand together on a pane of dense glass, floating above a sea of city lights. We stand together at a window and take a selfie, the night sky and Tokyo sparkling behind us. I smile a real smile.

The next morning, I receive a notice from my bank alerting me that five thousand dollars has been withdrawn from my account and my balance is four thousand five hundred sixty-three dollars in the negative. The owner of the bed-and-breakfast has charged me for everything, the whole house for the whole weekend, including the meals we wouldn't eat, three months in advance. I try to call him, but it's ten o'clock at night in New Orleans.

"It's okay, Elizabeth," my father says. "I'll give you the money."

"I don't want you to give me the money!"

"Please, Elizabeth. Don't let this ruin your vacation," my mother says.

"Mom, how can I not let this ruin my vacation?"

For the rest of the day, I'm gone.

1975

   He loves her. He chooses her. This is sacrifice. This is love.

2015

   We sit at a nice table in the nice restaurant of our too-nice hotel. We wait for Mori, my mother's nephew, the adopted son of Yoshi, her third oldest sister. He lives an hour by train outside of Tokyo. Mori is running late, and he calls my mother to tell her not to wait, to eat without him. My father orders sashimi, because it doesn't get cold, plenty for the four of us. We wait, eating sashimi with porcelain chopsticks and sipping top-shelf sake.

   When Mori enters the restaurant, I know he's Mori because my mother jumps from her chair and stretches her arms and smiles so wide I can see all the wrinkles around her eyes and mouth. She holds him tight and close. I'm surprised by this display, this amount of affection. I haven't heard of him until today. Or maybe I did hear of him, but don't remember. I try not to notice his shabby appearance. His tattered T-shirt and jeans. The grease on his clothes and hands, under his nails. He is missing four front teeth and the rest are yellow, rimmed with black. He stands at the table and bows. He doesn't sit until my father stands and shakes his hand, until I stand and shake his hand. As soon as he sits, the waiter brings him a steamed towel. Mori wipes his hands, but the grease doesn't come off. He says, "Sorry, sorry, thank you, thank you, hello, how are you?" My father and I say "Douzo, douzo, konnichiwa, genki desu ka?" *Please, please, hello, how are you?* And those are the only words we know how to say to each other.

   My mother and Mori talk, and talk and talk. They talk fast and easy. I have never heard my mother talk so much and so fast and so easy with anyone in my life. Not to my father. Not to me. Now that I see her with Mori, I feel like I see more of who she is and where she comes from. The way his posture shrinks, the way he presses his lips shut when he smiles. Until this moment, until seeing my mother with Mori, their ease and comfort, I couldn't fully grasp what it means for my mother to have grown up poor. Not "we can't go on vacation" poor. Not "we are late on rent" or "paycheck to paycheck" poor. But the kind of poverty that stays inside, shames and haunts, gnaws at the bones. My mother is also missing her four front teeth. I forget that, because she wears a set of false teeth. She brushes her false teeth every morning and every night, after taking them out to floss. When I was a child, she told me she lost her four front teeth in a car accident. Later this year, I will ask my mother again how she lost her four front teeth and she will say "Oh, it's very sad. Because I didn't get enough to eat."

I wish I could talk fast and easy with my mother and Mori. I wish I could understand.

My mother and Mori stop talking and look at me. I can tell by the way my mother says, "Kare-wa konakatta," *He didn't come,* that they are talking about Kendall. I look down at the napkin in my lap.

"Oboeteimasu," Mori says.

"Mori says he remembers you," my mother says.

I wish I could remember him, too. But I don't. So I smile and look down at my napkin and say "Thank you."

"Anata ga atachan no toki dakoshimashita," Mori says, and makes the shape of a cradle with his arms.

"He held you when you were a baby. Do you remember? From the photograph?" my mother says.

I do remember the photograph. "Thank you," I say.

He takes his phone out of his pocket and types. Then he reads to me, "You will always be in my heart."

Is that the right translation? The phrase seems too dramatic, too intimate for cousins who barely know each other.

"Thank you. Thank you." I force myself to look at him even though I want to look down at my napkin again.

"I'm sorry I don't speak English," Mori says.

"No, no. Please don't be sorry. I'm the one who should be sorry. I'm sorry I don't speak Japanese."

My father buys a bottle of whiskey and brings it to their hotel room. My father sits at the desk, I sit on a bed, and my mother and Mori sit on the other bed. They sit facing each other with their legs crossed. They haven't seen each other in twenty years but they're so at ease, so comfortable. What are they talking about? His mother, my aunt? Obaa, our grandmother? My father and I watch television. My mother and Mori talk, and talk and talk. We drink the whole bottle of whiskey. My mother and Mori drink most of it.

At approximately nine o'clock in the evening in Tokyo time and eleven o'clock in the morning in New Orleans time, I hug Mori goodbye and say good night. I take the elevator to the lobby and leave the hotel. I step over a row of hedges, nestle on the ground between two bushes, lean against the wall, and light a cigarette.

I call the owner of the bed-and-breakfast. "Please, five thousand dollars is a lot of money for me. Five thousand dollars is a lot of money for my parents. They don't deserve this," I say. I cry. I beg.

"It's not personal. It's just business," he says.

I hang up the phone. I chain-smoke cigarettes.

Then I see Mori. He walks past me, but can't see me. Then I see my mother. She chases after him, but can't see me. She grabs him, holds him tight and close. She tries to give him a wad of cash, but he clenches his fists behind his back. She shoves the cash into his shirt pocket and runs away from him, crying, covering her face with her hand.

And now I'm clutching handfuls of grass and dirt, trying to keep myself from screaming, furious at myself, ashamed of myself. For wasting more time. For talking on the phone to the owner of the bed-and-breakfast instead of my cousin who remembers me, who held me when I was a baby.

Stay here. Stay here, goddamnit. You need to fucking be here for this.

NIKKO
2015

Nikko is roughly seventy-five miles north of Tokyo, at an elevation of five thousand feet. Everywhere in Nikko, there is water. The clouds in the sky. The mist on the ground. The seventy-two waterfalls that descend from the lush green mountains. Three rivers, the Otani, the Kinugawa, and the Watarase, converge at the center of town. Everywhere in Nikko, there is the constant sound of water. Cascading, gushing, flowing, trickling.

We are staying at a ryokan, a traditional Japanese-style inn. All the rooms have tatami floors and paper-screen doors. Guests have access to onsen, hot spring baths, below the first floor, where they can soak in porcelain tubs and granite pools. They walk around the hotel, in and out of rooms, in their complimentary yukata and zori, their hair wet, their skin pink and glistening.

My mother and I stand in the lobby, enjoying the tapestries and plants. My father stands at the reception desk, speaking louder than necessary.

"Brina. B as in 'boy,' R, I, N, A."

"Hai, hai. Bu-ri-na-san. So desu." The clerk confirms the

reservation, looks at my father, then looks at me and my mother, then keeps looking, counting. "Only three persons?"

I roll my eyes at the clerk, as if she should know, and turn around.

"Don't cry," my mother snaps, as if she's trying to scare me from the hiccups.

At the moment, I feel offended, betrayed. But her trick works. I don't cry.

I recall her responses to previous breakups and heartaches. "Oh, come on. Why are you so upset? He doesn't like you. Just forget it." The bluntness I once mistook for mistranslation, for not understanding me and the depth of my emotional injury, was perhaps her way of provoking me to get over myself, to put my privilege in perspective, and focus on what I still had—what I still have. My youth, my freedom, my blank slate of a future.

1975

When my mother stepped off the train and onto the platform, she could feel the difference. Slower than Tokyo. Quieter than Tokyo. People walked without purpose. She breathed in the air. Moist, but it didn't smell like the ocean, and it wasn't warm.

My father grabbed her hand and led her to the station agent. He stammered and pointed, cheerful and confident, asking the questions, figuring out the answers. My mother watched the mist swirl and dissolve, and listened to the rivers. She saw a bridge across the street and wanted to look down from it, but when she tried to move toward it, my father wouldn't let go of her hand. He held her by his side until he was finished talking.

Nikko is most famous for the shrine of Tokugawa. A resplendent palace of a shrine, with hundreds of structures and sculptures. My father knew the history, explained the history. Three men were responsible for bringing the civil wars of Japan to an end. Nobunaga Oda, the first unifier of Japan, reigned from 1534 to 1582. Hideyoshi Toyotomi, the second unifier of Japan, reigned from 1584 to 1598. Tokugawa Ieyasu, the third unifier of Japan, reigned from 1603 to 1616. But Tokugawa was the wisest, the most effectual.

"Little cuckoo, if you don't sing, I'll kill you," says
    Nobunaga.
"Little cuckoo, if you don't sing, I'll force you," says
    Hideyoshi.
"Little cuckoo, if you don't sing, I'll wait," says
    Tokugawa.

My mother nodded as he explained, but she wasn't listening, couldn't understand. She was staring, eyes wide, at the gates, the pagodas, the fountains, the corridors connecting edifices, the carvings and etchings, all erupting with gold and silver, red and purple, blue and green. *How else would she ever get to see this? Who else in her family, in Okinawa, would ever get to see this?*

"It's heaven," my mother said.

"Yes. Heaven. We are here," my father said.

2015

We have to climb a series of stone steps to reach the tomb of Tokugawa. The stairs don't have a railing, just a long slacked rope. My father grabs my mother's hand and pulls her up each steep step. If she wobbles, my father holds tighter and pulls her closer to him. His caution seems excessive, paternalistic, and this annoys me.

Am I defending my mother? Am I jealous?

When Kendall and I hiked or rode bicycles, very often, especially in Norway, he would forge ahead and leave me behind.

"Take it easy, Dad. She can do it by herself."

"Don't mind us, Elizabeth," my father says.

I observe my mother's arm: muscular, flexed, strong. I realize that she's supporting him as well, that they're supporting each other, using each other for balance.

1975

On their second day in Nikko, my father wanted to see a waterfall, to show my mother a waterfall, but not just any waterfall, one of the most secluded, one that he read about in a book, one that the less informed tourists couldn't find, wouldn't visit. He pointed out the window, to the hills and the trees, then he pointed down to her feet and lifted a pair of his army-issued boots.

"We're going for a long walk today. You need to wear comfortable shoes."

My mother nodded.

She put on a pair of socks and sandals with straps that fasten around the ankles. My father shook his head. He rummaged through her suitcase. Only sandals. Only heels.

She didn't understand what he meant by "long walk." She didn't understand what he meant by "comfortable shoes." She didn't understand why he was so disappointed.

"We're going for a long walk to a waterfall," my father said. "Your feet are going to hurt because of those shoes. But it will be beautiful. I promise."

My mother nodded.

2015

On our second day in Nikko, my father wants to see a water-fall, to show me the waterfall he showed my mother forty years ago. I know about this waterfall. Since I was child, my father has told me the story of this waterfall many times. How he asked my mother to wear comfortable shoes, but she wore sandals. How he made her walk to the waterfall with him anyway, and the skin on her feet reddened and blistered and peeled. How even though she cried and yelled at him, yelled that she hated him, that she was leaving him, going back to Okinawa, my father knew, based on the description in the book, that as soon as she saw this waterfall she would forgive him.

When my father tells me this story, he chuckles at his own foolishness, but there is also a hint of pride, a hint of lighthearted rancor toward my mother. Sometimes my mother chuckles. Sometimes she shakes her head and rolls her eyes and says, "Your father is crazy."

1975

My mother didn't understand why my father wanted to walk through trees, through mud, up a hill, on purpose. This was what poor people had to do, what hungry people had to do. This was what she and her younger sister had to do when they foraged for berries and bugs. This was what scared people had to do, what hunted people had to do. This was what Obaa and her older brother and older sisters had to do when they fled from soldiers with guns. This was what soldiers with guns had to do when they hunted poor, hungry, scared people.

She limped and lagged behind my father. She wouldn't let him carry her or hold her hand, but when she sat on a boulder to rest, she let him rub her ankles, let him blow on the blisters. She didn't understand why he wanted to keep walking even though she was hurting. *Waterfall? Who cares about a waterfall? Is he mad at her? Punishing her?* Right then, she wanted to be done with him. She would take the train back to Tokyo by herself. She would take the plane back to Okinawa by herself. She wouldn't spend the rest of her life with this man.

2015

On our second day in Nikko, we wear sneakers. Except my father can't remember the name of this waterfall. He tries to describe this waterfall. My mother tries to translate. The receptionist at the hotel doesn't know. The driver of the taxi doesn't know. The driver of the taxi takes us up and down winding roads to the entrances of Ryuzu, Kegon, and Yutaki. We walk through parking lots, up and down long sets of stairs, through trees and mud to each one, and part of me wants to linger, to enjoy each one, but none of these waterfalls is the waterfall I have heard about since childhood. Too big, too close to the main road, not the right shape. The driver of the taxi drives us to Kirifuri and Jakukou and a bunch of smaller waterfalls along the way. My mother and father are tired and sore and they want to quit, but now I can't quit, can't stop. If we find this waterfall, then maybe it'll all be worth it. What "it" is, I'm not sure. The whole trip. Their whole marriage. If we find this waterfall, then maybe there is something in this world we can come back to, we can have again. I want them to have this moment. I want to give them this moment. I want all three of us to feel young and new again. I cross off name after name on the map.

The trail is steep and slippery and narrow. One side curves around a wall of rock; the other side is a precipice over a ravine. This is our most strenuous trek. This better be it.

"This is it!" my father shouts.

"This is it." My mother seems less certain. But she smiles anyway.

Maybe they're telling the truth. Probably not. I don't care.

The name of the waterfall is Urami, which is a strange name for a waterfall. "Urami" means "grudge," or "spite," or "bitterness." It also means "hours."

1975

Just as the book described. Just as he imagined, but better, because he found it.

"See? Wasn't it all worth it?"

The waterfall my mother saw wasn't sanctioned by literature, by her searching. The waterfall my mother saw wasn't hers, it was his. But she smiled anyway. She couldn't disappoint him. She couldn't shatter his confidence and trust. She understood what he was trying to give her, what he was trying to give himself through her. Right then, at that moment, she understood how much he needed her, that he needed her just as much as she needed him, maybe even more. And maybe that's when she began to fall in love with him.

2015

It is beautiful. The way the water spreads over the wall of rock like a veil. We stand at the edge of the pool and linger.

"Should I take a picture?" I ask.

They pose in front of the waterfall. My father, gentle yet awkward, eager yet bashful, wraps his arms around her waist and lowers his face. My mother, more reluctant, tenses and shuts her eyes, braces herself. They kiss. A quick peck. Like two kids on a dare. Then they let go of each other and want to be parents again.

I pose in front of the waterfall with my mother. I pose in front of the waterfall with my father.

As a reflex, almost as an obligation, I wish they could take a picture of me and Kendall in front of the waterfall. But that is no longer the point of this trip. It never was.

.

Later that evening, after a soak in the onsen, after a ten-course dinner of sesame tofu, miso soup, pickled vegetables, sashimi, tempura, broiled eel, baked squid, scallop dumplings, beef shabu shabu, and red-bean mousse, I sit on the balcony of our room to smoke a cigarette and watch the sun set behind the trees, the light bouncing off the ripples of the river below.

Through the glass door, I hear my mother say, "Elizabeth have more fun if Kendall come, don't you think?" I hear my father say, "Kendall's the one who's missing out."

I feel guilt. I feel sorry for myself, sorry for them, sorry that they have to worry about me so much, sorry that worrying about me is sometimes all they have in common.

1975

Later that evening, after a soak in the onsen, after a ten-course dinner, my parents sat on cushions on the floor and sipped sake. My mother brushed and combed her long dark hair. My father rubbed her ankles and bandaged her blisters.

.

Did they make love? Did their bodies want and need each other? Did they talk and talk until three o'clock in the morning?

2015

I don't know why my father tells the story of the waterfall so often, what the story means to him, what he remembers so fondly. Maybe it's the story of perseverance, a husband wanting to show his wife something beautiful, something she wouldn't have seen without him. Maybe it's the story of a newlywed squabble, a husband and wife getting to know each other, forgiving each other. Maybe it's the story of love overcoming misunderstanding. Of love resulting from misunderstanding.

1975

Little cuckoo, if you don't sing, I'll wait.

HAKONE
2015

We can't wear shoes anywhere inside the hotel, so a kid about half my age, with spiky hair and crooked buckteeth, scurries toward us in a dark blue kimono, bringing chairs to the entrance, so we can sit while we untie our laces. He carries our shoes to our own assigned cubby in a closet. He asks for our name.

"Brina," my father yells. "B as in 'boy,' R, I, N, A."

The kid confirms our reservation. The kid looks at my father, then looks at me and my mother, then keeps looking, counting. I already know what he's going to say.

"Only three persons?"

My mother bursts into laughter. Even my father cracks.

"Yes, yes, hilarious," I say.

.

Hakone is a small town in a national park on the coast of Lake Ashi, famous for its premier views of Mount Fuji. Kendall and

I were supposed to climb Mount Fuji. Summiting the mountain takes six hours, and our plan was to spend a night in one of the huts at the midpoint of the trail, then wake up before dawn to watch the sunrise from the top. I feel angry and deprived as I try to catch glimpses of the mountain from tour buses, ferries, sidewalks, the shoulders of roads, benches by the lake. I can't find it anywhere. A cluster of clouds. A bad angle. For a second, I see it, through the corner of the window, and then the bus turns and it disappears again. My father nudges me with his elbow.

"Twenty. Maybe ten."

"What're you talking about?"

"Twenty years ago, I could have climbed to the top of that mountain with you."

But that's how time and age mess with us, remain so ridiculously unfair to us. Twenty years ago, I was fourteen, and I probably wouldn't have wanted to climb to the top of Mount Fuji to watch the sunrise with my father.

1975

Forty years ago, my father didn't climb to the top of Mount Fuji, either. That was his original plan, to climb to the top with my mother, but after seeing her shoe collection, after seeing her limp and lag up the trail to the waterfall, my father yielded to more leisurely activities. He preferred historical sites and museums. My mother preferred to shop for omiyage, souvenirs, to send to her family in Okinawa. He was never hungry before five o'clock in the evening, a habit he acquired from his years in the army. My mother hated skipping meals. So he paced the aisles and held her bags while my mother browsed. He sipped tea while my mother ate, and when she complained of eating by herself, he ordered a snack and shared dessert. He didn't feel angry or deprived. He felt like a husband.

KYOTO
2015

Kyoto is a stunning and inimitable city. So stunning and inimitable that when Kyoto appeared on the list as a possible target for the atomic bomb, Henry Stimson, the U.S. secretary of war, who had recently authorized the internment of one hundred thousand Japanese American citizens, who had previously traveled to Kyoto while he was governor of the Philippines, implored President Harry S. Truman to remove Kyoto from the list. Surprising that a man capable of such callous policy could recognize the exceptional cultural significance of Kyoto, not only for the nation of Japan, but for the entire world. Kyoto is a city that ignites humanity.

This is not to say that what happened to Hiroshima and Nagasaki was anything less than abominable, criminal, anything less than pure evil.

.

We go to the Arashiyama Bamboo Forest. We go to Kinkakuji, the Golden Pavilion, with the boat-shaped pine tree. We go to the Ryoanji Temple, with the garden of fifteen rocks. We go to the Fushimi Inari Shrine, dedicated to the god of rice, with the tunnel made of one thousand torii gates. Dozens and dozens of temples and shrines, too many to keep track. We see a steel high-rise shopping mall a block away from a row of wooden cottages. We see a 7-Eleven right next to a traditional teahouse. We see lanterns hanging in doorways and electrical wires twisting and twisting like vines from pole to pole, rooftop to rooftop. We go to the ramen restaurant with six floors. We go to the Nishiki Market with tables of ice and fresh fish, barrels of fermented vegetables, carts of meats on sticks, and dumplings. We walk on the Tetsugakuno Michi, the Philosopher's Path, which follows a canal lined by hundreds of sakura. We turn a corner and see dozens of women sporting Coach and Burberry purses, Gucci and Prada sunglasses, all twirling parasols and waving folding fans. We walk the woven streets of Gion, the geisha district, and catch a glimpse of a woman with a painted white face and sculpted black hair, her long-sleeved silk kimono billowing as she glides across a dark alley into a limousine.

We're waiting for a train. It's nearly midnight. We're tired and sweating from a long day in the sun, in the heat and humidity. Tomorrow morning, we leave for Okinawa.

"My neck hurts," my mother murmurs.

"Hurts? What do you mean, hurts? Is it stiff? Sore?" My father has that tone. He's on alert, ready for action.

"No, no. Not stiff."

"Do you mean your throat? Would you like some water?"

"It . . . burns." She points to the skin between her chin and collarbone.

My father inspects. "Yes, it does look a little red." And without further warning or explanation, he charges to the end of the platform and down the stairs to the lower level, scanning, assessing, then out of sight.

"Where's he going?" my mother asks.

"I have no idea."

I'm already mad at him for missing the train that is supposed to be here in five minutes. I want to get back to the hotel to get enough sleep. I need to get enough sleep to be happy and cheerful for my uncles and aunts and cousins and second cousins when we meet them at our hotel for a dinner party. I need to get enough sleep to prove that I'm a good daughter.

My father sways up the stairs, arms folded over three bottles of water and a can of soda. He struts a little, head high, showing off his bounty. He offers me a bottle of water. He offers my mother a bottle of water and the can of soda.

"I don't want to drink that," she says, pointing to the can.

"It's cold," he says. "For your neck. Hold it against your neck."

My mother holds the can against her neck. She nods. Then she notices his shoes are untied. She kneels on the ground to tie his shoes.

.

I often complained to Kendall that he seemed impervious to my anxieties and discomforts. One of the many issues we discussed for hours and hours, spanning the three days after we broke up, before he left for New Orleans and I left for Tokyo.

"Well, how did you want me to react?" he asked. We were sitting on a bench in a park in the city of Bergen, sharing a paper plate of crab legs.

"I wanted you to feel bad when I felt bad. I wanted you to hurt when I hurt."

He talked about feeling bad at first. He talked about empathy fatigue. "And besides," he said, "isn't that selfish?"

No, I thought, but wouldn't say to him. *That's love.*

1975

They stood at the edge of the pond to gaze at the reflection of the Golden Pavilion, the koi fish, the mandarin ducks. My mother, leaning close to my father, her arm around his elbow. My father, standing straight, at attention. Then a horde of children dressed in their school uniforms, brandishing their notepads and pens, squealing "Sa-in! Sa-in!" *Sign! Sign!*

"Good morning!" one of the children said to my father, with concerted effort, as if he had just learned the phrase. "Sa-in, please."

My mother laughed and watched as my father smiled and shook his head, tried to explain to the children that he wasn't famous, wasn't a movie star, wasn't even an actor. She could have helped him explain, but part of her was still a child who also believed that anyone from the United States could be famous, could be a movie star, could be successful, could win. And now, soon, she, too, would win.

That night, their last night before they left for the United States, before they moved to the United States—America, this place that had been in her dreams all her life—she was too excited to sleep. Too excited to be afraid.

HOME
2015

The distance from Osaka to Naha is seven hundred and forty-eight miles. The flight takes two hours. The distance from Naha to our hotel in Chatan is eleven miles. The drive takes thirty-five minutes and passes four military bases. But I'm not thinking about the military bases, or the traffic, the roads confined, blocked on both sides by barbed-wire fences. I'm thinking about my mother, seeing her home again, seeing her family again, after twenty-two years. She sits with me in the backseat of the taxi, turned away from me, looking out the window.

The driver of the taxi speaks to us in English. He speaks mostly to my father, because my father is the one who initiates and maintains conversation. "There's an Eisa performance in downtown Ginowan today," the driver says, and then he looks at my mother through the rearview mirror. "But I'm sure your family will perform one for you."

"Eisa?" I ask.

"Drum dance," the driver answers.

I let out a chuckle. My family will perform a drum dance? He must be joking. The driver doesn't laugh. My mother doesn't laugh.

.

Genshin, my mother's second oldest brother, and Yoshi, my mother's third oldest sister (now the oldest because the first oldest died of pneumonia and the second oldest died of cancer), are waiting in the parking lot outside the hotel, waiting in the sun, in the heat of the late afternoon, just to be the first to welcome us. Genshin paces with his hands clasped behind his back, wearing a Yankees baseball cap and aviator sunglasses. Yoshi sits on a bench with her cane propped between her legs, wearing an "I ♥ NY" T-shirt and a towel around her neck. We haven't seen each other in twenty-two years, but we remember each other, recognize each other.

They comb their fingers through my mother's hair. Grayer now. They pat my father's belly. Bigger now. They pat my cheeks. A woman now. They ask many questions. My mother doesn't seem nervous or reluctant or even giddy with joy. Just comfortable. Just home. They talk fast and easy. I smile and nod, even though I don't understand.

Genshin has reserved a conference room at the hotel to host the party. He and Yoshi, my mother's only surviving siblings (except for her first older brother, who doesn't come to the party, who doesn't come to see her until the last day, early morning, still dark, just before the taxi arrives to take us back to the airport). My mother's nieces and nephews and their spouses and their children. My cousins and second cousins and third cousins. Dozens of them. Maybe fifty. I have never seen so much family, together, all at once. I have never seen so much family throughout my entire life, all instances combined. They gather around us in a circle. They smile, bow, shake our hands, introduce themselves, ask many questions. They apologize for not speaking English.

"No, no. Please don't be sorry. I'm the one who should be sorry."

I wish I knew the words in Japanese.

1975

The distance between Osaka and San Francisco is five thousand three hundred seventy-seven miles. The flight takes ten hours. The distance between San Francisco and New York City is two thousand nine hundred two miles. The drive takes days, and passes through mountains and desert and more mountains and plains and more mountains and more plains.

But they didn't drive straight from San Francisco to New York City. My father wanted to show my mother his country, his home, her new country, her new home. In San Francisco, he bought a new car, a Datsun B210 hatchback, and they drove south, to Disneyland, to Las Vegas, to the Grand Canyon, to Phoenix, to Amarillo to visit her friend from Okinawa, to San Antonio to visit his friend from the Special Forces, then drove along the Gulf Coast, across the Mississippi River, to Memphis, to Atlanta, then drove north, on I-95, where my mother encountered her first bliz-zard and she gasped and gasped, hand on her chest, amazed at the white swirling sky, amazed at my father, who drove and drove through the fierce howling wind and wasn't afraid.

"Were you afraid?" I would ask my mother many years later.

"No, Elizabeth. I wasn't afraid. I was very exciting. I left Okinawa."

"So you were happy?"

"Yes. I was happy then."

My mother had never experienced such immensity of dis-tance. She had no idea the United States was its own world, the size of a planet. She had no idea how long the drive would take. They drove for ten days, spending nights in hotels, going to clubs and bars, going dancing and drinking, being happy, being young. Being married.

They drove across the George Washington Bridge. She saw the big buildings, the bright lights, the busy streets, the fast cars. When my father parked his car at the corner of Seventy-second Street and Broadway, my mother wasn't afraid.

"We are here," he said.

I am here.

.

Mom, I am twelve years older than you were, and I still don't know how to be you. I still don't know how to not be afraid.

2015

We sit at a round table with my cousin Eiko, Chieko's daugh-ter, and my second cousin, Eiko's daughter, and my second cousin's two children, a boy and a girl, both fourteen years old, a set of gorgeous twins. We speak in fragments, with gestures and pictures on our phones. I ask my mother to ask the twins silly questions, like what their favorite subjects are in school and what they want to be when they grow up, because that's what silly adults used to ask me when I was fourteen years old. Totsu, Setsu's ex-husband, her first husband, the uncle who felt bad for me and brought me hot dogs and hamburgers on his way home from work twenty-two years ago, comes to the party late and greets us. My mother stands to hug him, holds him tight and close, and they weep together, holding each other, remembering Setsu.

I weep when I see my mother weep. Like I should have wept for Setsu, for my mother losing Setsu, when she died ten years ago.

1975

My mother told me she was afraid of my grandfather, my father's father. She told me my grandfather was rude to her, thought she wasn't good enough for my father. My father told me my grandfather asked him if he was sure about her, absolutely sure about her, because there were plenty of fine pretty girls from reputable Italian families who would jump at the chance to marry a retired soldier and captain, a former Airborne Ranger and Green Beret. My mother told me she would have returned to Okinawa, wouldn't have stayed in the United States, if it weren't for my grandmother. My mother told me my grandmother was the nicest person, most welcoming person, that she praised and combed her long dark hair, took her shopping at Macy's, taught her how to set the table, how to use a knife and fork. My father told me my grandmother always defended my mother, always sided with my mother, whenever he and my mother fought.

2015

Genshin carries his youngest grandchild—a girl, one year old—from table to table, pointing and introducing. The youngest grandchild rubs her eyes and hides her face. The second youngest and third youngest and fourth youngest follow him around the conference room and tug at his pants. Genshin has twenty-two grandchildren. Genshin carries his youngest grandchild to his wife's lap, then stands at the podium and speaks into the microphone. The whole room, my whole family, together, all at once, turn and look at me.

"What did he say?" I ask my mother.

She doesn't answer.

Together, all at once, the whole room, my whole family, rise from their chairs and gather around our table. They form a line behind me. Then, one by one, they put a bright red envelope on the table in front of me. Ten envelopes. Fifteen envelopes. Thirty envelopes.

"What are these?" I ask my mother.

"Wedding gifts."

"No."

I open an envelope. Five thousand yen. I open another envelope. Fifty thousand yen. The tradition is to give newlyweds five thousand or fifty thousand yen, because "go-en," five yen, sounds like "goen," which means "love." Five thousand yen is the equivalent of fifty dollars. Fifty thousand yen is the equivalent of five hundred dollars.

I think about Mori, the grease on his clothes and hands. I think about my uncle working seven days a week. I think about Yoshi walking with a limp and slurring, collecting disability benefits. I think about the rest of my family. Some of them I just met. Some of them I don't remember meeting.

"Do they know? Do they know the wedding's canceled?" I ask my mother.

"They know."

"We have to give the money back."

"We can't give the money back."

"What should I do?" I ask my father.

"Thank them."

"Thank you," I say. "Thank you. I'm sorry."

I can't look at them. I can't stop crying.

2019

I think about my family on my father's side. I think about the money my father and my two uncles inherited from my grandmother and my great-aunt, more money than most people in the world will ever receive, will ever earn, and how my father and my two uncles bickered and quarreled over the terms of the will and testament, which favored my father, the oldest, the one who lived with his mother and aunt, took care of his mother and aunt, until the end, held their hands as they breathed their last breath, because no one else did, maybe no one else would, not my two uncles, and how one of my uncles is suing my father for embezzlement and fraud because he wants more, wants everything, and how my father has spent everything he inherited on lawyers just trying to keep my uncle from getting everything. They're brothers. They both vow never to speak to each other again.

My mother and father live in a house my father bought with a portion of his inheritance, but the legal fees absorb his monthly Social Security checks. My mother is seventy-one years old and works at the restaurant three times a week to pay for groceries, for soil to feed her plants and garden, for seeds to feed the birds, for shelled peanuts to feed the squirrels, for ingredients to cook beautiful meals to feed her friends at church, for an occasional splurge for herself on a sale at Macy's, for a frequent handout to her spoiled daughter.

My mother says she likes working. She says she doesn't mind.

1975

Any room of the condo on the corner of Seventy-second Street and Broadway was bigger than her house in Okinawa. The living room had a grand piano. The dining room had a crystal chandelier. Embroidered sofas and chairs. Mahogany tables and cabinets. Oriental rugs. There were three bedrooms, and each bedroom had its own bathroom and a bed. My father was rich, really, really rich, and my mother would never have to worry about money again.

2015

Genshin, still standing at the podium, still speaking into the microphone, introduces his three oldest grandchildren, all girls, sixteen, fifteen, and thirteen years old. They rise from their chairs slowly, looking down, faces pink. They wear bright red yukata and bright red bandannas tied around their foreheads. Genshin reaches behind the podium and gives each of the three girls a wooden stick and a barrel-shaped drum. He smiles, like he's telling a joke. They smile, like they're playing along. Each of them holds a stick in one hand and hangs the strap of the drum from her neck. Genshin nods. They begin.

They beat the drums and chant in unison. They stomp and kick and spin and raise their fists in the air, looking at each other and giggling between chants. This time-honored dance, these awkward teenagers, the juxtaposition is adorable. The whole room, their whole family, watch, proud and charmed. We clap to the beat of the drums. We hoot and laugh. When they finish the dance, my mother leaps from her chair to offer a standing ovation. She runs to them, arms outstretched.

This is what my mother left behind.

1975

At first, they went to restaurants together. They went to movies, shows on Broadway, and concerts at Lincoln Center together. They saw *The Man Who Would Be King*. They saw *The King and I*. They saw *The Nutcracker*.

But after a few weeks, maybe a month, maybe two or three, the excitement and their newness to each other waned, and routine settled in. My father wanted to stay at home more. He wanted to read more. He wanted to spend more time with my uncles and my grandfather. He would stay up late with them, drinking bourbon, reminiscing, arguing and agreeing about politics, playing war board games. Night after night, my mother would stay in the bedroom, my father's childhood bedroom, with shelves of books she couldn't understand and a television she couldn't understand, with wall-to-wall closets, mirrors on the doors, and the reflection of her lying on the bed all alone.

That's when she felt the distance beyond the dark corners of the bedroom, beyond the horns honking and the voices shouting outside the window. That's when she felt the distance whirring and tightening in her chest.

One night, she sneaked out, tiptoed past the dining room, where they were sitting, drinking, talking—they didn't even notice her—and took the elevator to the first floor, walked down Seventy-second Street toward Central Park, and kept walking until she found a bar.

2015

My mother goes with Genshin and Yoshi to Gensho's house, the house he inherited from Obaa. She goes with Genshin and Yoshi to Eiko's house, the house she inherited from Chieko. In Okinawa, the oldest child inherits the house, the oldest child tends to the altars. The rest of the children, who move away, however far, must visit the altars as often as they can, must visit the altars as soon as they return. They must bring offerings. My mother goes with Genshin and Yoshi to Totsu's house. Setsu didn't have any children, so her altar belongs with him.

The altars are wooden cabinets or dressers, ashes in urns, and totome, tablets inscribed with the names of the dead. The altars are framed photographs, vases of flowers, bowls of fruit, platters of rice balls, individually wrapped cookies and candy.

My mother kneels and bows at the altar, lights incense, and says a prayer. She isn't praying to God or Buddha or any deity. She is praying to her mother, her father, and her sisters. She is talking to them as if they are in the room.

I don't go with my mother to visit the altars. Not this time. Not this trip. Maybe because I'm tired from travel, from the party, from staying up late to drink sake and sing karaoke with my cousins and second cousins. Maybe because I'm overwhelmed, not quite ready, not yet deserving to be a part of this family, who have shown me more kindness and affection than family I have known for years. Maybe because I want to go to the beach, lie on a towel on the sand in my new bathing suit. I want to get rid of the tan lines from my old bathing suit, these tan lines from the last time I went to the beach with Kendall and his co-worker, when I let my shoulders and thighs burn under the Gulf Coast sun as I watched them jump and dive through waves together, watched him look at her, examining his face, knowing that look on his face, knowing he was already in love.

.

Shortly after I return from Japan, I will see Kendall at a festival with this co-worker. He will apologize for making me feel "stupid and crazy" for accusing him of having a crush on her.

1975

After she had several drinks, after she sat for several hours and drank alone, getting drunker and drunker—a nice girl like her in a place like this—the bartender skimmed through the phone book and called the Brina residence. My grandmother answered and asked "Kyoko?" My uncles laughed and yelled, "Way to go, Art!" My grandfather heckled my father about what kind of girl sneaks off by herself so late at night. My father hung his head low as my grandmother scolded and pointed at the door, telling him to leave now and bring her back, telling him to apologize, to promise never to stay up late and leave her alone in that bedroom again. "You're a husband now," she said.

2015

We take a taxi to Yoshi's house. We sit on the floor of her living room, which is also her kitchen and bedroom, amid boxes of empty cans and bottles, stacks of newspapers and magazines, piles of clothes folded in bundles, pieces of torn fabric and spools of yarn that she uses to make key chains as gifts, and three large fans oscillating and stirring the hot air. Yoshi sits on her bed, fidgets and strains to bend to the table with a set of photographs. Of my mother. Of Chieko and Setsu. Of herself. Of Obaa.

They're dressed in school uniforms, dressed for parties, dressed for picnics, posing in front of a rusted gate, posing in front of a cinderblock fence, under a pavilion by the beach. They share the same high bulbous cheeks, the same kind serious eyes. Of course they're beautiful, as we're all beautiful when we're young, especially in black-and-white photographs. My mother stares and nods at the photographs. I can see by the way she stares and nods that she is no longer here, that she is somewhere else.

I wish I could help her dig for it, sift for it, hold it with her, whatever she's thinking and feeling at that moment.

Years later, I will ask my mother about her sisters, how they lived, how they died. She won't have much to tell me.

Maybe she doesn't have the words. Maybe she doesn't want to dwell in that place for too long. Or maybe she dwells in that place always and forever, therefore doesn't know how to extract it, look at it from the outside, and describe it. Because she grew up with death. Death was in her house. Death was in every house.

I think about how Kikuko died at the age of seventeen, how Chieko died at the age of forty-five, how Setsu died at the age of fifty-four, how Yoshi had a stroke at the age of fifty-eight. I wonder if that's why my mother wanted to get out, knew she needed to get out. I wonder if marrying my father and moving to the United States saved her life.

1975

Her face flushed red. Her cheek smooshed against the shoulder of a man with his arm wrapped around her waist. She couldn't sit upright by herself, so his arm held her upright on the stool. She laughed like a girl who had spun too many circles, like a woman who had had too much to drink. My father interrupted, peeled them apart, introduced himself as her husband. The man laughed, waving his arm in surrender. My mother toppled. My father caught her.

"It's time to go home now," my father said.

"Home? I not go home."

"We're leaving." My father grabbed her arm, lifted her.

I don't have to imagine what she did next, because I've seen it many times. My mother squirmed and pulled and slapped and punched, trying to free herself. She didn't want to be grabbed and lifted. She screamed, "Get away from me! Don't touch me!" But my father wouldn't get away from her, wouldn't let go of her. He held her arm, held her upright, while thanking the bartender and tipping him an extra ten dollars. Maybe my mother squirmed and pulled so hard that she fell off the stool. Maybe my father lifted her from the floor. Maybe he was gentle. Maybe he lowered his eyes to meet her eyes and remembered what my grandmother had told him.

"Please, Kani-san. I'm sorry," he said.

My mother leaned into him, letting him guide her, letting him bring her home.

She didn't know how to respond to an apology without forgiveness. She didn't know how to hear "I'm sorry" without being sorry.

.

Mom, I have been there. I have gone to a bar and let a strange man touch me, hold me upright, just hoping that someone I loved, even someone I wanted to love, would come and save me with an apology.

2015

We wander the streets of Kadena, but they hardly recognize the town anymore. So much has changed. The nightclub is now a supermarket. My mother's first apartment is now a parking garage.

We stand on the side of a road that used to be one of the only three roads. One road went south to Naha. One road went north to Nago. One road went east to Koza, now called Okinawa City. The road is busy, but no taxis. A man my age, gripping several white plastic bags, biceps bulging, walks out of the supermarket and sees us standing, waiting, dumbfounded, lost. He asks if we're okay. We ask if he could, please, if he wouldn't mind, call us a taxi. He offers us a ride to our hotel. We object that it's too far. He gestures—swinging the white plastic bags—that, no, no, it's not too far, and that we should follow him.

My mother sits in the passenger seat, which surprises and pleases me. Her immediate familiarity with him surprises and pleases me. They chat in Japanese, or rather, Okinawan. Perhaps about Kadena, how so much has changed. We ask him to drop us off at the curb. He does a U-turn and drops us off at the entrance of the hotel. My mother tries to give him a wad of cash. He shakes his head and clenches the steering wheel. They shove the money back and forth at each other until my father says, "Kani-san. Please. Let him do this for us."

"Kani-san" is my father's nickname for my mother. My mother was born in July, the zodiac sign of the crab, which is "kani" in Japanese. When my mother worked at the nightclub, she used a pseudonym, she introduced herself as "Kani," or "Connie," as English-speaking patrons would hear her say it. For six months, my father knew my mother only as "Kani," addressed her only as "Kani" before she told him her real name.

"Yes," the man says, looking at my father through the rear-view mirror. "Thank you."

This is what all three of us left behind.

RETURN
2015

The first night, I don't sleep. I'm home, alone, everything missing, everything gone except for the bed, my dresser, my desk. Too much of his stuff is still here: his end table next to the bed, which he must have thought was mine, a few shirts he forgot that were hidden in the back of the closet, a sock covered in feathery dust. I rummage through the drawer of the end table, smoothing wrinkled receipts, searching for evidence—of what, I don't know. I read the last eighty pages of *Interpreter of Maladies*, a book he loaned to me. I sign on to Netflix, and even though I memorized the password, my name and icon have been removed from his account.

At five o'clock in the morning, I get a text from my father, telling me that he and my mother just unpacked, that he had the best trip of his life, that he misses me already, that he knows I'll be okay, knows I'm strong, but he worries, and to give him a call as soon as I wake up.

At seven o'clock in the morning, I get a text from my mother, just a picture of me singing karaoke, one of my go-tos, either "Walkin' After Midnight" or "Me and Bobby McGee." I sang both songs and more that night, sang with my cousins and second cousins, who are mid-clap, mid-sip, all of us with the same drowsy grin, all of our faces flushed the same shade of red.

The first week, I move. My friends help me, friends I didn't even know I had. They send me links to Craigslist posts. They send me pictures of "for rent" signs. They lug my furniture into a U-Haul and then into my new apartment. When we're finished, we eat fried chicken standing at the kitchen counter, drink beer sitting on the living room floor. The apartment is a little above my price range, but it's in my favorite neighborhood of New Orleans.

The first month, I still can't sleep, so I ride my bicycle around the bayou, around and around, again and again, listening to music with my headphones, singing at the top of my lungs, not caring who hears, not caring that sound carries louder over water, the heat and wetness in the air softening the streetlamps. I ride my bicycle down Esplanade Avenue to the French Quarter and back to the bayou. Sometimes I go to bars. Sometimes I have sex with men I meet at bars. I can go wherever I want. I can do whatever I want. I can be sad. I can be lonely. I can make it look good. I can make it look bad, too. If I want. Sometimes I feel okay. Sometimes I feel strong.

The first year, I start to wonder about the reasons, the many reasons, why I am who I am, and that maybe a few of those reasons are greater than the sum of my actions, greater than me. I start to ask myself questions about my mother, about everything that had to happen for her to meet and marry my father, about their marriage, about being their only child, their only daughter. I start to try to explain myself to myself. Sometimes those reasons hurt. Sometimes those reasons comfort. Sometimes I forgive myself.

1975

Maybe he kissed her on the forehead as he tucked her into bed. Maybe she was too tired to cry.

"I'm alone," she said.

"You're not alone. You have me."
"I just have you," she said.
"I promise I'll do my best."

.

I believe he kept that promise. I believe my mother believes he kept that promise.

.

I used to deny my parents' love for each other, because I didn't understand it, because it didn't fit some mold, didn't align with some image of love I had conjured. I thought that love, true love, should involve something more than just commitment.

.

My father never thought of leaving. Only of letting her leave.

.

My mother never thought of leaving. Only of threatening to leave.

.

Maybe love is choosing to stay. Maybe love is choosing to stay every day until the choice becomes permanent.

$\mathcal{I}$ am sitting at the head of the dining room table, my father to my left, where he always sits, next to the window, and my mother to my right, where she always sits, closer to the kitchen. My grandfather has recently died of a heart attack, and we have just returned from the funeral, from driving for seven hours, and my father is leaving the next day, going back to Manhattan to keep my grandmother company for a few more days. We are having dinner, and my mother is drinking too much wine, and she says to me, "When we get old, you have to take care of us."

I am eight years old. I don't understand what she means. My father seizes the opportunity to explain to me that aging and dying are inevitable, that aging and dying would inevitably happen to them, my parents, and, yes, because I'm their child, their only child, the duty will rest on me to take care of them.

"But I don't know how!" I cry, genuinely terrified. My parents both chuckle at my response. They think it is so precious, so precocious. They tell me they are proud of me for taking the task so seriously, so far in advance.

"Don't worry, Elizabeth," my father says. "You'll know how when the time comes."

.

Only children believe they are exceptional. They believe they are the best at everything and the worst at everything. They are the most loved and most disappointing.

.

My parents are seventy-one years old. I still have no idea how I'm going to take care of them. I hope I don't have to do it alone.

*   *   *

I look for a love that surpasses the love of my parents, the love they have for each other. I look for a love that could replace the love of my parents, the love they have for me, after they're gone. Isn't that what children are supposed to do? Surpass their parents? Live and love beyond their parents?

.

Sometimes I'm afraid of settling. Sometimes I'm afraid of not settling.

.

Sometimes I crush blossoming relationships with my huge greedy hands.

.

Sometimes I can't stop resisting, can't stop doubting, even when he reassures, even when he makes me feel safe. I can't be sure about him. And therefore he can't be sure about me, either.

.

Sometimes I think it will never happen. Sometimes that doesn't bother me.

.

Sometimes I think I want a child—a daughter, fingers crossed—who can keep me company, take care of me when I'm old, who can speak to my mother in Japanese, help me understand her, help me understand her love for me.

Is that a selfish reason to want a child? Is there any other reason to want a child?

Maybe that's a milestone of human experience I'm going to miss, I'm already missing.

Like having a brother or sister.

But that's okay, we can't have all the adventures.

Maybe it was always supposed to be just the three of us.

On the plane, I sit next to my mother. I sit by the window, my mother sits in the middle, and my father sits by the aisle. On my small television and my mother's small television, I cue the same movie, a Japanese movie called *Shoplifters*. I press "Play" on my screen with my right hand and on her screen with my left hand at the same time. We watch the movie together. We watch many movies together. The flight is ten hours.

I am thirty-eight years old and we are going to Okinawa. My idea. My treat. I don't want to let another twenty years pass before my mother sees her family again, before I see my mother with her family again.

.

We rent a house in the town of Yomitan, a short walk to Toguchi Beach, the site of the landing of the invading Japanese forces in 1609, the site of the landing of the invading United States forces in 1945. But now it's just a beach: shallow, calm, green with seaweed, boulders basking high above the water, a place where Okinawan families, and American families, the husbands and fathers with crew-cut hair, come to walk and swim and picnic and watch the sun set over the East China Sea.

.

Every morning, my mother cooks breakfast. She sautés bitter melon, bacon, egg, tofu, garlic, and ginger in soy sauce, mirin, and butter, or brews a pot of miso soup with tofu, mushrooms, and scallions. Always with rice. She loves the rice here. She thinks the rice tastes better here. She sings while she chops, cooks, and washes the dishes.

I eat two portions. I scrape and scoop the last morsels into my mouth with chopsticks.

"Mmmm," I say.

"I like when you say 'mmmm,'" my mother says.

.

Every morning, my father probes the Internet for breaking news, reads out loud the latest report, and supplements with his commentary. The protests in Hong Kong and how Donald Trump was right to raise tariffs on China. The acquittal of the man who stabbed Jair Bolsanaro and how Hillary Clinton is exonerated despite her known war crimes and corruption; meanwhile, Julian Assange rots in prison. Sometimes what he says is more temperate: "We have to take care of the people who live in this country first. Everyone who lives in this country. We have to seal our borders." Sometimes what he says is just plain awful: "Elizabeth, why do you think it's a good idea for our whole country to turn black and brown?"

I don't engage. If I engage, my heart beats faster and my jaw clenches and my neck aches. If I engage, I'm indulging the worst of him. Not the father who is kind and caring. Not the father who gives financial advice when his neighbor's young son wants to invest in the stock market to save for college. Not the father who helps my mother's friend at church with her divorce, helps her look for a lawyer and understand the legal documents. I've asked my father not to read out loud the latest reports, and supplement with his commentary. But he thinks I'm burying my head in the sand, and this is what he wants to talk about.

"I can't go to Florida anymore," my father says.

I don't ask why. We've never been to Florida.

"In Florida, if you oppose any Jew or the State of Israel, you go to jail."

"Try some pineapple," my mother says, sliding a bowl across the table, setting the bowl between us. "It's very fresh."

My mother is the one who keeps the peace now.

.

Every morning, after breakfast, my mother and I walk to the beach. My mother is so light on her feet that she skips. She can walk for miles, slow but steady. I like walking with my mother. I like walking by the houses with terra-cotta roof tiles and tidy yards and healthy gardens. I like pointing to the flowers, hearing her tell me the names in Japanese as I try to recall the names in English.

"Ayame."

"Iris."

"Ajisai."

"Hydrangea."

"Tsutsuji."

"Um . . . azalea?"

I like being present, talking about the here and now with my mother. Better than talking about the irrevocable past, the doomed future.

.

When my father walks to the beach with us, he limps and lags behind. He sits on a bench while my mother and I walk back and forth along the length of the cove. His knees are swollen from arthritis. His feet are swollen from gout. We blame his weight. We blame his staying awake late at night, reading and watching the news, staying inside all day, reading and watching the news. We blame the lawsuit, the hatred and vengeance his brother feels toward him, the hatred and vengeance he feels toward his brother. We blame a whole lifetime of suppressed anger and sadness catching up with him.

"Come on, old man. You can do it," my mother says, walking backward.

"I'm coming, dear. Thank you," my father says, wincing and groaning.

My mother jogs back to him, jogs around him in circles, then jogs back to me.

My mother is the one who is stronger now.

.

Every morning, after breakfast, after our walk to the beach, Genshin picks up Yoshi and drives to the house. Sometimes they're already parked in the driveway. Sometimes they're already waiting in the living room because we left the door unlocked for them. They don't call. They live only two miles away. So they just come to the house.

.

Every day, Genshin drives us around Okinawa. He drives us to places he has never been before, places he thinks will interest me, places for tourists. He drives us in a van that he shares with the rest of his family, his three sons and three daughters. They keep bottles of water and tea, bags of rice crackers, blankets and umbrellas in the trunk.

He drives us to a cave where Okinawans hid from bombs and tanks and guns, where eighty-four Okinawans committed suicide. Bouquets and wreaths of one thousand paper cranes heaped at the mouth of the cave, beneath a sign that says "Do Not Enter." The flowers are fresh. The paper is new. The bones of the dead are still inside.

He drives us to the Himeyuri Peace Museum, a series of linked caves that were once used as a hospital, where two hundred forty high school students, all girls, nicknamed Himeyuri, "Princess Lilies," were sent to feed and fetch water for wounded soldiers, wash them and change their bandages. Two hundred seventeen of those girls died.

He drives us to the Okinawa Peace Memorial, a monument of one hundred sixteen black granite slabs, inscribed with the names of all those who died, soldier or civilian, regardless of nationality—two hundred forty-one thousand five hundred twenty-five names. New names are added each year. The slabs are arranged in the shape of waves, curving toward the cliffs, toward the ocean. Okinawans believe the ocean is a symbol of peace, a "bridge between nations."

On one of the days, Genshin asks my mother to ask me where I want to go next. I tell my mother to tell him that I want to see a part of Kadena that hasn't changed since the war. He drives us to a cemetery.

On one of the days, Genshin drives us to Gensho's house, the house he inherited from Obaa. It still has the rusted tin roof, the rusted tin gate. It still has the cinderblock fence. The holes of the cinder blocks are filled with dirt and flowers, the roots and stems sprouting through the cracks and edges. Genshin knocks and opens the door. Gensho is sitting on the floor, against the wall, watching a television that is two feet in front of him. When he looks up and sees my mother, his eyes turn red and wet, and his lips quiver. I try to look at him and smile, but he can't look at us for more than a second. He doesn't smile. He was the person who was so angry and cruel. He was the person who hurt my mother the most. But now he's just an old man sitting on the floor, afraid to look at us. My mother bends toward him and rests her hand on his shoulder, gently, tenderly. She grabs my wrist and pulls my hand toward him. We shake hands loosely, awkwardly. Later, I will ask my mother why she thinks Gensho cried. She will guess that he felt regret. I will guess that he felt shame.

"What's difference?" my mother will say.

"I'm not really sure. I guess shame is deeper, more painful."

My mother will nod.

My mother kneels and bows at the altar. She lights incense and says a prayer. She talks to her mother, her father, and her oldest sister, who died of pneumonia. She tucks an envelope of ten thousand yen under one of the urns.

I kneel and bow at the altar. I light incense and whisper, "Hello, Obaa." *I'm sorry this took so long.*

.

But not all of our excursions are about war and death. He drives us to Shuri Castle, the replica built in 1992. Three months later, a fire will destroy the castle again. It will have to be rebuilt once more. He drives us to Ocean Expo Park, a gargantuan resort, to visit the Churaumi Aquarium, the second largest aquarium in the world, with two whale sharks and one manta ray. He drives us to a cartoony Okinawa Fruits Land and a pineapple theme park. He drives us over suspended bridges, over turquoise water, to the port city of Nago, and then to the ancient village of Bise. He drives us to flat and sandy beaches, to shell and pebble beaches, to fishing harbors.

My mother does the heavy lifting of socializing and translating. We can't communicate without her. We depend on her. She is the center of attention.

.

On one of the days, my mother tells Genshin and Yoshi to come back to the house tomorrow. My father can't walk, can't move. Not without wincing and groaning. He hobbles, dragging his swollen feet, cursing loudly at himself: "Goddamnit, oh, goddamnit!" He snaps commands in the form of questions at my mother: "Where's my belt? . . . Where's my jacket? . . . What about my socks? No, not that pair. I need thinner socks . . . Is there any aspirin left? . . . The store? You'll go to the store for me? Thank you, dear." My mother starts counting yen and shoves the coins into her jeans pocket. "Your purse! Kani-san, bring your purse!"

"Dad, could you ask nicely?"

"She needs her wallet and ID."

"The store is five minutes away."

"I'm traveling with a bunch of flower children!"

"It's okay, Elizabeth," my mother says. "I used to it. I feel nothing."

I think of my mother at home, alone, suffering his commands and criticism. I think of her shutting down, tuning out the babble of his misplaced anger. I think of my father at home, alone, suffering the pain in his mind and body, unable to contain it, remorseful for unleashing it, for losing control.

He wasn't always this bad, though.

Or was he?

I can't trust myself to know for certain.

Does his mind constrict as his body weakens?

Does his pedestal crumble, erode, neutralize, as I become older?

Am I more critical of him, less tolerant of him, because I don't know how to take care of him, because he was always the one who took care of me, took care of us?

Am I gravitating more toward my mother because her body doesn't scare me, doesn't disgust me, her words don't offend and contradict me, because she is the one who is happier now, more in control and at peace with herself now?

Is my mother happier now because of me? Because I feel closer and more at ease with her? Because I admire her?

Even when she shuts down, tunes out, she can flip a switch and automatically turn back to being patient and forgiving. She sits on a chair in front of him, lifts his leg on her lap, rubs his feet, puts on his socks, puts on his shoes, and ties the laces.

"Thank you, my dear," my father says, squeezing and kissing her hand. "I feel much better." His voice is gentle.

.

My mother and I decide to take a trip by bus, by ourselves, to Naha, to Kokusai Dori, the shopping district, to buy omiyage for our friends in the United States. We wander the main strip and side streets. We see stores selling figurines of shisa, a pair of guardian gargoyle lion-dogs, a sort of mascot, an icon of Okinawa. We buy a few figurines. We see stores selling hand-sewn Okinawan versions of aloha shirts. We buy a few shirts. We see stores selling boxes of purple sweet-potato pastries. We buy a few boxes. We see stores selling tropical fruit, stores selling herbs, stores selling jade jewelry, stores selling drums and sanshin guitars, stores selling bottles of awamori (rice liquor) and jars of pickled habu (snake). We look but don't buy anything. We talk about my father, how we're worried about him. We talk about Genshin and Yoshi, how nice they are to us, how much they want to be around her, how much they miss her. We talk about her nieces and nephews, how their houses are bigger, how life is getting better, Okinawa is getting better.

We talk.

We see a store selling dresses in unusual tie-dye patterns. My mother sees my eyes perk, and she wants to buy me a dress. As we rifle through the racks, the clerk, perhaps the owner, an elderly woman wearing a face mask and an apron, asks me a question in Japanese, which hasn't happened before, because when we're traveling with my father they know I'm American. Her question startles me. Not because I don't understand, but because I do understand and I'm searching for the words.

"Sumimasen. Sukoshi wakarimasu." *Sorry. I understand a little.*

"Nihonjin desu ka?" she asks. *Are you Japanese?*

"Uh . . . Hai. Watashino haha wa Okinawa shushin desu." *My mother is from Okinawa.* I hear the words dribble out of me.

Her posture changes. She is lighter, giddier. I'm so excited I dash away from her in mid-sentence to look for my mother. "Kite, kite," I say to my mother. *Come, come.* "Kare wa watashino haha desu." I introduce my mother to the clerk. They become friends instantly, talking and telling jokes and helping each other pick out dresses for me. "Kore wa?" *This one?* My mother and the clerk weave through aisles, in between racks, exchanging patterns and sizes.

"Let's see," my mother says.

I pull open the curtain. They both oooh and ahhh and "kawaii desu ne" at me.

"Ikura?" I ask my mother. *How much?*

"Nisen-en," she answers. *Two thousand yen.*

"Takai!" *Expensive.*

"Ie. Yasui desu yo." *No. It's cheap.*

"Two hundred dollars is cheap?" I ask.

"No, nisen-en. Not, niman-en. Just twenty dollars." My mother laughs. She explains the misunderstanding to the clerk, her new friend. They both laugh.

The clerk sells us four dresses for yonsen-en. Forty dollars. My mother gives her rokusen-en. Sixty dollars. Before we leave the store, the clerk presses both of her palms to my mother's cheeks, leans close, noses almost touching, and says "Wakai okaasan." *Young mother.*

.

What if we had lived in Okinawa? My mother could have been the leader, the expert. She could have chatted and bonded with clerks, neighbors, teachers, and coaches. What if we had visited every summer, year after year? I could have learned Japanese. I could have spoken Japanese with my mother.

.

On our second-to-last night, we host a party. Genshin comes to the house hours early, bringing coolers and bags of ice, bottles of water and juice, cans of soda and beer, taking us to the supermarket to buy two bottles of awamori, four bottles of sake, eight platters of sushi and sashimi and tempura, enough to load two shopping carts. Yoshi comes to the house hours early, bringing plastic cups and paper plates, wooden chopsticks and napkins, watching us sweep and mop, rearrange tables and chairs. After I shower and dress, I sit on the floor beside Yoshi. She looks at me, keeps looking at me, then makes the motion of applying lipstick with her hand. "Should put on some lipstick?" She smiles and nods like *yes, definitely*. So I put on some lipstick. Genshin's oldest daughter and her husband take the day off from work and come to the house, bringing a rice cooker and rice, a charcoal grill, and pans of marinated steak and chicken. Then Genshin's wife comes with her two oldest grandchildren. Then Genshin's youngest daughter comes with her four children. Then Genshin's oldest son comes with his wife and two children. More nieces and nephews. More cousins and second cousins.

We sit on the floor. We eat and drink. The children eat and play on the floor. I point to each child and ask, "Onamae wa?" *Name?* and "Nan sai?" *How old?* The mothers advise their older children to answer my questions themselves in English, like they learned in school. But I won't remember their names and ages.

One of my cousins notices my empty glass, then points to the bottom of her empty glass, then says "Ho-ru," *Hole,* as she makes the motion of falling liquid with her hand.

"Oishi. Dai suki," I say, shrugging and laughing. *Delicious. I love.*

"Daijoubu," she says. *It's okay.*

She takes my empty glass and refills both of our empty glasses with more awamori.

One of my cousins explains the age gap between her two sons, ages thirteen and ten, and two daughters, ages three and two, by showing me the word "divorce" on the screen of her phone, then holding up two fingers and saying, "Tu-waisu," *Twice,* flinching in anticipation of my judgment.

"Kamaimasen," I say. *Doesn't matter.* "In America, we say no big deal."

"Ah. Yes. Thank you. Thank you. Anata-wa?"

"Me? Never been married. No kids," I say, making the sign of a zero with my hand and an exaggerated frown.

She smiles and says, "No. Bigu. Diru."

I announce in English that there is ice cream for dessert. My mother translates. The children look at their mothers as if they want ice cream. Their mothers nod and say yes. The children keep looking at their mothers as if they want ice cream but they're afraid to seem too eager, afraid to get up from the floor and get ice cream from me. Their mothers point at me and say, *go, go.* The children move reluctantly, timidly, forming a line behind me. I'm nervous, sweating, making sure each child gets enough, making sure each child gets the same amount, bending low to give them their bowls. I don't want them to be afraid of me.

We finish every last bite of food. We finish every last drop of awamori and sake and beer. We get drunk. Some of us get very drunk. One of my cousins has to call a taxi. Two of my second cousins have to drive two of my cousins, their mothers, home. Genshin and his wife have to drive their children and grandchildren home.

"Ho-ru! Ho-ru!" we all shout as they leave the house. "Daijoubu!"

·

The morning after the party, I'm hung over. I toss and moan in my bed. I crawl to the bathroom and puke five times. After each time I puke, my father pours a can of seltzer into a glass with ice and brings the glass to my bed. "I guess you still need to take care of me sometimes," I say, struggling to sit. "It's my pleasure, my dear," he says, kissing the top of my head. After the last time I puke, my mother cooks a broth with garlic, ginger, mushrooms, spinach, and a package of ramen. "Noodle soup is best for hangover," she says, blowing into the steaming bowl. "Yes, I know," I say. I remember when she used to cook noodle soup for her hangovers.

It rains all morning, all afternoon. As soon as the rain softens to a drizzle, my mother wants to walk to the beach. Our last day. Our last chance.

"I'll go with you," my father says, turning off the television.

"Me too," I say, moaning from my bed.

The fresh air feels good. The drizzle on my face feels good. We walk close together, huddle together, my mother and I walking at the same pace as my father, who is holding the umbrella. We sit under a pavilion, and stare at the gray waves spinning and stirring the green seaweed. We agree that we'll miss this beach, miss Okinawa. Then, of course, it starts to rain again. Pelting sheets of rain.

My mother stands. "I'm going to run."

My father grabs her hand. "No. Please don't run."

"Just let her run."

"Fine. But you'll need the key. Put the key in your pocket." He points to the zipper across the side of her sweatpants.

"Not a pocket. Just decoration. I don't need the key. I wait outside."

"Kani-san, take the key, take it."

"Oh my God, Dad."

"Just let me be, Elizabeth." He shoves the key into her hand. "Hold on to it tight." She shakes her head at me, rolling her eyes at him.

"I'm going to run with Mom."

He sighs. "Fine. Then take the umbrella, too."

"No. You need it. You're walking."

"Take it." He shoves the umbrella into my hand.

"Now I don't want to run."

"Jesus Christ," I say. "I'm running."

My mother and I run in the rain. She holds the key. I hold the umbrella. We look behind us, at my poor father. He limps and lags, his hair and clothes drenched in rain. We stop running. We start to run back. He smiles and waves, motions for us to keep running. We laugh. We can't stop laughing.

"Your father is a pain in the neck," my mother says. "But he has a good heart."

"Yeah," I say, laughing, wheezing, out of breath.

Kashikoi okaasan. *Wise mother.*

.

They come early, at seven o'clock. Our flight doesn't depart for four and a half more hours. Genshin separates the recycling and takes out the trash. Yoshi watches us clean and pack. We drink tea and eat leftovers. Then Genshin's wife, his oldest daughter and her husband, his youngest daughter and her four children come to the house. I think they have come to say goodbye, but instead they tell us they're coming with us to the airport. We caravan to the airport in the van and two cars.

They wait with us as we stand in a long line. They wait with us as we confirm our reservations. I don't understand why they're still here. I don't understand why they're still waiting with us. In America, when we take loved ones to the airport, we usually drop them off at the curb.

"Naha de, kaimono o shimasu ka?" I ask my cousin. *In Naha, go shopping?* She shakes her head. "Hirugohan wa?" I ask, trying again. *Lunch?* Now she looks even more confused. "Are they going shopping or out to lunch somewhere in Naha?" I ask my mother.

"No, Elizabeth. They come here just for us."

"Daijoubu," my cousin says to me. Now she understands.

At the security checkpoint, before we take off our shoes and pass through the metal detectors, we hug each other. My uncle. My aunts. My cousins. My second cousins. I kneel on the floor so I can hug the two baby girls with both arms. My mother and Yoshi cry.

I don't cry. I'm not sad.

This is my family. This is Okinawa.

I was here.

XXIV
FREE OKINAWA!

No matter how far you have gone down the wrong path,
turn back.
—Turkish proverb

*I*n 1879, on the day our last king was banished from Shuri
and exiled to Tokyo, the day he surrendered the castle, as Japanese soldiers surrounded and escorted him, he turned to us and
said "Nuchi du takara." *Life is precious.*

He didn't want us to fight to save him. He didn't want us to
risk our lives for him.

This phrase is now our motto, our moral code. We believe
in the sanctity of life, that life itself, above all else, above any
proposed ideology or reason or excuse, must be cherished. We
worship life. We worship peace. Yet wars still come to us.

.

During proceedings leading to that day, the day we were
annexed, Ulysses S. Grant, as a citizen, as a consultant, mediated
between representatives from Japan and China. He determined
that we, the Lew Chewans, soon to become Okinawans, exhib-
ited more "ethnic affinity" with the Japanese, therefore should
belong to Japan.

We were not invited to attend these proceedings. We were not asked for our opinion.

Since 1609, we had already been a colony of Japan, in practice, in secret. We bowed to the Emperor, obeyed orders, paid tribute, changed our names, changed the way we spoke. But we still had our land. We still had our beaches. We still had our forests and sacred groves. We still had our Seimei, the first pure water of the year, the first day of the new year of the lunar calendar, when we drew from the fresh spring wells and washed our hands together. We still had our fish, our prawn, our octopi, our seaweed. We still had our pigs and goats and cows. Our crops were few, but we had plenty to share. Because we always shared.

.

In 1945, the Americans burned all our land, crushed all our land, all our beaches, forests, and sacred groves. The Americans killed one hundred forty thousand of us. Those of us who survived were homeless for years.

But the war is not over yet. The attacks on Okinawa are not over yet.

.

After the burning and crushing, the Americans demolished and bulldozed and paved. For years we lived in camps, and when we returned to our towns and villages, we discovered that our towns and villages were inside iron gates and barbed-wire fences, inside military bases. Some of us were allowed to build houses and farm on our land inside the military bases, requiring identification each time we entered, and some of us were forced to relocate. Some of us were fortunate enough to get paid for our land with a lump sum at six percent of the value.

Chatan became Hamby Airfield. Dendo and Tamayose became Camp Zukeran. Toguchi and Sobe became Torii Communication Station. Uza and Gima became Bolo-Point Firing Range. Kuwae and Irei became Camp Kuwae. Kadena, Kudoku, Kaneku, Noguni, Nozato, Kininao, Mizugama, and Higashi became Kadena Air Base. Hijabashi, Kina, and Nagatamakihara became Kadena Ammunition Storage Area.

And so on, and so on.

But the war is not over yet. The attacks on Okinawa are not over yet.

.

We hear jets every day. We hear helicopters every day. On some parts of the island, we hear fire drills from six in the morning until eleven at night, Monday through Saturday.

On our commute, on the way to work, some of us take the bus. We pass by Camp Zukeran and Futenma Air Base. We pass by Camp Lester, which takes four stops. We pass by Camp Kinser, which takes six stops. We pass by parking lots full of camouflage jeeps and tanks with signs that say FLAMMABLE: NO SMOKING 50 FT. We pass by casinos and American car and motorcycle dealerships. We pass by McDonald's, Burger King, KFC, A&W, and Domino's. We see the sky and hills behind the bases, trapped behind the bases.

.

In 1951, the Emperor and President Harry S. Truman signed the Japan-U.S. Security Treaty, in which the agreement was made—again, none of us were there—that the use of portions of Okinawa would be leased to the U.S. military for ninety-nine years.

Will the U.S. military return these portions of Okinawa in 2050?

.

In 1951, an aircraft dropped a fuel tank on a house, burning the house, killing six of us.

.

In 1955, a soldier raped and murdered one of us—a girl, six years old. The soldier was sentenced to heavy manual labor, and the bereaved family received two thousand dollars.

.

In 1956, a soldier drove a car over one of us, killing one of us, a man, twenty-eight years old.

.

In 1959, a jet crashed into Miyamori Elementary School, killing seventeen of us, injuring more than two hundred of us.

.

In 1962, a jet crashed into a house, killing seven of us, injuring eight of us.

.

In 1963, a soldier drove a car over one of us, killing one of us, a boy, twelve years old.

.

In 1963, a marine strangled one of us, murdered one of us, a woman, twenty-two years old.

.

In 1964, two soldiers robbed one of us at gunpoint. They stole our taxi.

.

In 1965, an aircraft dropped a trailer on one of us, killing one of us, a boy, eleven years old.

.

In 1966, a jet crashed onto a beach, killing two of us.

.

In 1968, a B-52 bomber exploded, killing four of us.

.

In 1970, a soldier, drunk, drove a truck over one of us, killing one of us, a woman, thirty years old. The soldier drove over her and drove away.

.

These are a few of the thousands of incidents, the thousands of crimes. Most unpunished. Our police and our prosecutors had no jurisdiction. The U.S. soldiers and marines and sailors would retreat inside the iron gates and barbed-wire fences, inside the military bases, then be judged in U.S. military courts, then acquitted, then sent off the island. Free.

.

In 1970, on December 20, at one o'clock in the morning, in the city of Koza, a soldier, drunk, drove a car into one of us, a man, also drunk, crossing the highway. A hundred of us, working in the nearby restaurants and bars, heard the man screaming. We rushed out. We saw the man bleeding from his left hip and left knee. We watched the military police come to rescue the soldier, come to take the soldier back to the military base. We hissed and jeered. We threw bottles and bricks. Minutes later, another soldier driving a car came speeding down the road. He swerved to avoid us, crashed into one of our cars. We threw a brick at the windshield. We dragged the soldier out of his car. We beat him, punched him, kicked him in the back and chest. We smashed the windows of all the cars with military license plates. Three thousand more of us joined. We were stomping and dancing. We were smiling. The military police returned, fired warning shots into the air. We fled to the gates of Kadena Air Base. We tore down the fences. We set fire to the cars. We smashed the windows of buildings. We dragged a mannequin of Santa Claus into the parking lot and lit it on fire with bug spray and matches. We were stomping and dancing. We were smiling.

We stomped and danced until six o'clock in the morning, when they sprayed us with tear gas.

They refer to that night as the Koza Riot. We refer to that night as the Koza Uprising. They changed the name of Koza to Okinawa City. To make us forget. But we remember.

Forty years later, Bruce Lieber, the man we dragged out of the car and beat, came back to visit Koza, now Okinawa City. A news reporter asked him if he thought the Koza Riot was justified. "Absolutely," he answered. "Okinawan people were pushed around by the American military too much. My only question is what took them so long to rebel?" When we saw him on the sidewalk, we stopped to bow and shake his hand. He didn't have to pay to eat at restaurants or drink at bars that day. That is how we thank those who remember.

.

In 1972, on May 15, Okinawa reverted, or, rather, was sold back to Japan for the sum of six hundred eighty-five million dollars. Yet the United States still controls the assets it sold.

The bases remain.

Those of us who represented Okinawa in the Diet were outnumbered, eight to seven hundred twelve. We opposed the terms of the reversion. We refused to attend the ceremony in Tokyo.

.

In 1995, on September 4, three marines rented a car and drove an hour north to the city of Naha, plotting to "get a girl." After many failed attempts, the three marines, defeated and dejected, drove back to their base of Camp Hansen, in the town of Kin, which once thrived and bustled with business and activity, with bars and brothels and bright lights, but since the Vietnam War ended had become empty and dilapidated, hardly the "cross-cultural experience" and "opportunity to see the world" that the U.S. military advertised. Perhaps this false promise contributed to their false sense of entitlement. Perhaps this false promise contributed to their false sense of betrayal and vengeance. It was eight o'clock on the night of Labor Day, the last day of a long weekend, and time was running out.

She was one of us, a girl, twelve years old. She was walking home from the store, carrying a notebook she had purchased.

They pointed a knife to her throat. They dragged her into the backseat. They bound her hands and feet with duct tape. They taped her eyes and mouth shut. They drove her to a deserted beach and took turns. They threw her bloody underwear into a trash bin and left her to bleed on the sand.

She crawled through mangroves, up a cliff, to one of the houses.

Before they blindfolded her, she remembered the vehicle and rental number. She remembered their faces.

We stood outside the gates and fences. We wouldn't budge. We wouldn't take our eyes off them.

One of the marines said, "It was just for fun."

Admiral Richard C. Macke, commander of the U.S. forces in the Pacific, commented, "For the price they paid for the car, they could have had themselves a girl."

The defense minister of Japan referred to the rape as a "ranko," an orgy.

We stood outside the gates and fences. We wouldn't budge. We wouldn't take our eyes off them.

The three marines were transferred to local authorities. They were convicted in a Japanese court, the first crime committed by U.S. military personnel to be tried and convicted in a Japanese court. They were sentenced to seven years in prison.

.

In 1995, on October 21, eighty-five thousand of us swarmed the streets outside a park in the city of Ginowan, protesting and demanding complete removal of U.S. military bases.

.

In 1996, in response to the outrage, the Japanese and U.S. governments agreed to close Futenma Air Station on the condition that the base be relocated to the northern, more remote, still relatively unpopulated and pristine area of Henoko, within the Nago City district.

Any of our representatives who accepted these terms of relocation lost their seats in the Diet the following year.

We don't want relocation. We don't want substitution. We want removal.

•

Their plan is to build an artificial peninsula in Oura Bay, an extension of Camp Schwab. The plan is to build one thousand eight hundred meters of runway and a pier the size of two football fields, long enough to dock the assault ship U.S.S. *Bonhomme Richard*. At the same time, the plan is to build a heliport in the middle of our Yanbaru National Forest, a heliport used to land osprey helicopters, also known as "widow makers" because of their tendency to crash.

Oura Bay is the home of our blue coral reefs, our three hundred species of conchs, our forty species of crab and shrimp, our one hundred eighty species of sea grass, and our beloved dugong, the marine mammal, only ten left in Okinawa. Yanbaru is the home of our one thousand species of plants and our five thousand species of birds.

Since 1996, construction has started, stopped, and started again, as we file lawsuit after lawsuit based on the Environmental Impact Assessment Law.

•

In January of 2010, we elected the mayor of Nago City on the platform of anti-base.

•

In September of 2010, we elected the assembly of Nago City on the platform of anti-base.

.

In November of 2010, we elected the governor of Okinawa on the platform of anti-base.

.

In 2011, our governor wrote a letter to the U.S. Senate, pleading for them to "respect the will of the people of Okinawa. Please show us the true worth of American democracy."

.

Twelve thousand of us demonstrated on Tokushima Island. Ninety thousand of us demonstrated in Yomitan. Twenty-seven thousand of us locked arms, encircled Kadena Air Base in a human chain, calling for closure.

.

Since 2014, protests have been constant, every day, all day, all night. Every day, we tie blue, red, and yellow ribbons to the fences, spelling the words PEACE and NO BASE and GIVE US BACK OUR LAND. Every day, we sit in front of the gates, forming human barricades. Every day, we paddle in canoes and kayaks to the scaffolding towers. We chain ourselves to the towers. We greet the construction workers with cups of tea.

Many of us are old, grandmothers and grandfathers. Many of us were children who lost our mothers and fathers, brothers and sisters, aunts and uncles in the Battle of Okinawa. When we are dragged off the street and heaved out of our boats, some of our bones break, some of us are hospitalized.

.

In 2016, after several rulings and appeals and rerulings and reappeals, the Supreme Court of Japan concluded that erecting seventy-six thousand concrete pillars and seawalls, then dumping twenty-one million cubic centimeters of sand and soil into Oura Bay, would not have an environmental impact.

.

In 2018, we sent a petition with two hundred thousand signatures to the U.S. Senate.

That same year, we conducted a referendum, a referendum no one in the United States seems to know or care about. Seventy-two percent of us oppose the relocation. The prime minister of Japan declared that he was sorry, that he must ignore this result and continue with construction. He claimed that relocation was the only "solution."

.

America, you spend more money on military than half of the world combined. America, why? Who threatens you? China? North Korea? Russia? Iran? So far, you have used our island to bomb Iraq and Afghanistan and Iraq again. America, as we speak, you are dumping sand and soil into our ocean. Not for our defense. Not for our protection. America, it's not too late. No matter how far you've gone down the wrong path, it's not too late. Turn back. Turn back.

Free Okinawa!

XXV
MORE APOLOGIES

Some apologies are unspeakable. Like the one we owe our parents.
—Eula Biss, "All Apologies"

The most common and important word in the Japanese language is "sumimasen." If there is one word to learn in Japanese, it is "sumimasen." It is a form of apology, but also used in wider contexts. If someone holds a door open for you, say "sumimasen." If you need to ask someone for a glass of water, say "sumimasen." And when someone brings you a glass of water, say "sumimasen."

.

In Japanese, sometimes "thank you" and "I'm sorry" are the same expression.

.

In Japanese, there are several variations of apology, ranging in nuance and level of formality. There are words for apologies of anticipation, for a future discomfort, and words for apologies of regret, for a past infringement. There are apologies used casually, only with family and close friends, and apologies used only with superiors or in speeches and letters.

.

Before you enter a home or an office, apologize. Before you leave a party or meeting, apologize. If you are late, apologize. If you are loud, apologize. If you have to reach in front of someone or obstruct a view, apologize. If, for any reason, you have to touch a person's body—for instance, if you are a doctor or an airport security officer—apologize.

.

If you've caused an inconvenience or made a mistake in any way, then profoundly, profusely apologize. Ask for forgiveness. Beg for mercy.

*   *   *

In a telegram to the vice admiral, on June 13, 1945, just before committing suicide, Rear Admiral Minoru Ota, commanding officer of the Imperial Japanese Navy in Okinawa, wrote:

> . . . Since the enemy attacks began, our Army and Navy have been fighting defensive battles and have not been able to attend to the people of this prefecture.
>
> Consequently, due to our negligence, these innocent people have lost their homes and their property to enemy assault. Every man has been conscripted to defense while women, children, and elders are forced into hiding . . . Moreover, girls devote themselves to nursing and cooking, as well as volunteering to carry ammunition and join in attacking the enemy.
>
> This leaves the village people vulnerable to enemy attack

where they will surely be killed. In desperation, some parents have asked the military to protect their daughters, for fear that when the enemy comes, elders and children will be killed and young women and girls will be taken to private areas and harmed.

After military personnel had moved on, the volunteer nurses stayed behind to help the badly wounded move. They are dedicated and go about their work with a strong will.

The military has changed its operations, forcing people to evacuate residential areas. Those without transportation trudge in the dark and rain, without complaining, all the while searching for food. Ever since our Army and Navy have occupied Okinawa, the inhabitants of this prefecture have endured these constant hardships . . .

There are no trees, no grass, everything is burnt to the ground. The food supply will be gone by the end of June. This is how the Okinawan people have fought the war.

And for this reason, I appeal to you to give the Okinawan people special consideration from this day forward.

•

Was this telegram a form of apology?

•

There is no apology on record for how the Japanese treated the Okinawans during the Battle of Okinawa.

•

Japan gave Okinawa one billion yen in 1962, and then another forty-five billion yen ten years later, and hundreds of billions more yen as part of the Okinawa Promotion and Development Plan, and later the Resort Act of 1987. Was this guilt money?

.

Okinawa is still the poorest prefecture in all of Japan.

*   *   *

While we were traveling in Japan, the culture of apology was palpable. I could see it in their bows. I could hear it in their inflections. With every apology, they seemed to acknowledge that their actions affected me, that all of our actions affect each other. I felt like part of a whole. Like they were humbling themselves, making themselves small in order to make room for me. This culture of apology felt familiar, comforting, like I had found something I didn't know I was missing.

.

In English, "I'm sorry" indicates sympathy, guilt, a request to be pardoned. "I'm sorry," when used too frequently, too offhandedly, can be construed as "I'm not really sorry" or even "I'm weak" and "I don't matter." When we apologize in America, maybe we have to be careful not to be misconstrued or exploited. When we say "I'm sorry" too often in America, maybe we will get squeezed out; maybe someone else will assume the space we left behind.

.

Throughout my life, I've been told I apologize too often. I say I'm sorry for asking a question, for asking too many questions. I say I'm sorry for not knowing the answer, not having the answer that was wanted or needed, for wanting or needing too many answers. I say I'm sorry for thinking too much, feeling too much. I say I'm sorry pre-emptively, before a comment that could possibly be interpreted as offensive, before bringing myself to express a challenging opinion or a negative reaction. I say I'm sorry retroactively, scrutinizing deeds and comments and sending text apologies in the middle of the night. I've been told I should sound more confident, more assertive when I talk. I've been told I shouldn't apologize so often. But sometimes my whole body yearns to apologize and for someone to accept my apology, for someone to be sorry just because I'm sorry.

·

My mother never explicitly taught me this culture of apology. I learned it and absorbed it from her lowered head and hunched shoulders, from her soft voice, from how easily and repeatedly and boundlessly she apologized. For the soup being too hot, for the steak being overcooked, for forgetting to bring me a napkin, for hitting her elbow on the table, for a dress at a store not fitting, for the store not having my size. Her apologies used to bother me. My apologies used to bother me. I used to equate apology with weakness, with lack of importance. I used to feel bad for feeling bad for taking up too much space.

Now I am grateful.

So much wrong happens in the world, and there is never enough apology.

·

"Gomen nasai" is pure apology, used for more profound transgression and wrongdoing.

Gomen nasai, Okaasan. I'm sorry for all those phone calls I didn't answer. I'm sorry for all those nights I pretended to be asleep when you came home from the restaurant. I'm sorry for all those nights I watched television in the living room while you ate by yourself in the dining room. I'm sorry for all those times we shopped together in silence, all those times we drove together in silence. I'm sorry for all the silence. I would give anything to go back to those times and talk to you, to have the conversations I should have had with you. I'm sorry for calling you "stupid" to your face once. I'm sorry for thinking it more than once. You are not stupid. You are the opposite of stupid. You are wise and kind. You speak two languages. You make beautiful meals and beautiful gardens. You keep plants alive and thriving. You take care of birds and squirrels. You take care of my father. You take care of me. You love and love, and you forgive.

I'm sorry I couldn't have been a happier daughter.

I'm sorry I couldn't redeem your sacrifice.

I'm sorry, Mom. I'm sorry for everything.

*W*hen I hear my mother say my name now, I just hear it. Her pronunciation doesn't sound wrong or right to me. Erizabesu and Elizabeth. They're both mine.

.

I am an Okinawan story. I am an American story.

.

I wish I could locate a precise point of transformation, the pivotal moment when my mother and I finally reconciled. But that's not how we apologize and forgive. The healing is gradual, cumulative. It happens as we begin to recognize our mothers not as mothers, but as women who endure husbands and daughters. It happens as we begin to accept and appreciate our very own exquisite uniqueness, and everyone we hold responsible.

It happens now as I write.

*   *   *

I call my mother on a Sunday, after church, just to say hi, just to talk. She tells me that her friends are very excited about the book.

"Mom, I don't think you should tell your friends about the book."

"Why not?"

"I don't think you want them to know . . . what I'm writing about."

"What are you writing about? I thought you writing about Okinawa."

"Well, that's part of it. But mostly it's about me. But also about you. And Dad, how you met him, your marriage. And . . . how you—"

"You're writing about my hard life, huh?"

"Yes, Mom. I'm writing about your hard life."

"Do you think that's interesting? Do you think people will be interesting?"

"Yes, Mom. I do."

"That's okay, Elizabeth. I want people to know about my hard life."

.

I am practicing how to say "happy birthday" in Japanese, listening to a recorded voice on my translation app and repeating, over and over again. "Otanjoubi omedetou gozaimasu . . . Otanjoubi omedetou gozaimasu . . ."

I call her. I say the words.

"Wow! Pretty good!"

"Anata wa roku ju hachi sai desu." *You are sixty-nine years old*. I say it slowly. Painstakingly.

"Hai. So desu. You remember."

"Mada wakai." *Still young*.

"Tabun." *Maybe*.

"Kyoo wa shigoto e ikimashita ka?" *Did you go to work today?*

"Hai. Ju ichi ji kara yon ji." *Yes, from eleven o'clock to four o'clock*.

"Kyoo wa nani o tabemashita ka?" *What did you eat today?*
"Natto to gohan." *Natto and rice.* "Anata wa?"
"Uh . . . pizza."
"Itsumo pizza o tabemasu desu yo." *You always eat pizza.*
She laughs. I laugh, too.
This is our first conversation in Japanese.

.

I am visiting home for the weekend. It is summer in Fairport, New York, and the kids are splashing in pools and the adults are mowing their lawns.

We drive for half an hour to the city of Rochester. We have to go to the Asian market to get fixings for a dashi broth. She plans to prepare a dish of cold soba noodles and tofu for dinner tonight. A delicious warm-weather meal.

I listen to music on my phone, which is plugged into the car stereo. She asks me how this technology works. I explain that these songs are downloaded, a concept she doesn't quite understand, and also tell her she can listen to pretty much any song she wants by searching YouTube, another concept she doesn't quite understand.

"Here. I'll show you. What's your favorite song?" She tells me the name of the song, and I do my best to type the romaji letters. "Can you repeat that? . . . Say it slowly."

"Ginza no Koi no Monogatari," "Love Story of Tokyo," as sung by Yujiro Ishihara and Junko Makimura.

It's a song I've heard many times. First released in 1961. The most popular duet in Japan. My mother used to sing it while cooking and cleaning. She used to blare it through boomboxes from cassette tapes that Setsu sent her in brightly colored, carefully wrapped packages. I remember the basic melody, and try to sing along, but fumble over the verses.

"I guess I don't know the words," I say.

"That's okay. I'll teach you."

She bobs her head and pats her knee. She sings loudly and clearly, so I can hear her.

ACKNOWLEDGMENTS

First and most of all, my mother and father, for how you love and continue to raise me. Thank you for trusting me and allowing me to share your stories. I know my rendition of you will always be inadequate and incomplete. Words cannot express everything you are and everything you mean to me. Words cannot express my gratitude.

The Makiya Family, for your hospitality and generosity and warmth. I've never felt more welcome.

The UNO Creative Writing Workshop, those of you who taught me and learned with me, gave me feedback and encouragement, especially Randy Bates, for your gentleness and kindness and helping me become a better writer than I thought possible. Also, Richard Goodman, Erik Hansen, Ann Hackett, Tori Bush, Wilson Koewing, and Thad Lee.

Francisco Cantú, for believing in this project and vouching for it.

Rebecca Gradinger, my agent, for making my dream come true.

Diana Miller, my editor, for understanding what I wanted this book to be, what this book needed to be. I couldn't have asked for a more skilled and patient and thoughtful guide.

ACKNOWLEDGMENTS

Claudia Rankine, for words and ideas on page 29, which I quoted and paraphrased from her book *Citizen*.

Mitsuga Sakihara, for the poem on page 32, which I quoted and paraphrased from his translation of the *Omoro Soshi*.

Jamaica Kincaid, for words and ideas on page 38, which I quoted and paraphrased from her book *A Small Place*.

Bread Loaf Writers, Conference, New York State Summer Writers Institute, and Blue Mountain Center for financial support and crucial inspiration.

Everyone who made an appearance, no matter how brief, in this book, and whether you read this book or not, I hope you forgive me.

ACKNOWLEDGMENTS

First and most of all, my mother and father, for how you love and continue to raise me. Thank you for trusting me and allowing me to share your stories. I know my rendition of you will always be inadequate and incomplete. Words cannot express everything you are and everything you mean to me. Words cannot express my gratitude.

The Makiya Family, for your hospitality and generosity and warmth. I've never felt more welcome.

The UNO Creative Writing Workshop, those of you who taught me and learned with me, gave me feedback and encouragement, especially Randy Bates, for your gentleness and kindness and helping me become a better writer than I thought possible. Also, Richard Goodman, Erik Hansen, Ann Hackett, Tori Bush, Wilson Koewing, and Thad Lee.

Francisco Cantú, for believing in this project and vouching for it.

Rebecca Gradinger, my agent, for making my dream come true.

Diana Miller, my editor, for understanding what I wanted this book to be, what this book needed to be. I couldn't have asked for a more skilled and patient and thoughtful guide.

ACKNOWLEDGMENTS

Claudia Rankine, for words and ideas on page 29, which I quoted and paraphrased from her book *Citizen*.

Mitsuga Sakihara, for the poem on page 32, which I quoted and paraphrased from his translation of the *Omoro Soshi*.

Jamaica Kincaid, for words and ideas on page 38, which I quoted and paraphrased from her book *A Small Place*.

Bread Loaf Writers, Conference, New York State Summer Writers Institute, and Blue Mountain Center for financial support and crucial inspiration.

Everyone who made an appearance, no matter how brief, in this book, and whether you read this book or not, I hope you forgive me.

SOURCES

Crissey, Etsuko Takushi. *Okinawa's GI Brides: Their Lives in America.* Translated by Steve Rabson. Honolulu: University of Hawai'i Press, 2017.

Higa, Tomiko. *The Girl with the White Flag: A Spellbinding Account of Love and Courage in Wartime Okinawa.* New York: Kodansha USA, 1989.

Kerr, George H. *Okinawa: The History of an Island People,* rev. ed. Rutland, Vt.: Charles E. Tuttle Co., 2000.

Keyso, Ruth Ann. *Women of Okinawa: Nine Voices from a Garrison Island.* Ithaca, N.Y.: Cornell University Press, 2000.

Martin, Jo Nobuko. *A Princess Lily of the Ryukyus.* Tokyo, Japan: Shin Nippon Kyoiku Tosho, 1984.

McCormack, Gavan, and Satoko Oka Norimatsu. *Resistant Islands: Okinawa Confronts Japan and the United States.* Lanham, Md.: Rowman & Littlefield, 2012.

Okinawa Peace Network of Los Angeles. http://www.uchinanchu.org. Buddhahead Productions. 2005.

Rabson, Steve. "Perry's Black Ships in Japan and Ryuku: The Whitewash of History." *Asia Pacific Journal / Japan Focus,* vol. 14, no. 16, ser. 9 (Aug. 15, 2016), apjjf.org/2016/16/Rabson.html.

Sakihara, Mitsugu. *A Brief History of Okinawa Based on the Omoro Soshi.* Honpo Shoseki Press, 1987.

Zeiger, Susan. *Entangling Alliances: Foreign War Brides and American Soldiers in the Twentieth Century.* New York: New York University Press, 2010.

A NOTE ABOUT THE AUTHOR

ELIZABETH MIKI BRINA is the recipient of a Rona Jaffe Bread Loaf
Scholarship and a New York Summer Writers Institute Scholarship.
She currently lives and teaches in New Orleans.

A NOTE ON THE TYPE

The type used in this book was designed by Pierre Simon Fournier *le
jeune*. In 1764 and 1766 he published his *Manuel typographique*, a trea-
tise on the history of French types and printing, and on what many
consider his most important contribution to typography—the mea-
surement of type by the point system.

Designed by Maria Carella
Composed by Digital Composition, Berryville, Virginia
Printed and bound by Friesens Printing, Altona, Canada